Seeing Through Writing

WILLIAM E. COLES, Jr.
University of Pittsburgh

HARPER & ROW, PUBLISHERS, New York
Cambridge, Philadelphia, San Francisco, Washington,
London, Mexico City, São Paulo, Singapore, Sydney

Sponsoring Editor: Lucy Rosendahl
Project Editor: Jo-Ann Goldfarb
Text Design: Pencil Point Studio
Cover Design: Brand X Studios/Robin Hessel
Photo Research: Mira Schachne
Production Manager: Jeanie Berke
Production Assistant: Beth Maglione
Compositor: ComCom Division of Haddon Craftsmen, Inc.
Printer and Binder: R. R. Donnelley & Sons Company
Cover Printer: Phoenix Color Corporation

Photograph Credits

Figure 2.1 (page 32) "Whale Washed Ashore at Ancona," Anonymous Italian, 1601. Engraving. F. Muller Collection (1081A). Rijksmuseum, Amsterdam. **Figure 2.2 (page 32)** Albrecht Dürer: Rhinoceros. 1515, woodcut. Print Collection. Miriam and Ira D. Wallach Division of Art, Prints and Photographs. The New York Public Library. Astor, Lenox and Tilden Foundations. **Figure 2.4 (page 32)** Emil Schultess, (c) Conzett and Huber, Zurich, Black Star. **Figure 2.3 (page 32)** Rhinoceros of Africa, Heath, engraving from *Travels to Discover the Source of the Nile,* by James Bruce. (c) 1970, George Ramsay and Co. **Figure 4.1 (page 61)** Reprinted from *Sex and Fantasy, Patterns of Male and Female Development,* Robert May, by permission of W. W. Norton and Company, Inc. Copyright (c) 1980 by Robert May.

Seeing Through Writing
Copyright © 1988 by William E. Coles, Jr.

Library of Congress Cataloging in Publication Data

Coles, William E.
  Seeing through writing / William E. Coles, Jr.
    p. cm.
  ISBN 0-06-041332-8
  1. English language—Rhetoric. I. Title.
PE1408.C54365 1988
808'.042—dc19

87 88 89 90 9 8 7 6 5 4 3 2 1

Students, as they are increasingly posed with problems relating to themselves in the world and with the world, will feel increasingly challenged and obliged to respond to that challenge. Because they apprehend the challenge as interrelated to other problems within a total context, not as a theoretical question, the resulting comprehension tends to be increasingly critical and thus constantly less alienated. Their response to the challenge evokes new challenges, followed by new understandings; and gradually the students come to regard themselves as committed.

Paulo Freire
Pedagogy of the Oppressed

I know it is true that . . . all [beings] work perfunctorily until they understand the significance and difficulty of what they are doing within the context of whatever love or loves structure the cosmos for them, and that perfunctory work is the death of the soul.

Vicki Hearne
Adam's Task

For Seven Men Who See

Ted Baird
Robert Coles
Bill Dixon
Albert Kafka *(in memoriam)*
Marty Leyden
Jack Martin
John Watt *(in memoriam)*

And for the child in my father

CONTENTS

FOREWORD

Normally, we do not expect original contributions from textbooks: a good text is a statement of shared beliefs about the discipline at a particular time. But the more creative teachers of writing occasionally use the textbook to go beyond established thinking, and it becomes a creative form, not merely a reflection of the achievements of others. *Seeing Through Writing* is such a book.

What impresses me about this book is the way it addresses a major problem in teaching that has arisen with the modern interest in rhetorical processes. One way of stating the problem is to ask how students can be given a usable understanding of the complex psychological processes of composing and a usable understanding of the social processes that influence these psychological processes. Or to change the emphasis a bit, how can processes of thinking and writing be discussed in print so that the student sees that it is *processes,* rather than their outcomes, that are at issue? Proficiency in writing requires more than a knowledge of what constitutes good prose; it also requires knowing how to do something. But the processes that we group under the term *writing* are often exceedingly difficult to explain.

The traditional methods of teaching—describing and analyzing—tend to distort the wholeness and fluidity of these processes by freezing them and breaking them into parts. Although description and analysis are the conventional methods of the scholar and the textbook writer, they are, by themselves, clumsy methods when we want to explain to others what actually occurs in composing and help them engage in the processes more effectively. It's a little like trying to describe to someone how to tie a necktie or perform a complex dance step (though these are much simpler processes than those Coles is trying to teach). We can, of course, tell someone how to tie a necktie, but we would not ordinarily try. Instead we would demonstrate how to do it.

And that is essentially what Coles does. The method he uses—enactment—is the method not of the scholar but of the artist; Coles dramatizes the processes of composition. A story about a group of students and their composition teacher working through a semester of writing assignments, the book resembles a novel quite as much as it does a textbook. Coles creates persuasive lives, and shows us persuasive writing coming out of those lives. The novelistic passages of the book are not to be read as mere interpolations that are finally irrelevant to what is really important, i.e., the more conventional explanations. Coles is trying to model on a broad scale what effective teaching and learning look like in action.

In this simulated world, writing is not presented as an isolated, monkish act but rather as <u>something imbedded in a social context</u>, shaping it and being shaped by it. One of the motifs that runs through the story is a looping action from public discourse, spoken as well as written, to inner speech, to writing, and back again to public discourse—(an effort to model writing in a world that extends beyond the classroom.) In such actions we see not only texts growing but minds growing as well. The different voices, each with its own history, that play around the assignments, the dramatic confrontations over the problems posed by the assignments, the writing that comes out of the confrontations and the problems, all combine to give us a better idea of the complexity of the composing process than explanation alone could give.

Coles invites the students using this book to play the roles which he has modeled for them. If they take their roles seriously, they learn not just about the effective and proper management of standard edited English (the traditional conception of writing); they also learn how to write in a more expansive sense in which <u>writing is seen as an intensely personal and moral struggle that takes place in the midst of others.</u> Coles offers a more spacious place for them to carry on the struggle.

Richard E. Young
Carnegie Mellon University

PREFACE

Seeing Through Writing is a college composition text grounded in an assumption that I want to be sure my audience is aware I am making. Vicki Hearne, from whose work I have taken one of my epigraphs, and who writes about teaching and learning better than anybody I know, asserts that <u>human beings need nobility,</u> are born to respond to it. "I mean," she goes on to explain, that we are "born to the demands of the heroic, of a pleasure earlier than love and nearer to heaven, the pleasure of the heroic approach to the knowledge of form. Hence an ethic or a theory of justice or a theory or practice of education that makes no attempt to trick out the syntax and the semantics of the heroic as a central mode of being human is not an ethic"—and may not, indeed, be much of anything at all.

My central assumption in writing this text is that the activities of teaching and learning about writing have in Vicki Hearne's sense a heroic dimension, one that is noble as well as ennobling. I do my best to trick out the syntax and semantics of this dimension as a way of making clear my belief that it, finally, is what gives those activities meaning. Thus, though my focus in *Seeing Through Writing* is epistemological, on what it means to see, to learn, to know as a reader and writer, because I believe that all epistemological concerns fold inevitably into concerns that are ontological as well, my interest is in dramatizing also some of the many ways in which learning and knowing are connected with growth, new being. The title of this text, therefore, has a double meaning. To see something through—that is, by means of—writing is to have a chance of seeing whatever is looked at better as a result of one's engagement with the writing process. But to see through writing in another sense is to have a chance also to see beyond a particular piece of writing to what makes writing worth bothering with in the first place.

Purpose and Design

In purpose and design this book is really very simple. It consists of two mutually reinforcing structures both created to interest students in making a commitment to work at becoming better writers. One of these structures is a sequence of writing assignments, twelve reading and writing tasks on the subject of seeing. This sequence poses questions about what it means to see something (both literally and metaphorically) not in order to play games with students, to ask questions that have either correct or incorrect answers, but to raise issues that have to be considered by thoughtful people again and again and again. What can get in the way of our trying to see things clearly, for example? What can we do to reduce such interference; how, that is, can we go about learning to see things better? The second structure is a series of fictional sketches dramatizing the experiences of a group of students working with the sequence of assignments on seeing in an undergraduate composition course run by a teacher nicknamed (and known in the sketches only as) the Gorgon. These two structures are reinforcing in that the twelve writing assignments provide the occasion for the experiences of the Gorgon's students, at the same time the students' experiences with those assignments in the Gorgon's course are intended to clarify the importance of the issues raised by the assignments.

The Assignment Sequence

The twelve reading and writing assignments invite students to consider the problem of how we see from a variety of perspectives and in the process to develop a full range of cognitive and compositional skills. Students are asked to use writing in a number of different ways and for a number of different purposes, but always in order to enable them to develop facility with the process of critical thinking, with the handling of ideas. There are assignments that have students make models, take notes on readings, compose drafts, develop hypotheses, construct analogies, solve problems, address particular audiences—writing tasks, in other words, that involve students automatically in the writing of analysis, summation, description, argumentation, definition, in the processes of comparing, inferring, deducing, contrasting, and arranging things in patterns.

The assignments offer more than just variety, however. To say that they are *sequenced* is to refer to something they are constructed to do both generally and specifically.

Generally, the writing assignments move from relatively uncomplicated writing tasks to those that are more sophisticated, from a focus on informal discourse to problems calling for more formality, from having students draw broadly on their experience to having them reflect upon it more and more particularly. Also, students are steadily encouraged to draw from their experience with earlier assignments in addressing those that follow. Writing Assignment 7, for example, involves students in a problem of extrapolation and inference ("given your way of addressing *that* situation, how do you then address this larger question?")—a problem analogous to one they coped with earlier (at Writing Assignment 3), but somewhat more difficult. And it is the students' experience with Assignments 3 and 7 that prepares them to address the still more complicated inferential problems of Assignments 11 and 12.

Specifically, the twelve writing assignments are sequenced to help students consider, step by step, and from a number of points of view, how and why the question of what we do to see something is important as well as complicated. Pared to its bones, the structure of the sequence looks something like this. Students are asked first to write a paper in which they take a position on the meaning of a college education in the context of their own lives. What's a new way of seeing that they hope college will give them? What do they imagine it will cost them to get what they hope for? What do they imagine they'll gain in getting what they hope for? Assignments 2, 3, and 4 ask students to develop a model of the seeing process, to address some of the implications of the ways in which it would seem we "see" not as cameras, but through certain schema that certainly have some source in one's culture and may perhaps even have something to do with biology as well. However, to rely on what seems to be the tendency of the mind to interpret what it "sees" in the context of its acquired schema only, though this has certain benefits, has certain liabilities too (Assignment 5), liabilities that make it important to consider the possibility of alternatives to stereotypical ways of seeing (Assignment 6) and what can be done to develop them (Assignment 7). For to understand how developing a new way of seeing seems inevitably to involve new ways of naming the world is then to have a way of talking about how reading and writing can help us develop ways of seeing for ourselves (Assignments 8, 9, 10). To learn to see for ourselves is often offered as an ideal (indeed, it is one way of talking about what a college education is supposed to provide), but the process of such learning, particularly as it is formalized in and with the demands of a college curriculum, seems to carry certain risks as well (Assignment 11). What now then, the final paper asks students, do you have to say about the issues that you addressed in your first piece of writing for the course?

That, of course, is only the most obvious way to see the structure of the sequence, and in any case is worth no more than what an individual teacher teaching, a particular student writing, can make it mean.

The Sequence of Sketches

Each of the twelve reading and writing assignments of the seeing sequence is accompanied by at least one fictional sketch (Assignments 1, 4, 5, and 12 are accompanied by two). These in aggregate also form a sequence, though one that is narrative or novelistic in nature, and as noted focuses on the experiences of a class of 15 students with the twelve seeing assignments as taught by their teacher.

The individual members of this invented class are varied in life experiences, interests, and abilities. Some of them are traditional col-

lege freshmen, people somewhere around the age of 18 who are attending college straight from high school. But there are also other kinds
of students. One, for example, technically a sophomore, a married
woman with two small children, has returned to college after having
dropped out 16 years earlier. Another sophomore in this course is a
computer science major on a full scholarship. Still another student,
slightly older than the average, a one-time street tough, is an alcoholic
three years sober through the fellowship of Alcoholics Anonymous. The
class contains science majors, an engineering student, a pre-med, and
also students majoring in the humanities. There are both whiz kids and
students who are more average. There are people who exhibit—sometimes alternately—kindness, stupidity, sentimentality, pettiness, bril-
liance, generosity, nastiness—the whole range of stances that seems
inevitably to accompany any serious attempt to work with, to learn
from, other people.

Like the sequence of reading and writing assignments, the sequence of sketches is also constructed to do something generally and
something specifically at the same time.

Generally, the sketches are constructed to help students better
understand the working of the composing process by modelling it in
human terms, as something that people do. Alice Walker, in an essay
printed as part of Writing Assignment 8 in this text, explains the importance of this sort of modelling by noting that "models in art, in behavior,
in growth of spirit and intellect—even if rejected—enrich and enlarge
one's view of existence." "Even if rejected" is the important qualifying
phrase to bear in mind when working with the sketches in this book,
because all of them are created to demand that students learn as writers
by having to position themselves as readers with dramatizations of the
composing process that can be, will be, should be variously evaluated.
Whether a dramatization is of a single student in dialogue with herself
(Amy, John, Karen, Mark), or a pair of students in dialogue with each
other (Pat and Lou, Betty and Sandy), or a group of students in conversation (Study Groups I, II, and III), there is no teacher or any other kind of
authority trotted into a scene to settle things, no one ever brought into
any of the sketches empowered to declare definitively that one set of
observations about a piece of writing makes sense and another does
not, that a particular writer is working efficiently or is spinning her
wheels, that this way of talking about that arrangement of sentences,
either to oneself or to others, is valuable whereas that way of talking
isn't. Such judgments must of course be made in order for readers to
locate themselves with the material in the sketches, but it is important
to remember that what some teachers and students may consider an
example of good conversation about writing others may consider limited, useful only in a way, or even pointless in its entirety. This is in-

tended. The sketches exist in general only to provide terms for the sorts of conversations that can enrich and enlarge the conversationalists' understanding of the composing process.

What is true for the arguments in the sketches is true for the characters in them as well. Some teachers and students might find a character like Charles attractive, for example, bright and incisive. Others might see him as a wimp and a bore. And then of course there is the Gorgon.

The Gorgon, it must be remembered, like all the other "people" in the sketches, is not a person at all. He also is a character, and all sorts of judgments about him are possible. Possible at the same time they must be suspect. For the Gorgon never appears in person. All we really know of him is secondhand, and undefinitive in any case, a matter of hearsay, rumor, recollection, mythology, what's on the wire. We have his course description to be sure, but what do we have in having that? The utterance of an egotist, or an expression of care and caring? The students' money's worth, or idiosyncrasy, quirkiness ("What's he talk like that for?")? Is the Gorgon a monster who delights, as one member of his class seems to believe, in freezing students to stone? Or is he rather, as another student says that the etymology of his nickname suggests, someone in the service of Wisdom, seeking only to make brutishness plain for what it is? The Gorgon of this text, in other words, and deliberately of course, is knowable only as he is experienced, and the experience of different teachers and students with that will be different.

In addition to their general function, the sketches are constructed to provide teachers and students with the opportunity for conversations about the kinds of writing problems that serious writers have to address in one way or another over and over again. How do you go about finding something to say as a writer, for example? How do you develop a strategy for saying what you want to say once you've made up your mind what that is? Do you use notes, or construct an outline, or what? Or do you write drafts? And what exactly is a draft anyway? What can be said about good ways to take notes or compose drafts? How can you use such things to help you say what you want to say correctly, effectively, gracefully? How about editing? What's that and how and when do you do it? How do you write about something you read? That is, how do you quote or make reference to something, not just accurately but convincingly, with authority? How do you use other readers and writers to help you say what you have to say better? What's a good conversation about writing, in other words, and what isn't? And then of course there's revision, doing it over, doing it again, fusing sentences, tightening connections, making what's muddy clear, making what sounds dumb sound smart, recasting, rearranging, adding stuff. How do you go about doing all that?

These are real questions, it seems to me—and the list could be extended—about real writing issues for both teachers and students, but they are difficult to address in the abstract very helpfully, first because any one of them has a way of involving all the others, and second because there's no way of addressing any of them raised about a particular writer's particular writing situation that the specifics of another writer's writing situation might not invalidate.

For these reasons, the particular writing problems that the sketches are specifically designed to help teachers and students talk about are never considered just once in the sketches, or in just one way, or in isolation from other concerns. Take, for instance, revision.

In *Seeing Assignment 2*, a group of students work at revising a paper, in part to eliminate error, but also for organization and tone—and with different students taking different positions on what's really wrong with the paper and what ought to be done about it. In *Seeing Assignment 3*, a different group of students examine a paper that has already *been* revised, and not just once but twice. One of the sketches accompanying Assignment 5 shows a single student revising not a whole paper, but only a paragraph of it, and for a different rhetorical problem than those examined at Assignments 2 and 3. In *Seeing Assignment 6*, still another student is shown in the act of revising, but this time it is an entire paper being recast from a whole new perspective. Revision is also an issue, though differently, in the sketches accompanying Assignments 9 and 12. Similarly, clarity and conciseness are rhetorical issues considered in the sketches accompanying Writing Assignments 3, 4, 5, and 12. Prewriting is taken up in the sketches accompanying Writing Assignments 5, 6, 7, 8, 9, and 11; editing in *Seeing Assignments 2, 3, 4, 5,* and *12;* and so forth.

Flexibility of the Text

All of the material in *Seeing Through Writing* has already been taught several times by a number of teachers in addition to myself and revised on the basis of our experience with it. Some of these teachers were relatively new to the teaching of writing, whereas others had extensive teaching experience. The classes involved included honors sections and evening sections for continuing education students as well as traditional daytime undergraduate classes. The breadth of this testing of the assignments forms the basis for my confidence that teachers and students anywhere can use the material of this book just as it is written and with every expectation of educational success.

This does not mean, however, that the printed assignments ought to be considered canonical. Other teachers, working either in groups or by themselves, may well decide to revise the assignments further as the style of a teacher, the length of a term, the requirements of a course, or the level of a class determines. Some teachers, for example, may have their students focus on a single question in an assignment rather than on the assignment as a totality. Other teachers may find their purposes better served by asking different questions about the material provided, or by substituting different readings for those offered. And of course there may be assignments that some teachers may choose not to use at all.

The sketches written to accompany the twelve reading and writing assignments may be used as no more than deep background in a course. The sequence of assignments does not depend on them in any way. But if the sketches are considered in a classroom, it will very quickly become obvious that the same options are available with them as with any body of readings. They can be used in conjunction with other readings: essays, poems, short stories, novels. They can be used to emphasize or question issues raised in the assignments. They can be praised for what readers can find praiseworthy or helpful in them and objected to for what seems objectionable. The point is that discussing the sketches at all makes more reflective consideration of the composing process possible.

Sources and Acknowledgments

Everything in this book not specifically attributed to a particular someone—characters, events, pieces of discourse—should be considered fiction. The book is based, of course, on my experience as a teacher, but on experience that I have freely edited and adapted as I believed it necessary for pedagogical and dramatic clarity. I am indebted to my students for granting me permission to edit my relationship with them and their work in this way. With them and for them I have written the kind of book that, in Alice Walker's lovely adaptation of a remark by Toni Morrison, I'd like to read. And just for the record, in the sense that, as Alice Walker goes on to say, "to write the books one wants to read is both to point the direction of vision and at the same time to follow it," I want my students to know that the doing of *Seeing Through Writing* was a privilege, and is their gift to me.

Specifically, I am grateful to: Michael Albert, Sophia Andreasson, Julie Beley, Marcia Bisnette, Lisa Borman (A No Namus), Lisa Boyle, Ann Cifra, Jackie Corey, Waverly Deutsch, Lisa Falensky, Greg Febbraro, Patrick Freeman, Neil Glagovich, Diana Goubeaud, Richard Guszcynski, Fred Hann, Taylor Harrison, Michael Hughes, Brian Kane, Laurie Kaplan, Bonnie Kartzman, Mary Kelley, Steve Kisak, Beth Lazzara, Patrick Madden, Eric Maisel, Therese Mambuca, Paul Marcoz, Eileen Martin, Lisa Miller, Lara Mikulaninec, Maureen Morrissey, Mary-Alice Olson, Renay

Oshop, Maria Oyaski, Steve Parks, Sandra Perez, Monica Perz, Debbie Polignone, Cheryl Polkosky, Dan Punday, Sandeep Rahangdale, Carolyn Rapaport, Thomas Reape, Amy Reznik, Lyneé Richel, Frank Ricciuti, John Schulman, Mark Shreffler, Thomas Smuts, Carl Stachew, Sharon Strong, John Young, and Phil Zarone.

A great many other people were important in different ways to my thinking and writing about the issues I raise in this book, and it is a pleasure to acknowledge their assistance as well. I am grateful:

to Gail Albracht and Glynda Hull, who kept me on track and refused to lie to me about my writing, even when they knew I wished them to.

to Marianne Davis and Stephanie Dobler and Linda Robertson, to John and Tillie Warnock—good readers all, and good teachers and good friends. They gave me courage.

to Bob Holland who listened and listens to me, and who tells me straight what he hears me saying. Always.

to Phil Leininger and John Wright, who believed in this enterprise, and who bet on it and on me.

to Karen Miyares, lavender and silver, bringer of light, healer.

to Ivan. They endured.

to the Community College system of Minnesota, where real teaching and learning go on. Much of this book the faculties and administrators of the 18 colleges listened to and gave me a chance to refine. They are friends I value and will keep.

to Professors Donald M. Murray of the University of New Hampshire, John Warnock of the University of Wyoming, and Richard E. Young of Carnegie Mellon University for their thoughtful readings of the manuscript of this book.

to Rita Capezzi, Syd Coppersmith, Elizabeth Drescher, Don Dunham, Mary Hall, Bill Hendricks, Monette Tiernan, Jim Villani, and Margaret Wyda for teaching the assignments of *Seeing Through Writing* in their classes and sharing their suggestions for revision with me.

to the staff of Harper & Row for their help, support, and encouragement, particularly to Lucy Rosendahl, sponsoring editor, and to Jo-Ann Goldfarb, project editor, workers of magic.

And most of all to Janet, for most of all.

William E. Coles, Jr.
University of Pittsburgh

Seeing
English 101

THE COURSE

ENGLISH 101: COMPOSITION

A course designed to enable students to improve their abilities
as readers and writers. Open to all undergraduates. No prerequi-
sites. 3 hours credit. Staff.

The College Catalog of Course Offerings

THE GORGON'S SECTION

"I don't know for sure where he got the nickname. The Gorgon's a monster in some old Greek stories that was supposed to turn you to stone if you looked at it. But then I heard some guy say that that was only part of it, that it was more complicated than that. I really don't know."

*   *   *

She looked up quickly from her edition of the fall course offerings to look directly at her roommate.

"You're not really going to take old Gorgy on, are you?"

"I was thinking of it. Marilyn took his section of the course last year. She said it was good, that she got a lot out of it."

She just stared at her roommate for a minute.

"Marilyn runs too, did you know that? Every day. At six in the morning."

*   *   *

"Oh, you hear different stuff, depending on who you talk to. He's in there for real I guess, the Gorgon. Everybody says that. I do get a little sick of being told I just have to *experience* it all to *really* understand, though. Like it was sex or something."

2

*   *   *

"You know what Tess said when somebody asked her that about his class? This is what I *heard* she said anyway, up in the Honors Center. She said a month after the course was over she found she liked eating raw tomatoes again. She said she hadn't liked eating raw tomatoes since she was a little girl. Of course you know Tess."

*   *   *

"Oh there're all kinds of Gorgon stories. I heard one kid one time tried to get out of something saying he worked, or had to go to work, or something like that. Anyway, the Gorg told the kid—right there in class too—that maybe he ought to wear a little yellow sign like the ones that say BABY ON BOARD. That way everybody'd know how special he was."

*   *   *

"So this is the famous course description, is it? He gives you this on the first day? What makes him think people are going to read it all?"

"Oh, you read it. You read it if you want to stay in the Gorgon's section. He tells you when he gives it out, see, that he's going to give a true–false quiz on it the next period. He tells you he'll say how many answers you have wrong, but he won't tell you what ones. You have to find what you had wrong and write out why it was wrong. It's a little bastard of a quiz too. He calls it the first lesson in reading and writing."

THE GORGON'S
COURSE DESCRIPTION

English 101 is described in *The College Catalog* as a staff-taught composition course "designed to enable students to improve their abilities
as readers and writers." "Staff-taught" in this case means that those of
us who teach English 101 have elected to work with a common body
of material in the form of 12 writing assignments. But because as
individual teachers we will be handling these assignments very differently, be teaching in effect very different English 101 courses, it is a
Departmental policy that every English 101 teacher explain as fully as
possible, and in writing, the assumptions, procedures, and requirements of his or her section. The idea here—transfer from one section
of the course to another is a relatively painless matter—is to provide
students with the kind of information that will enable them to select a
section of English 101 to which they intend to make a commitment.

This statement then, in keeping with our Departmental policy, is my
way of saying something at the outset of our work together about both
the particular requirements of this section of English 101, and my
assumptions about the teaching and learning of writing. In one sense
this statement is a kind of contract, one that specifies what I am going

to expect of all of you who choose to remain in this section of the course, what those of you who do remain may, and may not, expect of me. In another sense this statement may be read as a declaration, my attempt to say some things I believe it is important for you to know about my relation to our subject. When I speak from here on of "the course," please understand that it is this section of English 101 I am referring to. This section only. My course just.

What you should not expect in here is the usual course in expository writing (often seen as the polar opposite of "creative writing," whatever that phrase may mean) in which the student haphazardly writes book reports, impressionistic sketches, essays on international affairs; analyzes the artifacts of pop culture; studies examples of what is called "academic discourse" (whatever *that* phrase may mean); reads bits and snippets of Great Books; and in general goes on doing what she has already done in school. The course you are taking has a subject as well as a structure.

Neither should you expect a course in which the writing assignments are no more than randomly yelled short orders: "Gimme a theme about your summer vacation"; "Describe a tree"; "Construct a well-made argument on the nuclear arms issue, abortion, gay liberation." No. You are beyond the point now where it is enough to assume that knowledge, your knowledge, is a matter of information only, or of Personal Opinion regurgitated at the level of whatever first comes to mind—in response to what you read, as a response with what you write. The assignments in this course you will do best to see as assisted invitations to learning, as ways of modelling the question-asking process intended to help you get better at posing more useful questions for yourself.

Nor should you think of English 101 as only the introduction to other courses given by the Department of English. Rather, our course is part of the college curriculum which is concerned with your general education. It is designed to provide you with a training in method and certain basic approaches to the formulation and addressing of problems. It is designed to increase the range and power of the work you do as a reader and writer. This, after all, is why the faculty as a whole requires English 101 of all students, and recommends that they experience the course early in their college years. No matter what department of knowledge you are concentrating in, this course will have, it is hoped, relevance to your study.

The subject of this section of English 101 is writing, writing understood as an activity of language using that can become a special way of thinking and learning, of someone's coming to know.

I have several reasons for putting things that way.

I want to acknowledge first of all that there are other ways of understanding writing. Writing can be, and has been, seen as the revelation of character, for example, or as a mark of breeding; or at the other end of the scale as a form of communication—sometimes called the Name of the Game. The important thing to bear in mind about the way we are going to be seeing writing is that it does not necessarily deny any of the others. It's a question of focus.

Second, when I say that we will be considering writing as an activity, as that which involves a process as well as a product, I am calling attention to the fact that it is something people do. In a sense it is something people know about, of course, but only in the same more or less general way they know about health or growing up or the ballet. We know, for example, that Good Writing should be Clear, Coherent, and somehow Pleasing to the Reader. But how to make writing clear, coherent, and pleasing is another matter altogether. Many of us know various rules—for the use of the comma, even perhaps for constructing a paragraph (as if it were a building made of building blocks). And many of us know that such knowledge is useless beyond a point. Or that it may sometimes even get in the way.

This is not to say that there is nothing to learn about writing, no rules a student must know. Writing is in some ways a craft, in some ways a skill, and you may not expect to complete this course successfully without demonstrating a certain knowledge of convention and mastery of technique. For this reason, and in addition to what else they are designed to do, the assignments are constructed to enable you to develop a full range of cognitive and compositional skills by putting you in a position to use writing in many different ways. You will write in a number of different modes or forms, for a number of different purposes and audiences. For some assignments you will take notes from which to write a paper, or notes from which to write a draft from which then to write a paper. There are assignments that will require you to make models, to solve problems, to develop the implications of propositions, to compare and contrast, to analyze, describe, argue, define—to do the sorts of things, in other words, that every education, every career, every life demands you be able to do intelligently if you are to happen to the world rather than the other way around.

But you must also bear in mind that no one knows infallibly how to teach another to succeed as a writer, or knows enough to pronounce absolutely that this or that example is a Success. A teacher may praise something that a student has written. Another teacher might well make a different judgment. This may not seem fair, but such is the world once you leave childhood behind. Lawyers, no matter how clearly they present their cases, do not always win. Medical doctors sometimes make diagnoses with which other doctors would disagree. As for literary judgments, there are critics who do not praise *The Faerie Queen* by Edmund Spenser (1552?–1599). There is a wide difference of opinion about Norman Mailer, Joyce Carol Oates, Kurt Vonnegut, and so on. Because these are the givens of our situation in English 101, the best we can do is treat writing—and the writer—with respect and imagination, and, in our conversations about writing and the writer, hope to say something that matters. In the classroom we shall have good moments and moments not so good. Do not expect too much. On the other hand be sure you expect enough.

Third, to focus on writing as a process that can allow a writer to test what she believes in order to discover and develop what she knows is to involve us automatically in the consideration of the activity of reading as well. What it means to write a sentence in English cannot be separated from how one makes words make sense in sentences.

And finally, my referring to writing as an activity of language using is born of my reason for valuing writing in the first place. I value it as a form of language using that can be a uniquely powerful instrument for learning, for change. By "language using" here I am referring to the employment of any system of symbols in order to make sense of the world—the primary means by which all of us run orders through chaos, thereby giving ourselves the identities we have. As language users we name with symbols, creating ourselves as either down we fall or up we grow, moment by moment, in rain and fire, month by year by lifetime, but always with and through the various arrangements of the various languages we have at our command. "The limits of my language," one philosopher has said, "mean the limits of my world." Another has asserted that to command a different language is to be able to inhabit a different universe.

To see writing as a form of this world-ordering, self-ordering process gives me a way of seeing the ability to compose in sentences as an ability to conceptualize, to build structures, to draw inferences, to develop implications, to generalize intelligently—in short to make connections, to work out relationships—between this idea and that idea, words and other words, sentences and other sentences, language and experience. And from this point of view also I have a chance of offering writing to students as an activity of language using that can enable them to become better composers, better conceptualizers, better thinkers in whatever other languages they may work with: mathematical formulas, chemical equations, pigments, gestures, speech. Thus I have a way of offering writing as an avenue to a very special kind of power: the power to choose with awareness, to change and adapt consciously, and in this sense to be able to have a share in determining one's own destiny. And I have a way of suggesting that this power is available not just to those students who *become* writers, whatever may be meant by that, but even to those who are willing to do no more than work at it, to work at imagining what they could do if they were writers. I value writing in the first place because powerlessness is an invitation to victimization.

This way of seeing writing you will experience through a sequence of 12 writing assignments you will be given, one by one. The assignments are referred to as a sequence because each is designed to build upon your experience with earlier assignments in such a way as to help you cope effectively with a present writing task at the same time it prepares you for those of the future.

The nominal subject of the assignments this year is Seeing. This subject will provide you with something to think and write about, and will serve also to give our class conversations a focus, the day by day movement of the course a shape and direction. But the real subject of the assignments as we will be working with them is language, and their real function is to involve you with the activity of language-using, of *composing* in the largest sense of the word: selecting and arranging, putting together, taking apart in order to put together differently. In order to deal with the assignments you will be supplying your own information and material. After all, you have held various jobs perhaps. You have played games. You live in a variety of communities. You read. And for a number of years now you have had your own thoughts and feelings about things. This is your experience and from this entirely individual source you will derive whatever it is you have to say. In this sense, all of the questions of all of the assignments may be understood to involve the same issues: where and how with this problem do you locate your self? To what extent and in what ways is this self definable in language? What is this self on the basis of the language shaping it here? What has it got to do with you?

You should understand that the self being spoken of above, and the one that we will be concerned with in the classroom, is a literary self; not a mock or false self but a stylistic self, the self construable from the way words fall in a conversation or on a page. The other self, your identity as a person, is something with which no teacher as a teacher can have very much to do. That there is a relation between these two selves, between writing and who's doing it, a particular display of mind or sensibility and someone's intellect or being, a very complicated and involving relation indeed—this is undeniable. But the nature of this relation, that of the self to the roles or styles in which it finds expression and through which it grows, is one that only an individual writer or thinker has the right to work out.

Each writing assignment you will find is constructed on what is known as a reflexive principle. You're asked to do something. Then you're asked to do something, or more often some things, with what it is that you've done: to extend the implications of it perhaps, or to see how whatever position you may have taken on one issue enables you to take a position on some other issue. In one assignment, for example, you are asked to present a sketch of parents and children having a difficult time trying to understand each other. Then you are asked to analyze the source of the difficulty. Finally, you are asked to say what you think can be done about the difficulty parents and children seem to have understanding each other—to judge from your sketch, to judge from your analysis of your sketch.

One way of understanding why the assignments are constructed as they are is to see them as putting you in a position to learn something from what you do as a writer—thereby helping you, it is hoped, to develop the habit of self-consciousness (in the most literal sense of the term) that is at the heart of all educational processes. Another way of understanding their construction is to see the assignments as our doing what we can to frame a subject for conversation, an extended, term-long conversation that I will need your help to keep going at a level that is worth our while to maintain. Just as it is difficult to see the value of an extended conversation in which no contribution is imagined to be any better or any worse than any other, it is hard to imagine anyone's getting very much out of a conversation in which all of the real questions, the tough ones, are routinely ducked or trivialized. We have all of us, to be sure, had times in our lives when what we wanted out of Talking Things Over was simply to be agreed with, but a conversation on such occasions was not what we were after. This is to say that if you do your best to see the papers you write as something other than final pronouncements, less a way of closing questions than of keeping them open, you'll put yourself in a position to learn more. The point, after all, of anything anyone would want to call a valuable conversation is the dialogue it forces you to have with yourself.

Though the assignments for this course are arranged, I want to say emphatically that they do not constitute an argument. Beyond assuming that language using (in its broadest sense) is the means by which all of us run orders through chaos thereby giving ourselves the identities we have, they contain no doctrine I am aware of, either individually or as a sequence. Beyond offering writing as an activity of language using in order to provide you with a way of seeing how getting better at writing can have something in it for you, there is no Philosophy in them, either homespun or highflown, that I expect you to become aware of and give back to me. In fact, those of us who put the assignments together were careful to arrange and phrase things precisely to make impossible the discovery in them of anything like a master plan. We put things together in such a way as to mean only and no more than what the various responses they evoke can be made to mean, a meaning that will be different for different teachers and students as well as differently come by. It was only by acknowledging and making allowances for such differences that it was possible for us to develop a common set of assignments for English 101 to begin with.

This is not to say, of course, that every pattern, every way of addressing a question, is as good as every other, but it is to say that whatever continuity you construct from assignment to assignment, from one paper to another, from one class discussion to the next, is your continuity and yours alone. It is this continuity, this meaning, which will express also what you make your experience with the subject of composing mean to you. Whatever you learn from your experience with these assignments, you learn. Whatever you make of your awareness of the activity of writing as an activity of language-using is up to you.

I'll read your papers, comment on them, and bring examples of your writing to class to talk about (students' names will never be used either on or in conjunction with any of the writing we consider in class—by you or by me). In your attempts to improve yourself as a writer, to enlarge your understanding of the nature and function of language in your life, I'll help you where possible. But do not expect to be given a formula with which to improve your writing. When it comes to a subject like writing, the best a teacher can do, a course can do, an education can do, is to put you in a position to improve yourself for yourself—and be ready to acknowledge your effort. My regular policy, by the way, is to invite you to rewrite—as many times as you want—any paper with which you are disappointed. (Please, however, do not attempt to revise a paper until you have written at least four.) This is a standing invitation; I will read as many versions of as many papers as you have the energy to produce. When you hand in a rewritten paper include with it the original.

A word on error. I will mark all errors, all non-negotiable mistakes in your papers, the same way, with an X in the margin alongside the line in which a mistake appears, or in the case of a sentence error, with the sentence bracketed and an X alongside that. All errors of this sort must be located, corrected, and the paper returned with your next due writing assignment. You cannot receive credit for this course without demonstrating your ability to write—in your prepared papers—reasonably error-free prose.

One further commitment will be expected of you. At the beginning of the second week of the course you will be assigned to a study group, a group to be made up of you and several other members of this class. Together you will be expected to arrange a time and place to meet at least once a week and for at least an hour and a half throughout the term. At your first meeting each study group will elect a recorder who will be responsible for turning in to me a weekly statement of where your group met, for how long, and who attended the meeting or meetings.

The study groups are probably best thought of as a class within a class. They provide you with an opportunity for an ongoing conversation about writing with fewer participants than in regular class meetings and according to a format that you and the other members of your group design. I will from time to time be giving you material—student papers, quotations—that you may find it profitable to focus on in your study group; occasionally, I may specify that you use your group in a particular way. Most of the time, however, what you consider in your study group and how you go about having a conversation together will be left to individual groups. Though there has been a lot of variation in how it is done, most groups in the past have found it most profitable to focus on the writing of their members in the context of the issues of the writing assignments. Under ordinary circumstances, you will not be permitted to change membership in a study group.

Because so much of what you will be doing in this composition course will be connected with what other people do, it is important that we share some distinctions about how to be responsible to this involvement.

"To present, as one's own work, the ideas, representations, or words of another" is to plagiarize. As everyone knows, plagiarism is a form of cheating. At most colleges and universities such cheating may be punished by failure in a course as well as by suspension or dismissal from the institution. To allow someone else to pass off your written work as their own is another form of the same crime, punishable in the same way. Most cases of deliberate involvement with the act of plagiarism are detected more quickly and dealt with more summarily than the desperate might imagine. Moreover, in most colleges and universities it is not enough that you do not *intend* the representation of ideas or words originating from someone else as originating from you. Even the *appearance* of such misrepresentation can result in the charge of plagiarism. Because the charge of involvement with the act of plagiarism is so serious, then, it is important you learn how to work with the ideas of other people responsibly.

Fortunately, being responsible is largely a matter of following certain conventions, the main principle of which is that when you get something from someone else, you say so. You say what you took, from whom, and under what circumstances the borrowing took place. Recording your indebtedness to the work of others, whether printed or otherwise, means knowing how to quote accurately, to paraphrase responsibly, and to cite sources correctly, all of which you will have the opportunity to learn in this course.

I want to stress, however, that plagiarism is *not* to be confused with the sharing of ideas. All writers get advice from friends and colleagues. In your composition course, for example, as you work at writing a paper, as you move from an initial draft to intermediate drafts to the draft you hand in, I want strongly to encourage you to solicit your classmates' reactions to what you are doing. For most of the term I encourage you also to exchange papers with another student and copyedit each other's work for errors. You are not asking others to do your work for you when you train yourself to copyedit better by going over the work of a fellow student while he or she goes over yours. When you discuss your writing with friends, ask for their comments and suggestions about a draft of a paper, you are not being dishonest. You are not being unoriginal when you develop an interpretation of something as the result of a conversation about it—either in class or out of it. A college, after all, is a place where people are expected to talk about their work and the work of other people, about books and ideas. Evidence of your ability to learn from others, when you are responsible to what helped you learn, is in fact a sign of intellectual vitality and strength. Be sure to indicate your indebtedness to the people who have taken time to talk with you about your work, to read and comment on your paper while it was in progress, on an acknowledgment page attached to your paper.

*Remember, you can never be accused of cheating in a composition course if you take care not to violate the conditions of a particular writing assignment; if you are scrupulous in indicating precisely what form of help you received to write a paper and from whom you received it; and if you observe whatever conventions apply for working with the material of others.**

So far as grades are concerned, though no one with any sense would pretend they are unimportant, I am just as convinced that it is not possible to have an intelligent discussion about them—particularly in a course like this where our subject is a process and where evaluation is necessarily a subjective response to someone's development with the process. Does it help very much to say that excellent work receives an A or that if your stuff comes in late and you don't show up for class you run the risk of being asked to withdraw from the course? This is, after all, a college. You are, after all, a college student.

I can tell you that no one can receive credit for this course without turning in *all* of the written work assigned for it and showing up for class regularly. I can say also that though a record of your written work will be kept, I won't place grades on individual papers.

Talking over your work with you, having a conversation about your development as a writer, doing all I can to make you aware of where

---

*For the distinctions above between plagiarism and the sharing of ideas I am indebted to a document written by my colleague, William Hendricks of the University of Pittsburgh: *Your Written Work and the Work of Others.*

you are in your work—these of course are different matters, and I'll be glad to arrange conferences with you to discuss them. If you think that using conventional grading terminology in such a context would help you, fine. I'll do the best I can. On the other hand I'd like to be on record as saying that I think we have better ways of talking to one another.

Finally, some practical matters. Provide yourself with a snapback binder. Put in it the mimeographed specimen papers, the assignments, and your own papers, and bring it to class regularly. For all submitted work, use ink on widelined looseleaf paper (I will not read anything written on paper torn out of a spiral notebook) or type double space. Use only *one side* of a page and leave a good margin on all four sides for possible comments. In class, I'll describe a handbook you are to purchase. No other texts are required for this section of English 101.

Assignment 1

WORKING PAPER

Preparation For Writing

There are several purposes for this first writing assignment, or in-class paper, that you will be given about an hour of class time to work on. It will be used in part as an evaluative instrument, as a way of determining, that is, whether your ability to write what is known as edited American English is at a level that will enable you to take on the course successfully. Even though your paper will not be returned to you until later in the term then, it will be read by your instructor the day you have written it and we will consider examples from such papers at our next class meeting.

This writing assignment is also evaluative in another sense, for a second purpose of it is to provide you with the beginning of a record of your development as a writer, a development that you yourself will have a share in gauging. Where you come out as a writer with this course will in some senses have to be measured against where it is you are as a writer now.

Finally, this writing assignment is a way of our starting a conversation about our subject, an extended, term-long conversation in which all of us are participants and that all of us are responsible for maintaining at a worthwhile level.

The relevance of this notion of conversation to the paper you are about to write is to emphasize that you'll do best talking with something other than final pronouncements. Indeed one of the reasons this paper is called a working paper is to suggest that if you consider it a way of keeping questions open rather than an invitation to close them, you'll put yourself in a position to learn more.

You will have 50 minutes to work on this paper. Be sure to give yourself time to prepare and to proofread. Feel free to cross out or make corrections, but do so as neatly as possible. Don't bother spending time recopying your essay.

Writing Your Paper

Although before coming to college most if not all your formal education has been required of you by law, you now have a choice of whether to continue with it or not. And even though you may not have been in college very long, you have possibly speculated, however remotely, on why you are now attending an educational institution instead of doing something else, on what it is you imagine you are doing here, and on the meaning of a formal education in the context of your own life. In fact your presence in this classroom could be said to be based on your assuming that there is something in it for you to attend college, that you are at some sort of A with the intention of moving to some sort of B in a more or less upward direction.

In other words, you are in college because you choose to be here. And you choose to be here, presumably, because you subscribe in some senses to the idea that change is possible, that betterment is possible. For you.

Write a paper in which you do three things:

1. Single out and describe any one positive change that you expect or hope your experience with college will make possible.
2. Explain what you think you're going to have to pay for this change, for your moving from your A (wherever that may be) to your B (whatever that may be).
3. Say what for you, in spite of what you think you're going to have to pay, makes B worth shooting for, makes B worth it to you. When the change is effected, what specifically do you think you'll have gained?

If you make up your mind to try to write this paper intelligently (speaking of what makes things worth it), to face what you know and what you don't, you may find yourself puzzled, uncertain, frustrated.

The first stances it may occur to you to take with the issues here, on reflection, may seem to be less self-explanatory than they appear at first. "I expect to become a thinking adult." Or, "I want to get a good job." Or even, "My desire is to obtain a position upon graduation that will utilize to the fullest the knowledge and skills I . . ." And so forth. For while surely there is nothing wrong with wanting as a result of college to be a better thinker than you are now, or with wanting to learn what you might one day be able to use to earn a comfortable salary, no one with any sense would pretend that the issue of your individual relation to college was that easy to articulate intelligently or that cliches say what needs to be said. Perhaps it might help to remind yourself that just as this is not the first time you have been asked to define yourself as a particular person in a public context, neither will it be the last. And who would you have to become to imagine that the subject of this paper is not one you're going to have to deal with, and for yourself, sooner or later?

Seeing Assignment 1

WORKING PAPER

BETTY

"... any one positive change that you expect or hope your experience with college will make possible."

Oh my God.

And she was to "make up [her] mind to try to write this paper intelligently" when all she really knew was that she hadn't much more than a vague idea of why she'd decided to come back to college at all—particularly given all she had, and knew she had, and after all these years.

Did she *need* to be in college?

No. Not really. She'd worked as a paralegal clerk for one of Pittsburgh's biggest law firms, but a college education without a law degree, or even with one, wouldn't have helped her there very much. Buchman and Buchman's one very showpieced female associate had graduated from Harvard. The firm had no full partners who were women, let alone one that was Black. Besides, she'd already been at the top of the pay scale, college or no college, when she'd quit the firm 8 years ago after the job had run out for her somehow. But Michael had been doing just fine then, and he was doing even better with Westinghouse now. They could plan their finances these days. They didn't have to worry about money the way they once had.

Did she feel she *ought* to be in college?

Because at one time she *had* felt that way, she knew now that that wasn't it either. Not "ought" in the sense she felt she owed somebody something she could pay in no other way. Oh, there had been "oughts" of that sort in her life all right, but she'd made terms, if not peace, with them a long time ago.

She *wanted* to be here then?

Well yes, but there were different kinds of wanting. She didn't want college the way she'd wanted her home, her children, or the way she'd wanted her husband Michael. Had wanted and wanted still, though it had been 16 years since she'd dropped out of college to live with him, to go to work for their lives together while he finished his degree in engineering. She'd been nineteen. It was a want she'd never really understood, fierce as a fever, driving her in shame and quiet terror and in incomprehensible rebellion straight up against and through her father's disapproval, his hurt clawing at her, his bewilderment a twisted image of her own. Her father liked Michael too. He admired him: his dignity, his quickness, his easy sense of humor. And things had been all right at the wedding the summer after Michael's graduation, though she could still remember her father's queer half smile, it had torn her heart for some reason, at Michael's joke during the reception about her being Black. It was something her father had never joked about.

"Well, baby," Michael had kidded her in dialect, "you Black *almos'*. Almos' some*times,* you Black."

Her skin was the color of creamed coffee, her eyes blue. Michael had been raised in an all-black section of Swainsboro, Georgia. "Swines boro" he'd had to hear in the army a lot more than once.

No. She couldn't say she wanted college the way she knew she'd wanted some other things in her life.

Still, she'd wanted to come back.

It wasn't career. She wasn't a career woman (or "career person," as her male personnel manager had learned to say it, and who'd made her smile to herself every time he did). She'd been good at her job, had worked herself up from legal secretary to paralegal clerk, in fact, and with a degree would have been made a paralegal immediately. At least that was the way the firm told her they saw it. But it was law itself that had gone dead for her. Or maybe law as practiced by the lawyers she worked with. The difference didn't seem to matter much. She'd quit her job without a regret.

Nor was she coming back to college to Find Herself or anything like that. She knew all the phrases, had heard them enough, read them enough. Identity Crisis. Self-fulfillment. Self-discovery. Liberation. If you had to go to college to find yourself, Michael used to say, you were in for one hell of a disappointment the day you did.

Why then? What was she doing here anyway?

What she knew for sure was that she loved what she could remember of being a student, had loved it from the beginning in Greeleyville, South Carolina, where she'd gone through fifth grade, loved it through high school in Pittsburgh after her family moved north, loved her year and a half in college. The very things that had driven so many of her classmates crazy had been a source of satisfaction to her. She had learned to rely on them. The measured periods of class and study, meeting deadlines, reducing lectures to neat legible notes that in tandem with her textbooks could be highlighted at exam time in yellow and blue. Showing her command of the recommended outside readings. Answering questions from her homework, which she'd always done. The cool underwater feel of libraries in hot weather. Finishing books. She'd loved preparing her papers, typing them into finality on creamy, sacred-looking bond, late at night usually, though never at the last minute, and always with a title and a title page, all three of her names centered toward the bottom.

So what was she going to say about a positive change she hoped for from college? That she didn't think of school that way, of college in those terms? That was about as much as she knew of the truth given the queerness of what had decided her to come back finally, what had made up her mind somehow, an event that had nothing to do with the question she was supposed to be dealing with, and that she hadn't even been able to tell Michael about, not completely.

It was coming on that old drawing of hers, done when she was in second grade in Greeleyville, that had got her then from some kind of A to some kind of B.

She'd just got back from taking Carrie to her first day of school. Their second daughter. Their last child. She'd cried on the way home in the car of course—though not, thank God, on the way there—as she'd known she was going to, as she had over Rachel too, laughing at herself both times even as she wept.

What she had not expected and had no way of accounting for was remembering the box. Out of nowhere the thought had come to her while she was waiting at a stop light, and the moment she got home she'd taken the box down from the top of her closet. She'd had to stand on a chair to do it. It was a box full of her own school things, things her mother had saved and saved and given her . . . when? Seven years ago?

Eight? It had been at Thanksgiving anyway. She was pregnant with Rachel. Eight years ago then. "Your children will want this one day," her mother had said, "even if you don't," and Michael had carried it to the car and later put it on the shelf in her closet for her. She'd never opened it. She'd forgotten it even existed.

It was heavier than she'd thought it was going to be, filled to the top with pages and pages of completed arithmetic problems marked with huge A pluses, with mimeographed poems and stories, with word lists copied in huge penciled capital letters:

B A T

B A L L

B A B Y

Her kindergarten diploma, rolled up and tied with a piece of black wool, had been tucked upright in a corner. All her report cards through fifth grade were together in a manila envelope.

And there were pictures, stacks and stacks of pictures.

Most of them were on dittoed sheets made up for children to color in, purple stencil outlines of nursery rhyme characters, or cities, or gardens. Her crayoned responses were predictable. Very neat and predictable. The muffin man's face was orange-yellow, his pastry the color of cornbread. Her skies were blue. The grass of her parks a steady green. Her coloring was always carefully inside the lines. She could remember having worked at that; it had been important to her.

But there were other pictures too, mostly in crayon but sometimes in watercolor or pastels or crayon in strange combinations with smudges of charcoal, pictures that she could not remember, not even vaguely, having done at all. They were freely drawn, all of them, no lines to follow here, and in every instance filled the entire page. They had a rawness about them, a suggestion of violence that shocked her. Some were subjectless so far as she could tell, no more than great savage masses of color that swirled and marched straight to the edges of the paper. But there were pictures of animals too, and of people. In one, an enormous pair of round-eyed, carnivorous-looking cows towered redly over a group of tiny mouthless stick people. In another a flock of serenely flying pigs, lavender and pink, were headed into a net. There were pictures of dogs with mountain peak teeth, of men covered with stars who tended fires that roared black and orange and yellow heat. There were pictures of buttercups and daisies, but coiled like snakes, lethal looking, and taller than houses. And there were many forests and swamps, impenetrable, flowerless, their trees filled with staring eyes.

She had done these? These were hers?

On the backs of many of these pictures she was puzzled at first to see writing, her writing, childish of course but neat and legible, even then.

One set of sentences stopped her for some reason, rolling back her life, rolling her back to the all Black school, her all Black world in Greeleyville:

The white clouds are pretty. There are only 15 people in our room. We will go to gym. We have a new poster. We may go outdoors.

And then she remembered. She refelt the warmth of the occasion of the sentences, of many such occasions, how her teachers had made learning wonderful for her.

"I want y'all t'write fihve senences that make a statement. Anybody git done 'fore the rest kin color."

Standard English taught with Black English. It was the way you learned to speak and write correctly in Greeleyville along about second grade. There was kindergarten. And then there was little first, and then big first, and then there was second grade. "We say," her Black teachers had said, " 'The white clouds *are*,' not 'De white clouds pretty.' We write 'There *are* only 15 people,' not 'Th' ain't but 15 people in our room.' " There had been no disjunction in any of that for her, nothing unnatural.

Her sentences were perfect. They had made her smile that morning sitting on their bed, her past spread out around her like a sea. Five perfect sentences in perfect English, finished she was sure before any of the other children had finished theirs, because she could remember always finishing her work before the other children. She'd worked at that too, at finishing first, earning the right to color. Still smiling she'd turned the paper over.

It had come inside her like a fist, what she had drawn there. Enclosed in a circle in the middle of the page were three hearts and a sun, the hearts a riot of blues and greens and oranges and gay reds, the sun smiling, radiant, embracing the hearts in rays of yellow-purple love. But the whole of the rest of the page, everything outside that frail circle of protection, was covered with a blood black rain of darts, driving in on the hearts and sun from all sides, from every direction, terrible in their fury it seemed to her, relentless, inescapable, annihilating.

What was this? Oh, what was this?

And then she had fallen as from a blow, straight across their bed, in a flood of tears, sobbed out of a part of her she hadn't known existed, tears from a depth she could not have begun to explain, not to Michael, not to herself, not then and not now. It was that night at dinner though, that she had told him she wanted to go back to school. She had explained it by saying only, and somewhat guiltily, feeling as though she were lying even though she knew she wasn't, that she felt like studying again. She hadn't mentioned any of the rest of it, not the tears or the pictures or even that she'd opened the box her mother had given her. And here she was, here, now, with the subject of one positive change she hoped college would produce in her life. Well, she could say what she knew. She could try anyway. She began to write.*

BETTY'S PAPER FOR ASSIGNMENT 1

Though it probably seems strange to say so, the change I hope for most coming back to college has to do with an attitude toward myself. I don't mean that I consider myself stupid or ever uninformed. It's just that it's important to me to finish what I start.

I am the mother of two small children, the second of which started school just this September. My husband has a job at Westinghouse that he's good at. Westinghouse seems to like him. I don't have to work now the way I did when we were first married. I could just stay home now if I wanted. I don't think I'd get fat or just disappear either. I'd probably watch some television, but I've never been addicted to it and I've always liked to read.

~~But it~~ On the other hand, my being here doesn't

---

*For the details of my description of the teaching of English in Greeleyville, South Carolina, and for her permission to make use of her experience with them, I am indebted to my colleague, Barbara Mellix of the University of Pittsburgh.

come for free for sure. We've had to cut some corners financially. I have to arrange my day so that I get time away from both my kids and my husband to study. I'm not preparing for a better job than I could have right now if I went back to work as a paralegal secretary.

So why am I back after leaving college the middle of my sophomore year over ten years ago to get married and build a home? That's a good question. It is a better one than I thought it was when I started this paper. I need ~~entirely~~ ~~pro~~ discipline. I read, yes,

but ~~I need to~~ (time)

talk (people)

~~To somebody to my~~

~~security~~ (for me

color in my

Time!

LOU

"... in a more or less upward direction."

I wonder what you'd say if you knew the half of it, Gorgy, which I got no intention of spilling my guts over not because *I* particularly give a shit one way or another, but because they told me not to—that I had to remember that the flip side of the ego that kept you out of AA for so long is the guy who can't talk to anybody without having to tell them how solid he is in the Program and what a star he is now that he's got sober and humble and all grown up, and what about you, pal? How about a little help with *your* life from the guy who's been there and gone?

You don't play wooden leg out there with your alcoholism, Marty my sponsor tells me. But you don't play superman either.

I feel sometimes like I want to remind Marty that I've already been sober almost three years in AA, and that there are *some* things I understand. But I know how he gets when I get like that. When he asked me about the tutors I hired last year to get me ready to take the tests to get into school, I told him that now that I was sober I figured I was ready to step into life. Oh you're sober all right, he said, stark raving sober. And then he told me I had the best half-assed understanding of life he'd ever seen. But that's O.K. That's just the way Marty talks. I wouldn't be back in school if he didn't think it was a good idea. I know I need him the same way I know I need AA.

Hey. How about this Gorgon? Would you call a miracle a move in a more or less upward direction? Because that's what it was in my case, plain and simple.

I was bad. I was no punk ass kid fresh out of the burbs stoned in somebody's game room on Saturday night with a bunch of chicks in cashmere sweaters who brushed their teeth with Top Job. No way, Jose. I was a punk a long time before being a punk was fashionable. Sometimes I even think I invented it. I could palm cards and shoot dice and pool and shoot hop too, and I rapped shit and had that glide in my stride and I could steal and fight and all that noise. By ninth grade I was a professional. I mean, I worked at it all, the same way I once worked at little league and for a while, real early on, at being a straight A student. Can you believe that? Me, Lou Smuckbagger Rozetti, Angle-oo on the street by name and reputation. Can you believe I was once a straight A student? It's true, though. It was always important for me to be something. Even Marty says I spent half my life making myself up. He says I spent the other half changing my mind.

Anyway, I was bounced out of ninth grade twice and then bounced around a couple of schools on the north side. As a discipline problem they called it, which I was, which was easy to be when you hated school the way I did, and your teachers hated school, and everybody hated school, and so they threw me into vocational. Vocational was a joke, a garbage can without a lid and everybody knew it. They sent all the misfits there. All the losers. And all you had to do was show up occasionally for a couple of years and then they told you you'd done your time and they threw you out so they could bring in more garbage. That's where I got with The Cemetery Gang.

I worked at that too. I got the bandana and the engineer's boots and the wallet on the chain and the bunch of keys at my belt and I became bad, man. We were bad together, me and B-B Eyes and Fast Fang and Jimmy and the rest. The kings of the losers. The cream of the scum. We were The Cemetery Gang.

I was headed no where, of course, a victim of my own beliefs (Marty says I was a victim of not having any), but it didn't feel that way because we had each other. I mean it felt like we had each other: I know now we didn't really. Marty says that all we had was the idea of having each other. But it *felt* like we had each other stealing, wheeling and dealing, because we had the wine and we had the cemetery and that's why they called us The Cemetery Gang. I mean we lived there in the summertime. All night we'd hang there sometimes, just sitting up against the side of this one vault in a little hollow there, just listening to the summer in the woods down at the bottom of the hill, watching the stars, drifting on Thunderbird or whatever we'd scrounged. It felt good. It felt like nobody knew where we were and all there was was sky and all you could smell was the grass. B-B Eyes always wore a pair of handcuffs up there. He'd even pass out and sleep wearing them. He said they made him feel alive somehow being right there in the middle of all those people who weren't.

It didn't last though. Eddie got the jerries one night up there. F M Eddie we called him because he used to wear those earphones all the time until he got to where he said he didn't need them anymore, that he could hear music all the time without them. So we called him F M Eddie. He got the rams right there in the cemetery and we got the cops and they took him to the hospital. He was blue then, and the doctor kept saying I don't believe it, I don't believe it. This young? I just can't believe it. And we just laughed and spit and told all the nurses *they'd* better believe it and stood around with our thumbs hooked in our back pockets and then they told us he was dead. Who's his family they wanted to know. Where's his family? And B-B Eyes told them Eddie's family was lost, that all our families were lost and that that's why we lived in the cemetery where you knew where things were, so we wouldn't get lost too.

They took us to the slammer then and kept us apart. Detention. And so what the hell, I figured. All it could mean was court again and another goddam disposition. One more system to psych out and crash. I didn't think I gave a shit one way or the other then, because I'd been through so much of it all before. My mother was only in court because she had to be. All she did was shake her head. She told me later that for a year she'd tried to imagine me dead. Just like your father, she said. It was easier she said than trying to think of me alive.

I see now that a lot more of all that was eating me up a lot more than I could admit to anybody, myself included, especially myself, which I guess is why I listened to Marty. Maybe I'd have listened to anybody then, but it's hard for me to believe that, because it was the way he started with me that caught me.

You know, he said, the worst part for me about drinking wine when it was nice out and I could get off where nobody would bother me, was remembering to save some for the morning. I mean I could *remember*, he said, but I could never do it. And every time I was sorry in the morning. My God was I sorry in the morning. But I still couldn't ever save any.

A guy talks like that has been there.

But he was somewhere else too then, and somebody, and I could feel it, and that's where I started.

And it was a miracle.

Because Marty told me later that he'd talked to all of us that same morning after court, all of us separately, and all of us the same way, he said. And B-B Eyes didn't hear him. And Jimmy is dead now; I hear he hung himself up at Hawthorne. And Fast Fang is crawling around Federal Street somewhere. And I don't even know about the others. I opted for White Deer Run rehab and it's three years later now and I'm still sober and I'm in college. Marty says that it's not *just* disrespectful for me to say I'm lucky. In your case, he says, that's downright stupid. I know he's right.

I catch onto things fast, as you'll see, Gorgon. I got on good in AA right from the start and it's been good to me. It wasn't even so bad doing what they told me to do, though none of it made any sense, because my M.O. has always been to start things that way, pretending to listen, pretending to fit in, all the time just wanting to run my own number. Marty says I'm a good speed reader. Well, what the hell. They didn't call me Angle-oo for nothing. What's really unbelievable though is that I've stayed with it, and that the things they told me I'd come to believe I've started to believe. Just bring the body, Marty says. The mind will follow. And it happened. It's happening. AA is the only thing in my life that ever worked for me just the way people told me it would. I finished high school living in a half-way house. I got tutors to get me through the College Boards, which is how I got here: Angle-oo Smuckbagger Rozetti, college student. Can you believe it? Marty says I may be the only guy ever to go to college convinced he already knows everything he's supposed to be there to learn, but I know he's proud of me. And I'll make him prouder. Him and my mother both. This place can't be as hard to do as White Deer Run or the Butler Half-Way House, and the Program got me through them just as slick as oil. I'm on my way Gorgon pal, and you bet in a more or less upward direction. And it's a lot more than just one positive change I have in mind.

He began to write.*

LOU'S PAPER FOR ASSIGNMENT 1

[handwritten notes]

dependant → individ.
lose security → freedom/adult
pain

sheltered dep. → free, self-reliant, control
(per. authority)
means / pain / stress from change.
but / Adulthood worth it →

One positive change that college will help me to work in my out life will be to the th transition from a chil sheltered dependant to a fre self-contai fully cognizent, self-relia free individual. This change will enable me to fully control my own life. I will no longer be regulated by the authority fig of my

---

*For some of the phraseology in this sketch, I am indebted to the work of Mr. Courteney Wayshak as represented in Coles and Vopat, *What Makes Writing Good: A Multiperspective,* D. C. Heath and Company, 1985, pp. 21–22.

parents & and relatives. This change, however, will be accompanied by &n a sacrifice

The payment for the transition into individual adulthood will be the loss of the complete security of childhood. Once total freedom is acheived, one becomes fully accountable as an indivdual for his actions. There will be many more payments, x I am during the transition, in the form of stress and agonies caused by stress. These payments will be the inevitable results of changing, and of realizing that one has changed too much or that one is not changing quickly enough. These payments undoubtedly will be painful, yet the promise of self-awareness makes the goal of adulthood worth attempting.

Adulthood with its full freedom and responsibility, and cognizance, is a goal worth any price to me. When adulthood is attained, I will have the ability to live life fully and to be totally self-aware. This property of being self-aware is what I most desire from adulthood, and what makes the phase of change worth enduring.

Assignment 2

We are all familiar with the cliches that suggest that the same things can look different to different people. "Depending upon one's point of view," we hear, or "Well, I see it another way." Variants of the metaphor come easily to mind. "Different strokes for different folks." Talk of "bags" or "scenes." Being "into" this or that. And so on. Advertising, the object of which is to make everybody buy what is bought by everybody else, often ingeniously asserts that to allow one's self to be manipulated in this way is really to be an individual, someone who is said to "think for him or herself." A number of popular songs, designed, of course, for mass consumption, do much the same sort of thing. No wonder that variants of the idea come so easily to mind. We're assured enough, and in enough ways, that we see differently simply because we *are* different— an assumption that such talk would not be such talk were we supposed to question it.

The assumption is one we'll be considering later.

In this assignment, however, we're going to be considering some of the ways in which the process of seeing may be said to be the *same* for all of us of normal physiology.

You are going to be working with a statement about how we see.

Chances are you will have to read it more than once. Such is the case with many of the worlds of discourse you will be experiencing in your years as a college student. Particular disciplines often make use of special ways of talking about particular phenomena, ways of talking that are not always easy to understand immediately. It is, of course, possible to seek to evade the difficulties of such special ways of talking by reducing them to catch-phrases, cliches, but for such an evasion a reader pays a price.

One function of a college education, an education in which composition is usually a required course, is to enable you to read such texts without cheating yourself of their richness, but without putting you in the position of having simply to give up in the face of the difficulties that richness often involves. This is done in part by helping you to see that you are not as stymied by such difficulties as you may at first be tempted to think, and in part by enabling you to understand the value to a reflective person of being able to read and to write such texts with confidence. Here is the statement about how we see:

> Information about the world enters the mind not as raw data but as highly abstract structures that are the result of a preconscious set of step-by-step transformations of the sensory input. Each transformation step involves the selective destruction of information, according to a program that preexists in the brain. Any set of primary sense data becomes meaningful only after a series of such operations performed on it has transformed the data set into a pattern that matches preexisting mental structure.*

Suppose a friend of yours said this to you about that paragraph:

> I'm not sure I understand what's being said here, but if I do, I don't see how it could be important to know about. How does this person know, first of all, that there is "a program that preexists in the brain"? What is this "program" anyway? What principles does it seem to work on? Is he saying that the brain is a computer or what? And finally, if there is a "program," so what? What difference could knowing about it or how it works make to anybody?

---

*Gunther S. Stent, "Cellular Communication," *Scientific American* 227, no. 3 (September 1972), pp 50–51. Reprinted by permission of *Scientific American.*

Your assignment for this paper is to use the following information to write a response to your friend's question.

Here is a simple three-step experiment:

1. Stand before an ordinary bathroom mirror. What would you say is the relationship (in size) of the shape of your head in the mirror to your actual head? Is the head you are seeing larger than or smaller than or the same size as your actual head?
2. Now, allow the mirror to become clouded with a little steam. Trace the outline of your head on the surface of the mirror with your finger and then clear the steam from the area inside the outline of steam. What is the relationship (in size) of the shape you have made on the mirror to your actual head?
3. Clear the mirror and again stand before it. What do you know about the relationship (in size) of the shape of your head as you see it in the mirror to your real head now? What do you see?

This experiment makes clear that when it comes to looking in a mirror, though we can know perfectly well that our eyes are seeing a world that is exactly half the size of the world being reflected in the mirror, our brains will insist that we are seeing things full size. We're having what's called an illusion. We can know that. It can even be explained with a geometrical proof. But when we look in a mirror we go right on having the same old illusion anyway. In spite of the evidence. In spite of what we know. Our brains seem to have done something with what's Really There in order that we may "see" something else.

Just what this "something" is that the brain seems to have a tendency to do when confronted with new information is taken up by a famous art historian named E. H. Gombrich. A number of famous ancient artists, Gombrich points out, have made a mistake in their drawings of horses. They portray horses with eyelashes on their lower eyelids, a feature of the human eye certainly, but not of a horse's eye. Similarly, a famous engraving of a whale washed ashore at Ancona, Italy in 1601 (see Figure 2.1), a picture that the artist claims to have drawn "accurately from nature," shows a whale not with flippers, but with its flippers turned into a pair of gigantic ears.

And then there is the strange history of the rhinoceros as represented in art and also in zoological literature. One of the most influential drawings of the animal, done by Albrecht Dürer in 1515, shows a

Figure 2.1   Figure 2.2

Figure 2.3   Figure 2.4

member of the Indian species (one-horned) with a small extra dorsal horn, spiraled, as the horns of unicorns were traditionally represented, and dressed in plated armour (see Figure 2.2). The mistakes are understandable. Dürer had never himself seen a rhinoceros but was working from a rough sketch and brief description of someone who had. (The Indian rhinoceros, unlike the African, has a heavily folded skin. Perhaps this is the source of Dürer's armour plating, or this in some combination with the many pictures Dürer must have seen of dragons who were represented as having armoured bodies?) Yet Dürer's representation of the rhinoceros with its two obvious mistakes remained the model for most other drawings of the rhinoceros in Europe for well over two hundred years—even in natural history books and even when the drawings were done by people who *had* seen rhinoceroses.

In 1790 an explorer of Africa, James Bruce, published a drawing of the rhinoceros (see Figure 2.3) and proudly announced his awareness of Dürer's influence. He is very harsh, not only in his criticism of Dürer's woodcut ("ill-executed in all its parts"), but of what he calls the "prejudices" and inaccuracies of all other representations of the beast (many modeled on Dürer's). People simply hadn't been attentive enough, he suggests disdainfully, simply hadn't seen what was there to be seen. Here, however, in the engraving done for *his* book *(Travels to Discover the Source of the Nile),* Bruce is making available to the public a picture to be trusted, one of an African or two-horned rhinoceros to be sure, but "designed from the life," the real thing, and for the first time. And there the rhinoceros from Bruce's book is, just as advertised, an African, free from Dürer's dorsal horn certainly—but an African rhinoceros with an *Indian* rhinoceros's body, still wearing, that is, the same nonexistent armour plating that Dürer had clothed it in originally! (See Figure 2.4, photograph of an African rhinoceros.) (See also E. H. Gombrich, *Art and Illusion,* Phaidon Press, London, 3rd edition, 1968, pp. 69–72.)

NOTE: As you plan your paper, please bear in mind that "friend" here means friend. Not boob. Not blackboard. You'll want to say something to your friend about *what you conclude from* having done the experiment you perform with the mirror of course, about *what you conclude from* looking at the pictures you are being given in the context of what you are told about them. But it's only fair to assume that your friend wants a conversation rather than to be put down with a lot of talk that will suggest only that you've read and done some things he or she hasn't. You're being given some information in the paragraphs above. In writing your paper, however, the important thing will be what *use* you make of this information, what you see such information amounting to or meaning so far as your friend's questions are concerned.

Seeing
Assignment 2

STUDY GROUP I

It was almost 3:15 and Karen still hadn't arrived. Nobody yet had enough of a sense of what they were supposed to be doing or knew anybody else in the group well enough to be anything but uncomfortable.

They'd agreed right after the class in which the study groups had been assigned to hold their first meeting in Lounge C of the Tower on Wednesday from 3:00 to 4:30. It was Charles who'd proposed the lounge, saying it was usually pretty empty late in the afternoons on weekdays. Charles was a sophomore (along with Betty), and was living in the Tower for his second year. The rest of them were first term freshmen.

"Why don't we meet just to talk about Assignment 2," he'd said, "and see how it goes?"

It wasn't going at all.

"Well," Charles said nervously, "I guess maybe Karen isn't coming." He then gave each of them a copy of a paragraph from a book he'd been reading, one that seemed to him, he said, to have to do with the same thing the assignment was talking about.

"Of course we don't have to go at things this way," he said. "I knew about the Gorgon's study groups when I signed up for the course but

I've never been in one before. I just thought this might be something to get us started. So, see what you think."

Mature awareness is possible only when I have digested and compensated for the biases and prejudices that are the residue of my personal history. Awareness of what presents itself to me involves a double movement of attention: silencing the familiar and welcoming the strange. Each time I approach a strange object, person, or event, I have a tendency to let my present needs, past experience, or expectations for the future determine what I will see. If I am to appreciate the uniqueness of any datum, I must be sufficiently aware of my preconceived ideas and characteristic emotional distortions to bracket them long enough to welcome strangeness and novelty into my perceptual world. This discipline of bracketing, compensating, or silencing requires sophisticated self-knowledge and courageous honesty. Yet, without this discipline each present moment is only the repetition of something already seen or experienced. In order for genuine novelty to emerge, for the unique presence of things, persons, or events to take root in me, I must undergo a decentralization of the ego.

Sam Keen,
To A Dancing God

They were in the middle of reading the paragraph when the door of the lounge burst open, and Karen swept in, as distracting as a rattle of hail. She was blond, very pretty, and knew it.

"Hi guys," she said flouncing to a seat. "I'm really sorry I'm late. I get totally lost in this place. I thought we said Lounge D. I'm really terrible about new places. Did I miss anything so far? What's this?'' she said, picking up one of Charles' photocopied sheets from the coffee table. ''Whose is this?''

Charles explained.

''Super,'' she said. ''O.K.'' and turned herself to the paragraph, holding and reading it as though it were a menu.

''Wow,'' she said after reading the paragraph through quickly. ''Far out. I can see why Chuck says this is about the assignment though. In fact I say a lot of the same things in my paper.''

Everyone was looking at her.

''Um, look,'' she began, and then paused, and then began again. ''Look,'' she said brightly, ''does everybody know everybody else's names? I'm just terrible with names. Chuck I remember and let's see, you're Betty, aren't you?''

Betty said she was.

And then Lou told her he was Lou and Charles said he was Charles. Or Charlie. Not Chuck, please.

Pat, who was smoking, simply waited, half smiling, watching her.

''And you're . . . you're Pam?'' Karen asked her.

''I'm Pat,'' Pat said, stubbing out her cigarette.

''Was anybody else freaked out by this assignment? I mean it totally freaked me out, really.'' She pronounced it ''rilly.'' ''All that stuff about the rhinoceroses and mirror. It just blew me away at first. I mean I couldn't even find the topic for a while, could you? I think the Gorgon's just showing off.''

''Well,'' Charles said, ''that's not just the Gorgon. They use the same assignments in all the sections of English 101. It's supposed to be a course in reading and writing both sort of, do you see?''

''I don't see why the topics have to be this blah, blah, blah though,'' Karen sniffed. ''I think these 101 teachers are just showing off. We don't need to be impressed with all this stuff in here. I mean come on.''

''I thought the rhinoceros thing was interesting,'' Lou said. ''And I never knew that about the mirror. Did you try it? I went and tried it. I even told my roommate about it.''

''Well, I've got better things to do than stand around in front of bathroom mirrors,'' Karen said sniffing again. ''You can have people be creative without all this, if that's what the Gorgon thinks he's doing. I had a teacher in high school who could make you really creative. In AP English.''

''In AP English,'' Pat said drily, looking at her nails.

''Really,'' Karen went on. ''He could just totally blow you away. He really made you use your imagination. Like this one time he just drew a square on the board and told us to write about it? Really far out things like that. Another time he took and threw a handful of pennies against the wall and we free wrote about that. I mean that was the topic. It was a neat class."

"You free wrote?" Charles asked her.

"Yeah. You know, you just put down anything you wanted, whatever came to you. But you really had to use your imagination. Some really weird stuff came out of it too." She rolled her eyes. "Some totally weird stuff. But you could really get into the class."

"Pennies against the wall," Pat said with the same dry tone, still not looking at Karen. "Like pennies from heaven, sort of. I wonder why the Gorgon hasn't thought of that one? Maybe we could get back to Charles' paragraph here?"

Lou was grinning broadly. Betty just stared down at the paragraph Charles had passed out to them. The silence was tense, uncomfortable. Even Karen had felt the tone that time.

They read.

"Look," Karen said finally. "I for one really appreciate Chuck's hunting up this paragraph here—"

"It's Charles, please," he interrupted her politely, smiling. "Or Charlie. *Not* Chuck. O.K.?"

Karen reddened, but pushed ahead, already committed.

"Look, I'm not trying to take things over here or anything. I know I was late, but I couldn't help it and I tried to say I'm sorry. And I really do like *Charlie's* paragraph too." She smiled engagingly at him. "I really meant it when I said I try to say some of the same things in my paper. See, I'm new here. I'm just a freshman. And I'd like some feedback on the paper I wrote for this assignment, which I already finished. So because I discuss some of the same ideas Charlie's paragraph does, maybe we could discuss Charlie's paragraph that way, I mean if that's O.K. with you guys. The Gorgon said we should use the study groups to help our writing, remember? So I don't mind being first. I have my paper with me. It's all typed and everything. Part of the reason I was late is that I wanted to Xerox it for everybody. I'd like you all to be very honest with me about it too. You can just tear it apart if you want to."

"Charles gave us his paragraph before you got here," Pat said to her. "I think we ought to talk about it first."

"No," Charles said. "It's O.K. I was just interested in the idea in the assignment, I mean as a way to get us started on it. If Karen's already done her paper, and particularly if she's using the same idea Keen does, then maybe we'll see more if we look at it. Go ahead, Karen. Pass out your paper."

She did. And they read what she'd written.

Well, I'm not sure I understand either--I seriously doubt that I ever completely comprehend events about me because I think I miss so much that I don't even realize I delete occurrences.

I really have trouble accepting that he knows that there is "a program that preexists in the brain". He may believe he knows, but who can say such with certainy; no human being truly knows, in my opinion. Theories and lab experiments may support hypothesis, but who is to say the results are occurance of chance parelleling the expected outcome?

The way I understand this program, quite simplified, is that we already have beliefs so obdurate that even when evidence proves our conceptions false we either continue to seek justification for what we believe or simply delete new information in favor of existing patterns.

I think there may be some truth to this program, but then I could probably say that of just about anything. But anyway, take for example the mirror experiment. Until reading this experiment I believed the size to be an accurate sizeable reflection, the distorted depth I noticed. If questioned whether the image is larger or smaller than actuality I would have answered smaller because I know I would prefer being small so it seems logical to conclude I view myself as being real proportioned even thought this is false.

So this brief experiement may have some symbolic meaning. Consider how often our brain distorts reality; we are ignorant to the deception. How can we be sure of what is real?

Recall the unicorn, rhinocerous and the whale with
ears, the artists after being exposed to a false
picture were programmed, if you will, just like a
computer, and ignored what they were actually
viewing, replacing werity with illusion. Is this
possible to do with common everyday events? The
entire world could be a misconception. Our brains
are nothing more than giant computers and they
could be programmed wrong.

Betty was the first to speak, after nervously clearing her throat. "I assume you'll be fixing the errors in here before you turn this in," she said.

"Oh thanks, Betty," Karen said sweetly. "I'm really terrible with mechanics and that kind of thing. Sure I'll fix them. Can you help me see where they are?"

"Well, you have some misspellings. 'Occurrence.' 'Experiment.' I think I saw some others too, but I'd have to read the paper over to find them."

"You've got a run-on sentence in your last paragraph," Charles said. "You need a period after 'ears.' Or a semicolon."

"Oh *sure*," Karen said ostentatiously making the corrections on her paper. "Of course. Thanks. Any others anybody sees?"

"In that same sentence you have 'werity,' " Betty said. "Is 'werity' a word? Don't you mean 'verity'?"

"Oh, of course," Karen said happily, again correcting her paper. "Thanks again, Betty. Is that it then? Pat, do you see any boo-boos?"

Pat, who had lighted another cigarette, just looked at her, and then looked at everybody else.

"Of course I'm only a freshman, too," she said, "but I'm wondering what the hell we're all doing."

Everybody just stared at her.

"What are you getting at?" Lou asked her.

"I mean that I don't see that the point of these study groups is to sit around and clean up somebody else's messes for them—particularly when they damned well know how to do it for themselves."

"Look, Pat," Karen said, her voice rising. "I really am a terrible speller. I really do have trouble with mechanics. I'm asking for your help."

"Crap," Pat said shortly. "You just batted this paper out at the typewriter, is what you did. You didn't take any time with it at all. Most of the words you misspell in it you get right other places in the paper. You show you know how to use stuff like the semicolon too. You don't have 'trouble.' This is just lazy. You better start getting serious, girl."

"Now let's take it easy, people, O.K.?" Charles tried.

"I *did* take this paper seriously, Pat," Karen yelped, "the idea of it I really worked on. My third paragraph says just what Charlie's paragraph out of a book says, doesn't it, Charlie?"

"Not exactly, no," Pat retorted, leaning in front of Charles to cut him off. "And even if it did, what would that prove? You're sloppy: sloppy in the way you use evidence, sloppy the way you try to make your points. You sound like a teeny-bopper the way you say *you* prefer being small and the whole world could be an illusion. Tra-la-la. You know what the Gorgon will do to a paper like this?"

"Betty," Karen appealed, stiff with outrage, turning to face her directly, "Betty, do *you* think my paper is just sloppy?"

Betty, reluctant, ill at ease, shifted a bit before responding.

"Well. Sloppy. I don't . . . oh, . . ." And then finally, "I did wonder about your using the unicorn the way you do in your last paragraph, Karen. I don't think the unicorn in the assignment is an example the same way the whale and the rhinoceros are, is it? I mean unicorns are mythical, so the artists couldn't have been programmed with a *false* picture of them. I think the unicorn's being used in the assignment a different way."

"One other thing while we're on the last paragraph of your paper, Karen," Charles said, grateful for the neutral ground. "This is a real tick with me I guess, because I'm a computer science major, but I think you'd better not say that the brain is nothing more than a big computer. It isn't you know."

"What do you mean?" Lou asked him.

"Well, you hear it all the time that the brain is a computer, the brain is a computer. It's a false comparison. As a matter of fact the stuff in the assignment shows why. See, when you program a computer you can predict how the program is going to work. And if you want, you can erase it. But did *everybody* see whales as having ears? Did *every* artist put eyelashes on horses? And how do you erase the brain's program? I mean how do I see myself only half size in the mirror? My point is, the brain is different from a computer. It has a *tendency* to do certain things maybe, but it doesn't always do those things."

"Then how come the psychologist, or whatever he is—he sounds like some kind of psychologist—" Lou persisted, "how come he talks about a program in the brain?"

"I don't think he means 'program' the way we use it in computer science exactly, I think he means—"

"Well then I think *Mister* Gorgon should have told us that," Karen said interrupting him. "This is a very confusing assignment. *I* thought the psychologist was talking about computers."

Pat made a quick derisive hissing sound.

"Hey, Karen," Lou said, who had had a good deal of some rather rough-edged rehab group therapy. "Quit being so defensive. *You* gave us the paper, remember. You asked us to be honest about it. You even said we could tear it apart if we wanted, didn't you? O.K. then. You're getting just what you asked for. Now, tell me what you're saying in here about the mirror experiment. It seems to be the main point of your paper and I can't get what you're saying exactly."

"I said what I wanted to say," Karen said sulkily.

"O.K." Lou said. "Maybe. But I don't know what that is yet, see? What do you mean in your second paragraph when you say, 'Theories and lab experiments may support hypothesis, but who is to say the results are occurance of chance parelleling the expected outcome?' What do you mean there?"

"What she meant to write," Pat interjected coldly, "is that 'the results *are not the* occurance of chance'; 'who is to say the results are *not* the occurance of chance.' She left the 'not' out because that's one of the little boo-boos Karen seems to have trouble with, like misspelling 'occurrence' and 'paralleling.' "

Betty looked more and more pained. Charles bit the corner of his lower lip.

"Is that right?" Lou demanded. "You just forgot to put the 'not' in the sentence? So you're saying that the results of the mirror experiment are just chance then, that they don't mean anything?"

"Ask Pat," Karen said, sullen now, hostile. "She seems to know everything I meant to say."

"Look, it's your paper, Karen," Lou said in exasperation. "Stop feeling so damned sorry for yourself, will you. I think you *did* leave 'not' out of the sentence. No wonder I didn't know what it meant. And down the way here you go on to make some big point about the mirror thing, but I can't get what you're talking about there either. What do you mean when you say because you'd like to be small you'd have thought your image in the mirror was smaller?"

"She's being cute there," Pat said, "don't you get it?"

"And," Lou drove on, "what sort of 'distorted depth' do you see in a mirror? It doesn't make any sense. And you know if we can't make any sense of this, the Gorgon sure as hell won't be able to. Pat's right, you know. He plays a pretty deep third base, this guy does. I've checked on him. If he thinks you can do better than you're doing, that you're just screwing off or something, he'll tear your head off."

Mouth set, chalky, Karen stood up quickly, as though jerked on a wire.

"Excuse me a minute, Lou," Charles said quickly and then, "wait a minute, Karen. I think I see something here. I've been thinking that if you see this paper as a kind of rough draft, it really has some possibilities."

She just stood, blinking back tears, blinking hard, staring at him grimly.

"No, I mean it," Charles went on anxiously. "Sit down a minute, will you? Just give me a minute. I know we're almost out of time, and we still have to get a recorder and all that, but this is important. Just give me a minute here. How about you see the first part of your paper as a type of, well, as a type of free writing, like the kind you said you did in high school, where you're writing to loosen yourself up sort of, where you write more about yourself than about the issues of the assignment, O.K.? Then, if you did that, you might not feel so bad about cutting it maybe, or . . . ah. . . ."

He trailed off, stopped, but then picked up decisively.

"See, the third paragraph of your paper makes a lot of sense. It really does. It's like what Keen says, I think—in the paragraph I brought, you know? Why not just start your paper there, with the third paragraph? Just cut the first two paragraphs and start with the third."

"It would cut out all that bubbleheaded bouncing around at the beginning, anyway," Pat muttered, but audibly, and Lou laughed.

"And if you did do that, Karen," Betty said to her quickly, "maybe you wouldn't need to just throw away everything in your first two paragraphs. If you started right off with what you think the program is, *then* you could say you're not sure you accept it all but you accept it some, and then you could go on to say what it *is* you accept. Do you see what I mean?"

Karen, still standing, just looked at her, swallowing convulsively.

Betty tried again. "Look, I'm not too sure here, but maybe the trouble with the way you talk about the mirror experiment now is that you work against yourself. You seem to say first, in your second paragraph, that there's no truth to the experiment. But then later on you seem to say there may be some. Why don't you set things up so you say something like, here's the program. Start with your third paragraph the way Charles said. Then say, I don't see complete truth in it, and why you don't. Then you could say that you do see *some* truth to it, however, and what that is and what it implies. Do you see what I mean now?"

Karen nodded, but mechanically, her face still very white.

"And that, of course," Pat said as she was standing up, "will make everything wonderful."

Lou laughed again.

"I'm sorry to say so, folks," Pat went on, but it *is* getting on to 4:30 of the clock."

"Look, it won't fix everything in the paper maybe, Karen," Charles said, "but it will give you a place to start. It could make you be clearer."

Lou had gotten up also and moved to Pat's side. They were whispering to each other.

"Karen," Betty said to her, "Karen, listen. It is 4:30 and I've got to go too. I've got kids to pick up. But walk me to my car, will you?"

Assignment 3

"The familiar will always remain the likely starting point for the rendering of the unfamiliar; an existing representation will always exert its spell over the artist even while he strives to record the truth" (p. 72), says E. H. Gombrich. And he later says, "Without some starting point, some initial schema, we could never get hold of the flux of experience. Without categories, we could not sort our impressions. Paradoxically, it has turned out that it matters relatively little what these first categories are. We can always adjust them according to need" (p. 76).

Modern novelist and essayist Walker Percy, however, is not so optimistic about the possibilities of adjusting categories:

Garcia Lopez de Cardenas discovered the Grand Canyon and was amazed at the sight. It can be imagined: One crosses miles of desert, breaks through the mesquite, and there it is at one's feet. Later the government set the place aside as a national park. . . .

Why is it almost impossible to gaze directly at the Grand Canyon under these circumstances and see it for what it is—as one picks up a strange object from one's back yard and gazes directly at it? It is almost impossible because the Grand Canyon, the thing as it is, has been appropriated by the symbolic complex which has already been formed in the sightseer's mind. Seeing the canyon under approved circumstances is seeing the symbolic complex head on. The thing is no longer the thing as it confronted the Spaniard; it is rather that which has already been formulated—by picture postcard, geography book, tourist folders, and the words Grand Canyon. As a result of this preformulation, the source of the sightseer's pleasure undergoes a shift. Where the wonder and delight of the Spaniard arose from his penetration of the thing itself, from a progressive discovery of depths, patterns, colors, shadows, etc., now the sightseer measures his satisfaction *by the degree to which the canyon conforms to the preformed complex.* If it does so, if it looks just like the postcard, he is pleased; he might even say, "Why it is every bit as beautiful as a picture postcard." He feels he has not been cheated. But if it does not conform, if the colors are somber, he will not be able to see it directly; he will only be conscious of the disparity between what it is and what it is supposed to be. He will say later that he was unlucky in not being there at the right time. The highest point, the term of the sightseer's satisfaction, is not the sovereign discovery of the thing before him; it is rather the measuring up of the thing to the criterion of the preformed symbolic complex.

Seeing the canyon is made even more difficult by what the sightseer does when the moment arrives, when sovereign knower confronts the thing to be known. Instead of looking at it, he photographs it. There is no confrontation at all. At the end of forty years of preformulation and with the Grand Canyon yawning at his feet, what does he do? He waives his right of seeing and knowing and records symbols for the next 40 years. For him there is no present; there is only the past of what has been formulated and seen and the future of what has been formulated and not seen. The present is surrendered to the past and the future.

The sightseer may be aware that something is wrong. He may simply be bored; or he may be conscious of the difficulty: that the great thing yawning at his feet somehow eludes him. The harder he looks at it, the less he can see. It eludes everybody. The tourist cannot see it; for him it is only one side of the space he lives in, like one wall of a room; to the ranger it is a tissue of everyday signs relevant to his own prospects—the blue haze down there means that he will probably get rained on during the donkey ride.*

Percy's assertion that it is almost impossible for the sightseer to see the Grand Canyon as it is because it "has been appropriated by the symbolic complex which has already been formed in the sightseer's mind" can provide a way of understanding more than the problems of tourists. This assignment is an opportunity for you to discover what light Percy can be made to shed on why members of different generations (parents and children, for example, or teachers and students) often have such a difficult time understanding one another—even when they really try to do so.

First, write about a time in your life when you experienced what you would call an example of members of different generations having a difficult time trying to understand each other. "Trying to understand" is the important notion to work at dramatizing here. Don't waste your time, in other words, rendering a Monster Parent's abuse of a Saintly Child—or any of its innumerable equivalents. (Though this may, it does not have to be something you went through yourself. You are a reader. You've seen plays and movies. You move in a world with other people.) Give all the relevant particulars. Who was there? What was said and done? Do this part of your paper in no more than a page or so and as though it were a scene in a novel or short story, one in which particular people act and speak. That is, rather than just *saying* what the difficulty involved ("There was a misunderstanding over . . ."), try to *show* the difficulty actually taking place.

Beginning on a separate sheet of paper, locate in the sketch you just wrote what Percy calls the "preformed symbolic complexes" through which the characters in this instance seem to have seen each other. What are these "preformed symbolic complexes" made up of? Where do you think they come from? How do they seem to influence understanding?

You have written a sketch showing members of different generations having a difficult time understanding each other. You have located the "preformed symbolic complexes" through which the characters in your paper seem to have seen each other. Now, on still another sheet of paper, address this final question: to judge from your analysis of your

---

*Walker Percy, "The Loss of the Creature," *The Message In The Bottle*. New York: Farrar, Straus and Giroux, 1975. Reprinted by permission of Farrar, Straus and Giroux. pp. 46–8.

sketch, what do you think can be done about the difficulty members of different generations seem to have understanding each other? Consider very carefully whether it is going to help very much to say such things as: "Well, we can close the generation gap with mutual understanding." "Well, we can solve the communication problem by communicating better." "Well, we can make an effort to share the same value system." Etc.

The direction above, incidentally, "beginning on a separate sheet of paper" (you will meet it again in this sequence of assignments), is to help you do justice to what is often the most difficult, but in some ways the most important of tasks in an assignment: the task of synthesizing your experience with an issue or a problem, the task of putting things together.

Seeing Assignment 3

STUDY GROUP II

"Well, what did he give it to us for then?" Sally asked him.

"Look, I'm not saying the paper doesn't have *anything* to do with Assignment 3. All I'm saying is that it's not on the same topic."

"In a way it is," Sandy said. "Our course is about seeing and the girl writes about an eye operation."

"I can see that, for heaven's sake," John said. "I just don't see how going over this paper is supposed to help us write our sketches or talk about the generation gap, that's all."

"The Gorgon says in the assignment you're not supposed to talk about the generation gap," Sandy persisted. John reminded her of her older brothers. Living with them had taught her a lot more than just how to defend herself.

"I know, Sandy," Sally said before John could retaliate, "but all the Gorgon means is that we're not supposed to use cliches. We *are* supposed to talk about people of different generations, and that's what we have in this paper, isn't it? And besides, didn't the Gorgon say that what happens in this paper is the whole point of the course?"

"Yeah, he did," Frank said, leaning forward quickly. "He did say something like that. What did he mean by that anyway?"

"I don't know about you folks," Amy said, smoothing her khaki skirt, "but I've got work to do, and I wonder if we could go at things a little more efficiently this time." None of the members of her study group knew that Amy had used the occasion of her reporting to the Gorgon as her group's recorder to complain that their study sessions were a waste of time. They'd had two meetings, she'd told him, and both of them had been swallowed by John and Sandy's needling each other. And while Sally seemed O.K., Frank was utterly hopeless. All the Gorgon had done was smile and tell her to focus people on a text. "The course is about what it means to write sentences," he'd said. "So force people to stay with sentences." As for changing her study group, his answer, much to her annoyance, had been a cheerful, "Oh no."

"Why don't we just look at the paper first," Amy went on. "I think Sally's right. The Gorgon must have had something in mind giving us this particular paper. Maybe if we talk about it the way he said, we'll see what it has to do with the assignment."

"He didn't say we had to talk about it," Sandy said. "He said we could talk about it if we wanted to."

"He said 'locate yourselves with it,'" Frank said. "Did you guys hear him say that? What's he talk like that for? What did he mean by that?"

"Maybe," Amy said evenly, "if we just look at the paper we'll see what he meant."

"I've got a good thing for the generation gap," Frank said. "I'm going to write about how my mother wouldn't let me get a car. She was going to stick me with the whole insurance. Can you believe it?"

"O.K., Amy," John said, "we may as well look at the papers. There was a story connected with them, though, remember?"

"Paper," Sandy corrected him. "Not papers. These are three different versions of the same paper. You said papers. And the Gorgon said the girl wrote version A, had it trashed in class, and then wrote B and C. That's the story."

"Well, not the whole story," Sally said, before John could respond.

Amy saw her chance and moved quickly. "Let's look at the three versions of the paper first. Then we can get the story."

A

The examining room is cold and sterile and makes me feel isolated and alone. There are cabinets of instruments as though in a torture chamber. The doctor finishes peering indifferently at my eyes

and then, without paying me the least bit of
attention, scribbles urgently and brutally on a
piece of paper clipped in a clipboard. He has on a
frightening looking white jacket that comes to
just above his knees. His trousers are brown
corduroy and his shoes are a sickening looking
black. From time to time his blue eyes look up at my
brown eyes again, at my brown eyes only, brimming
with tears. Not in any way does he ever think to
look at me. And then he says callously, "I'm going
to recommend that you have another operation,
young lady." He does not care about me as a person.

And I *knew* there would have to be another
operation on my eyes! I just knew it! I had
expected this all along because I'd already had
three operations. Still the news exploded in my
face like a hand grenade.

I had almost gathered the courage to ask whether
this operation would be the last one, but I was
never *given* the chance. I can tell the doctor
doesn't really care anything about me, because he
leaves the examining room so quickly. The hard,
bright, enameled metal door stares at me like a
giant accusing eye. I'm cold from sitting on the
hard metal table under the unfriendly stare of the
harsh fluorescent lights. I feel more lonely and
afraid than ever. He's busy, I know with all those
"really" sick people to make him feel important. I
know also that the condition I have afflicts only
babies and young children mostly. But maybe if the
doctor took just a minute to think, he'd
understand that though he is unused to questions

from his other patients, I'm a young woman of 17
and not just a child and I could use some
reassurance. Do doctors care only about their
fees?

I stare down at the floor through a mist of
tears. The orderly pattern of alternate green and
white checkerboard in the hard tile floor is
hardly any more reassuring than the doctor has
been. Its orderliness in fact seems to mock the
crazy quilt of my emotions which have no order at
all. I watch my tears splash down onto the hard
cold tile, one by one.

B

~~The examining room is cold and sterile and makes
me feel isolated and alone. There are cabinets of
instruments as though in a torture chamber.~~ The
doctor finishes peering ~~indifferently~~ at my eyes
and ~~then, without paying me the least bit of
attention,~~ scribbles urgently ~~and brutally~~
on a ~~piece of paper clipped in~~ a clipboard.
~~He has on a frightening looking white
jacket that comes to just above his knees.
His trousers are brown corduroy and his shoes
are a sickening looking black.~~ From time to time
his ~~blue eyes~~ look up at my ~~brown~~ eyes again, at
~~my brown eyes only, brimming with tears.
Not in any way does he ever think to look~~ at me.
~~And then~~ he says ~~callously,~~ "I'm going to
recommend ~~that you have~~ another operation,
~~young lady." He does not care about me as a
person.~~

And ~~I *knew* there would have to be another operation on my eyes! I just knew it!~~ I had expected this ~~all along because I'd already had three operations. Still the news exploded in my face like a hand grenade.~~

~~I had almost gathered the courage to ask whether this operation would be the last one, but I was never *given* the chance. I can tell~~ the doctor ~~doesn't really care anything about me, because he~~ leaves the examining room ~~so~~ quickly. ~~The hard, bright, enameled metal door stares at me like a giant accusing eye. I'm cold from sitting on the hard metal table under the unfriendly stare of the harsh fluorescent lights. I feel more lonely and afraid than ever.~~ He's busy I know ~~with all those "really" sick people to make him feel important. I know also that~~ the condition I have afflicts ~~only~~ babies and young children mostly. ~~But~~ maybe ~~if~~ the doctor ~~took just a minute to think, he'd understand that though he~~ is unused to questions from his ~~other patients, I'm a young woman of 17 and not just a child and I could use some reassurance. Do doctors care only about their fees?~~

~~I stare down at the floor through a mist of tears. The orderly pattern of alternate green and white checkerboard in the hard tile floor is hardly any more reassuring than the doctor has been. Its orderliness in fact seems to mock the crazy quilt of my emotions which have no order at all. I watch my tears splash down onto the hard cold tile, one by one.~~

C

The doctor finishes peering at my eyes, and scribbles urgently on his clipboard. From time to time he looks up at my eyes again. At them, not at me. He says, "I'm going to have to recommend another operation."

I had expected this.

The doctor leaves the examining room quickly. He's busy I know. And the eye condition I have afflicts babies and young children mostly. Maybe the doctor is unused to questions from his patients.

I stare down at the floor. The orderly pattern of green and white tile is hardly reassuring.

"Now," Amy began, "Version A was criticized in class. The next day the girl showed up in the Gorgon's office with B, right?"

"With Versions B *and* C," Sally said. "Version B is just version A crossed out. Version C was what she wrote after crossing out A. She wrote it from B, I mean. And she told the Gorgon she wanted the class to see her rewrite, wasn't that it? She wanted them to read C?"

"You got it," Frank said, "and the kid did all this because she was pissed and that's what we're supposed to locate ourselves with."

Amy was determined to maintain a direction. "O.K. then. The girl wrote a description of an event. That's A. The class discussed it and found certain strengths in it and one main weakness. And yes, then the girl crossed out most of A because she was angry about what the class had said. But then she did C from B because she said she got interested, right?"

"Yes," Sandy said. "She got interested in the effect of B. That's what the Gorgon said she said in his office. So she did version C on her own."

"Then the Gorgon didn't make her do C?" Frank asked.

"The Gorgon didn't make her do B *or* C, Frank," Sandy informed him. "That's the point. She did them both on her own. And she said she was glad she had."

"Actually," John said archly, "Actually it was a little more complicated than that. What the girl *really* said" . . . he shuffled his notes. "O.K., here it is. Just as the girl was leaving the Gorgon's office, she said: 'I don't know whether I can say I'm *glad* for what the class said about my paper, but I'm grateful for what they made me do to it. I see a lot of things now I didn't see before.' We're supposed to work out what she might have meant. The Gorgon said there was no right answer, by the way. He said he never asked her what she meant."

"I bet he never asked her," Frank said with heavy sarcasm. "He asked her all right. And she talked about having *seen* something, you guys notice that? I bet that's the whole point."

"That's what *I* said," Sandy reminded everyone. "But John didn't seem to think it was important."

"Look," said John, "that *isn't* what you said. Anyway, the Gorgon *said* he never asked her what she meant."

"Actually, John," Sandy said in parody of his inflection, "you didn't say a *thing* I didn't already say. The girl said she was glad she did C. That's just what I said."

"The point is," John snapped at her, "that *isn't* what she said. She said she *wasn't* glad. She said she was grateful. There's a difference."

"Glad. Grateful. What's the difference?"

"Why don't we look at version A of the paper," Amy said, "and see what the class might have criticized?" Her tone was sharper than she'd meant it to be, but the timing of her suggestion was just right.

All five of them stared hard at the paper.

"Jeez, three operations," Frank said, after a bit. "What a bastard that doctor was."

Again they were silent, reading.

"Maybe that's what the class didn't like, though," Sally said speculatively.

"I was thinking the same thing, Sally," John said.

"What, that a doctor can be a bastard?" Frank hooted. "Doctors can be bastards. And besides, the point is the girl's feelings about the doctor."

"Maybe John doesn't like human feelings," Sandy sniped. "Maybe because the kid cries over having to have a fourth operation he thinks she's being a baby or something."

"Look get off me will you?" John said heatedly. "What's with you anyway?"

"You can call me Sandy. I have a name."

"Will you two cut it out?" Sally said sharply. "This is supposed to be a study group and I have work to do too. We're supposed to be looking at what the class said was wrong with this paper."

John was flushed, Sandy, seemingly, as cool as milk. Neither of them looked at the other.

"I *was* talking about the paper," John said defensively. "And I know the girl is writing about her feelings. But don't you think this doctor's a little much? I mean his shoes are sickening, and his tie is vomit green and he's just a machine, and she's this poor little thing all pushed around and nobody cares about her. She doesn't sound much like 'a young woman' to me. She sounds like a little kid. In fact, none of this sounds realistic. It's like a comic book or something."

"And maybe that's how the paper connects with the assignment," Sally added. "I mean the assignment says we're not supposed to deal with monsters in our sketches."

Sandy was still looking hard at the paper. "I don't see where it talks about his tie."

Again, Amy moved in quickly. "John's got a point, I think. John and Sally both. This girl does overdo things a bit. The lights are harsh, the door is accusing, the doctor scribbles brutally. And there are a lot of tears."

"But those are concrete and specific details she needs," Frank said. "I think her vocabulary is excellent. It really shows her true feelings."

"But it's the *way* she uses the details," John went on, Amy having given him courage. "She sounds whiney, overdramatic."

"What do you want her to do, lie?" Frank demanded belligerently. "This is what she feels. How would you feel having to have a third operation on your eyes? Maybe you'd be a little dramatic too."

"Fourth operation, Frank," Sandy said. "She's already had three. The one coming up is her fourth."

He turned his whole body to her.

"Don't try that with me, Sandy," he said flatly.

The group froze.

Oh my, Amy thought. Ohmyohmyohmy.

"Maybe that's not the point though, Frank," John said, finally. "Sure I'd feel bad. I just don't think this is believable the way she talks. For instance she doesn't know the doctor leaves the room just because he doesn't care about her. Nobody could know that."

"Look," Amy said. "Maybe we could look at what this writer thought. I mean she was the one who crossed out almost everything in her paper because of the class."

"But she was angry when she did that," Sandy said.

"I know," Amy went on. "But she did it. She did it on her own too. I mean the Gorgon didn't make her do it. So she must have agreed with *some* of what the class said, don't you think? And because she crosses out so much, somebody must have said she overdid things, don't you think?"

"Well," said Frank, "she was really pissed when she did B all right. You can tell that. She cut out everything."

"Well, not quite everything," Sandy said, but then she added quickly, "I know what you mean though, Frank. I mean it *looks* like she cut out everything, but C shows she didn't, don't you think, Frank? I mean it's like C is a clean copy of B? C is B copied over, isn't it?"

"Actually Sandy," John said distinctly, as though addressing a child, "version C is *not* just version B copied over. Version C in fact came *out* of the crossed out B, Sandy, because the girl got interested in the effect. Remember the Gorgon saying that? I think Sandy, if you look *closely* at C, you'll see that it's not the same as B at all. We have three different versions of one paper here."

Sandy, white, her mouth a line, flipped from B to C and back again, reading hard. "O.K." she said. "The final paragraph of B and C are different. She crosses it all out in B, but then puts part of it back in C. But the rest of the paper is word for word. Listen: 'The doctor finishes peering at my eyes and scribbles urgently on a clipboard.' That's B if you read around the crossouts. C has the same first sentence."

"Wrong," John said decisively. " 'A clipboard' has been changed to 'his clipboard.' And don't give me what's the difference. The difference is important."

"How?"

"Because she changes her whole interpretation of the doctor in C is how. Well, in B and C. It's like what she did in B made her see that 'a clipboard' made the doctor too business-like, sort of. *'His* clipboard' makes him more . . . , well, more like he sounds in C when he tells her he's going *to have to* recommend another operation, like he's sorry. In B he says just 'I'm going to recommend another operation.' "

"Yes," Sally said. "The doctor in B and C sounds a lot more human."

"But," Frank said, "if he really was a bastard that means she's lying making him more human in C."

"But we don't know he *was* a bastard," Sandy said quickly, and then, less abruptly, "do we, Frank? I mean maybe she was lying in version A."

"At any rate," Amy said, "he's certainly a lot more believable in B and C than he is in A, the doctor I mean. The girl says in A that when the doctor leaves the examining room quickly that means only that he doesn't care about her, the way John said, that the doctor is just a money grubber. In B and C she says the doctor may have left quickly because he's busy."

"The way I took it," Sally said, "is that the doctor leaves quickly because he *does* care about her. He doesn't get many questions because his patients are so young. So when he has to deal with this older girl, who's already had all those operations, he's embarrassed or in shock or something. I think he leaves quickly because he can't stand to see her hurting. He's upset I think."

"Maybe her eye condition was like an emergency," Frank offered. "Maybe he left fast because he had to set up an operating room in a hurry or something like that."

"Which would still mean he cares about her, wouldn't it," Sandy said, "if he was acting like a good doctor? That's a good point, Frank."

"Yeah," Frank said, rubbing his chin reflectively. "I wonder what was the matter with her eyes. I wonder if she was O.K. after that last operation."

"We don't even know . . .," Sandy started, and stopped.

"Right, Sandy," Amy picked up. "We don't even know if it was the last one. I wonder why she sounds braver about the operations when she doesn't tell you how many she's had. Does she sound braver to any of you folks in C than she does in A?"

"She does to me," Sally agreed. "She sounds a lot more grown-up in C than she did before. More mature. She cuts out all the tears she had in there earlier for instance. All of them. Even in her last paragraph. But even though there aren't any tears in C, I feel for her more there. Maybe that's the way it is with the number of operations cut out."

"She sounds braver to me too, Amy," John said, "not so much like a little kid jumping up and down screaming. 'I had expected this,' is all she says. That's a really powerful line somehow."

"Yes," Frank said. "It's really neat the way that line jumps right out at you the way it's all by itself. It's like that guy. . . ." He searched for the name while everybody waited. "You know the guy who writes the poems with the words all over the place, with all that weird punctuation?"

"e.e. cummings?" Amy offered, softly.

"That's the guy. Wrote a poem about Buffalo Bill. We read it in high school. He's got this word 'Jesus' all in a line by itself and you don't know if he's swearing or praying or what. Super poem. You guys know that poem? Anyway, this line here is like that."

"So is what we're supposed to work out that the girl got honest in this paper, is that it?" Sally asked. "We're supposed to see she was glad she got the chance to look grown-up—glad or grateful or whatever she was? What exactly did the Gorgon say, John? You copied it down."

"She didn't say she was *glad*," John said, picking up his notes. "She said, let's see now . . . O.K. Here's what the Gorgon told us to copy down. She said, 'I don't know whether I can say I'm *glad* for what the class said about my paper, but I'm grateful for what they made me do to it. I see a lot of things I didn't see before.' What we're supposed to do is work out what she might have meant. There's no right answer, remember. The Gorgon said he never asked her what she'd meant."

"That's what we're supposed to locate ourselves with," Frank said. "O.K. So it's obvious isn't it? This kid lied about what she went through the way she told it first. She didn't like being called a liar by the class, but she's glad she had a chance to tell things straight. What else could she have meant?"

Nobody said anything for a while.

Amy cleared her throat and said, "I thought we agreed that what really happened in the examining room might have been very much like the way she describes things in version A. I mean that it *could* have been that way."

"You mean then that what she sees is how to lie about herself in writing and that's what she's grateful for?" Frank was belligerent. "You guys really think that that's what she meant?"

"Well, no," Amy said lamely, "not lie exactly, but. . . ."

She stopped. Again nobody said anything.

"But what then?" Frank demanded. "What did she mean?"

"Well," said Sally, "she could have meant that this was how she *wished* she'd acted."

Frank just stared at her.

"I mean maybe she really did whine and cry in the examining room. Maybe she even screamed at the doctor. Maybe all she means is that version C gave her a chance to play the whole thing over."

"So she could act better in the future, maybe, and she's grateful for that," Amy put in.

"You're crazy if you guys think she meant that."

"Look, Frank," Sally said, "I don't know *what* she meant. I just don't think it's as simple as saying first she lied and then she told the truth or first she told the truth and then she lied, that's all."

"You know," John said, "she might even have meant that doing version C gave her a chance to see that the doctor was *worse* than she thought he was. Version C might be a way of saying what she wished *he'd* been, too."

"Or," Sandy suggested, "maybe all the girl meant was that she was glad, grateful I mean, to make something good out of a bad scene, I mean the bad scene of the *class* where everybody trashed her paper. Or where she thought everybody was trashing her paper. Maybe she meant that she saw they weren't doing that really. I mean if she wrote C then some good came out of the class, didn't it?"

Everybody just sat.

"So where are we?" Frank grinned. "How have we located ourselves? The Gorgon said this paper was the whole point of the course, or something like that. So what's the whole point of the course?"

Nobody looked at anybody else. Nobody said anything.

"Well does anybody see how we're supposed to do Assignment 3 better now? Does anybody see *that* at least?" Frank asked emphatically. "Because I think John's right that we have to write a dialogue and this kid's only describing an event. So what's the connection?"

"Maybe it's the other stuff in the assignment the paper is connected with," Sandy ventured, "this stuff about 'preformed symbolic complexes.' "

"You mean you think this kid's paper has something to do with 'preformed symbolic complexes'? Like what?" Frank asked her. "How?"

"We aren't going to have time to get into that now," Amy said rising. "At least I can't. I have to get to my biology lab."

"I have to leave too, but wait a minute, Amy," Sally said. "You know we could get together again once more this week if you guys want to, I mean just on this paper and the preformed symbolic complex thing. Does anybody want to? We got a good start on the paper and the Gorgon did say it was the whole point of the course."

"I'm in," John said. "I want to hear Sandy on those preformed symbolic complexes."

Assignment 4

Behind the eyes with which all of us see is a brain or mind or sensibility that operates in such a way as to make a difference in what it is we say that we see. This it would seem is what the social scientist quoted in Assignment 2 is taking into account in speaking of the brain's tendency to selectively destroy sensory information "according to a program that preexists" in it. It is what Walker Percy addresses by speaking of all of us carrying around in our heads "preformed symbolic complex[es]" against which we "measure" what we look at. Each of us can be said to have a "program," or rather a number of programs with which and through which we have a tendency to see the world. Each of us, it would seem, is a good deal more complicated than a camera recording Reality as it Really Is.

Things become more complicated still when we consider *whose* mind or sensibility is operating on what "raw data" under what circumstances. More complicated how and what difference it may be said to make is what you'll begin to explore in the paper you write for this assignment.

A psychologist presented a picture of two trapeze artists, a man and woman in mid-air (see Figure 4.1), to a number of men and women in the United States and asked them to write out the story that the picture seemed to suggest to them:

Figure 4.1

Here are three pairs of such stories, the first in all instances told by a woman, the second by a man:

I
(woman)

They are a very famous man and wife trapeze act. They have been unable to perform on the high wire because of certain marital conflicts. They have tried many times to regain their previous skills, but each time they are in the air, ready to catch one another, either the husband or the wife realizes something about himself or his wife and finds themselves unable to reach out for the other. They have tried desperately to come to some sort of answer, and tonight they feel they've reached it. But they both wonder if they will be able to reach each other, and by clasping hands, become man and wife again. They reach each other, and eventually learn to communicate and to enjoy one another.

(man)

Sam gripped Martha's wrists, tensed, and flipped her into the air. She turned in the air much as a leaf turning during that second in which it hangs suspended upon the wind. The audience was silent except for scattered gasps and an occasional licking of lips. Again Sam caught her by the wrists, thrilling to the sensation of strength which violently surged from his arms into hers. Sweat formed in glistening beads upon the bulging sinews of his thickly corded arms, "Sam, I love you," sighed Martha. "And I you," said Sam, releasing her wrists with the steel-trap reflexes for which he was famous, watching her fall towards the upturned faces.

II

(woman)

Husband and wife who've been given an opportunity in a first-class circus after many discouraging months in carnivals. She's discovered she's pregnant after having had several miscarriages. She's been warned not to indulge in strenuous physical activity. However, knowing that this would be an opportunity for her husband, she goes ahead without his knowledge. She feels joyous, being partner to his success and suppresses thoughts of a possible miscarriage. They're a standing success. They perform with discipline and artistry. She does not lose the child.

(man)

This is a husband and wife team flying through the air before a packed house. He has just caught her and they both feel a thrill of excitement. He met her as a young girl and fell in love with her and trained her to fly with him. He was very anxious for her at first but now he feels a sense of pride and relief. But too soon—in the next pass he reaches for her hands and misses. She falls to her death. He spends the rest of his life feeling guilty. He loses his confidence and his ability to fly.

III

(woman)

This man and woman had climbed a mountain. They reached a certain point where no gravitational force existed and went flying off into space. Now they are concentrating all of their energy into trying to hold on to one another. They are not fighting their flight into space, but just kind of being carried by some strange unknown forces. Again their only concern is that they remain together. The lights in the bottom of the picture are just some kind of satellites sent up by some country on earth. They get carried into a place where there is no past, present, or future, and remain transfixed there together.

(man)

How would you like to be a trapeze artist and constantly catch your wife in the act? Well, Joe was sick of the circus life, the make-believe, the shiny costumes, the fake smiles, the drama of the drums as they came to the final triple somersault. He had to get out. He had to escape from Liz. She was so possessive. She didn't let him do anything. He had to get rid of her to be free. Tomorrow, yes, tomorrow, when they came to Gary, Indiana, they would work without a net. The daring Dariuses would cause great excitement in the crowd with their courage. Then he'd drop her. He would miss and she would fall on the ground, a crumpled body in gold lamé.

The psychologist claims that most of the stories told about this picture by women in the United States are similar in pattern to those told by the three women whose stories are reproduced here. The same is true, he says, of the stories told by men. (These patterns he calls "fantasy patterns.") "This sort of sex difference is typical of men and women in our culture." As men and women in the United States, he claims, we have a tendency to look at things differently.*

Now, prepare yourself to write the paper you are going to do for this assignment by first developing a set of notes. On one sheet of paper take some notes on what seem to you the points of similarity between the three stories told by women. On another sheet of paper do the same thing with the three stories told by men. These notes are to help you see what position you may wish to take on the issues of this assignment, and are to help you also to develop the most complete and compelling argument you can in explanation of whatever your position is. Please bear in mind that the quality of your paper will in large part depend on your ability to handle the texts you are working with authoritatively: to

---

*Robert May, *Sex and Fantasy, Patterns of Male and Female Development*. New York: W.W. Norton and Company, 1980, pp. 15–33. Reprinted with permission of W.W. Norton and Company.

quote accurately and effectively, to paraphrase responsibly, and to observe the conventions that apply to both. Be sure to turn in these notes with your completed paper.

Use the notes you have developed to write a paper in which you do three things.

First, create a pattern from the points of similarity you have noticed in the three stories told by women. What possible interpretation of the pattern you have created can you imagine? That is, what do you see the pattern you have created amounting to or meaning?

Next, do the same thing with the stories told by men that you did with those told by women.

Finally, and this is the most important part of your paper, to judge from what you see in these sets of stories told by women and told by men, what value do you see in assuming that these stories are, as the psychologist claims, typical of the different ways in which men and women in our culture have a tendency to look at things? That is, what benefits might there be to assuming what this psychologist claims is true? What liabilities might there be to assuming the same thing?

Seeing Assignment 4

SALLY AND CHARLES

She'd found out from one of her dorm counselors that he was a sophomore, a Chancellor's Scholar and "a real hotshot in computer science." He was as thin as a wire and awkward looking but with a habit of holding his mouth pursed slightly as though in a silent whistle that made him seem vulnerable to her. He had the period after the Gorgon's class free she knew because she'd seen him twice in the Burger Chef having coffee, both times alone. It was simply a matter of waiting around a couple of days until one morning he got in line.

"Hi, Charles," she said stepping up behind him. "I'm Sally. From your English course? We're experiencing the Gorgon together."

He turned quickly.

"Oh sure," he said. "How are you? How are you, Sally?"

"Well," she smiled, "I could use some talk about the course from an old timer, O.K.?"

They got their coffee and found a table.

"How's your study group going?" she asked him.

"Oh, fine," he said and then, nervously, "well, better now. We had a sort of rocky start, I guess."

"Yes," she said, "I heard about it. Pat can be a real piece of broken glass when she wants to be. She's in my dorm. She rooms alone. I hear you got called 'Chuck.'"

"Well," he laughed. "She didn't know. Karen, I mean. She's really come around though. I didn't see how we'd ever get anything going after that first session, but we did. Lou really helped, surprisingly. I mean, what he did surprised all of us. At our next session, he apologized to Karen for laughing at her. He did it in front of everybody too. He said he still thought her paper had been awful, but he apologized for losing his temper with her. He said he'd broken some code he had, but he didn't sound stuffy the way he said it. I think even Pat was impressed. And of course Betty's been wonderful. She's some lady."

"She really is," Sally agreed. "Our group's been going better too. We just sort of slopped around at first. Nobody knew what to do really. But then we got arguing about that examining room paper the Gorgon gave us, and we even set up an extra session to talk about it—tying it into the Percy thing and the quote from the psychologist. Everybody came too."

"I wish our group had been able to get to that paper. There's just so much to talk about in the course. We decided to give first priority to what people in the group are writing, though. That's one thing our first session did. We made some ground rules the second time we met. All we're going to look at for a while in the group is stuff that we're writing, but it can only be stuff that you know you haven't finished yet. That way, see, we can talk about drastic changes if we want to and nobody has to get upset. We'll see how it goes anyway, and at least we all agreed to try it. Even Pat. She's really very smart, you know."

"That's one thing we hadn't been doing enough, talking about our own stuff. So we agreed to do that this week. John's up first. It means we won't be able to talk about the poems the Gorgon gave us with 4 at all, though, which I'm really sorry about. Have you looked at them?"

"The poems? Yes," Charles said. "I sure have. I'm not sure I understand them." He laughed self-consciously. "I'm never sure I understand poetry. I guess I'm your basic computer science major. But yes, I read them. I like them."

"Which one," Sally asked him, taking the poems out of her notebook and laying them side by side on the table so they could share her text, "which one do you like best?"

I Learned about Sex

I learned about sex from Dunc and Jenny
Who moved down the street into the duplex
Made of red almost black ridged bricks

Under cedar trees whose bark peeled
In strips of ivory undersides.
They moved in married that afternoon
As we watched
Pleating blades of grass
Stringing clover chains
Biting tender weeds
Tasting their juices
Feeling their crunchy forms.
We marked their comings and goings
Up the sloped path across the gravel walk
Through the screen door into where we could not see.
She wore white short shorts and carried small items
While he in levis only hoisted tables and chairs
Climbing six steps up as she moved aside a bit
Before descending again for another belonging.
Later, together, they crossed the dividing driveway
Introduced themselves by first names only
Sat down close brushing hands
As we stretched round them on the grass
Her tan thighs puckering near the cuff
His matted frame keeping time
To all our breaths and dreams.*

A Man and a Woman

Between a man and a woman
The anger is greater, for each man would like to sleep
In the arms of each woman who would like to sleep
In the arms of each man, if she trusted him not to be
Schizophrenic, if he trusted her not to be
A hypochondriac, if she trusted him not to leave her
Too soon, if he trusted her not to hold him
Too long, and often women stare at the word men
As it lives in the word women, as if each woman
Carried a man inside her and a woe, and has
Crying fits that last for days, not like the crying
Of a man, which lasts a few seconds, and rips the throat
Like a claw—but because the pain differs
Much as the shape of the body, the woman takes

---

*"I Learned About Sex" by Tilly Warnock. Copyright © 1978. Reprinted by permission of Tilly Warnock.

The suffering of the man for selfishness, the man
The woman's pain for helplessness, the woman's lack of it
For hardness, the man's tenderness for deception,
The woman's lack of acceptance, an act of contempt
Which is really fear, the man's fear for fickleness,
Yet cars come off the bridge in rivers of light
Each holding a man and a woman.*

Sally's copies were heavily underlined and annotated.

"Oh my God," he said laughing. "I feel like I'm being tested."

"No," she said. "You're not really. I'm just curious which one you like best. Remember, the Gorgon said there were no 'hooks' in his giving them to us, one good and one bad or anything like that. He said that they were just poems about male–female relations and we could see what we thought of them, remember? That's all he said."

"I know," Charles said good naturedly, "but that's not all you're saying, is it? I mean look at your notes on these things. Don't you want to see whether I think like a man because I like one poem or the other, or something like that?"

She laughed. "O.K." she said. "I'll tell you what. You write down the one you like best and I will too. Then we'll exchange names. _Then_ we'll talk about it. Fair enough? That is," she said, her tone a bit uncertain, "if you do like one best. You do, don't you? I'm right about that?"

"Well, yes," he said. "I do. Is that part of the test too?"

"Write, mister. The truth. Now."

He did and she did. Both wrote the name "Tilly Warnock."

They exchanged papers.

He read and looked up at her. "Do I pass the test?"

"That's really the truth for you?" she asked him, serious. "No kidding now?"

He nodded.

"You thought I was going to pick the other one, didn't you?"

She started to nod and then said, "You know, honestly, I'm not sure what I thought. I think one part of me thought you'd like the Feldman best. But another part of me . . ." She trailed off, puzzled, and then said with a fierceness that was close to anger, "these stories about that damned picture in Assignment 4. . . ." She stopped herself. She began again, as though in explanation, "Three of us in my dorm were up Sunday night till two in the morning talking about this assignment. I don't mean in a study group either. Just three women in the dorm. One of them isn't even in the class." Again she stopped.

"And?" he asked her. "Where do the poems come in?"

She didn't answer.

He watched her for a bit and then said, "Well, I guess we do have some things to talk about, don't we?"

JOHN

He supposed it served him right.

The only reason he'd volunteered to be the first to bring a paper for his study group to talk about (though it was supposed to be only the opening of his paper; no more than a page—that was Amy's suggestion) was that Sandy had made it clear there was no way she was going to start things off and he hadn't been able to resist the temptation to show her up. "Well," he had heard himself say grandly, "we're all here to learn. I guess I could go first." She'd jumped like a spider:

> Great, John. You know, I think the rest of us would learn a lot if you could show us how you're trying to deal with the Gorgon's criticism of your stuff so far. I mean you could show us how you're working on the weaknesses in your writing. We'd really learn a lot that way. We all have weaknesses in our writing you know, John.

She had had him.

If he'd said that the Gorgon hadn't *been* critical of his writing, he'd have looked like a liar—and Sandy would probably have demanded to see one of his marked papers just to make sure everybody in the group knew it. If he'd said that he couldn't do what she'd asked, he'd have looked dumb. If he'd said that he wouldn't, he'd have looked like a wimp. Damn the girl.

Damn her to hell anyway.

The Gorgon, of course, had indeed been critical of his "stuff so far." He had spoken sharply in fact in his final comments on the two papers John had gotten back in pretty much the same way about exactly the same thing. Not that the full comments were *totally* negative by any means, but what had been positive in them John, a former editor of his high school yearbook, had found less than intoxicating. "Any jerk can quote," had been written at the end of his paper for Assignment 3, for example. "Any jerk can learn to quote accurately. Quoting effectively, however, is an art, one you show you can learn to master." ("Oh yeah," a joker in his dorm had said to him about the remark. "That's vintage Gorgon, all right. Praising with faint damns.") The main trouble with his writing, however, according to the Gorgon, was that it was "too bloody loose. Leaky. You *sprawl.*" He needed to "tighten" things.

It wasn't an incomprehensible complaint, he'd had to admit. In fact the Gorgon had edited the opening paragraph of John's paper for Assignment 2 in order to show him what he meant. Then he'd drawn a line across the paper and had written: "See? Can you *hear* the difference these changes make? Now *you* do it from here on—make your changes right on these pages—and then come see me with them."

John hadn't felt stupid in the conference. Some of his changes the Gorgon had liked ("Yes, here you go. Do this more. Write more like you do here"). But he'd missed more than he would have believed he could have, and his memory of the conference fastened on the Gorgon's talk about "jumbled paragraphs still," "junk yard arrangements," of John's need "not just to cut, but to cut and then recombine." *"Listen* to this, John," he could remember the Gorgon's saying before reading a string of his sentences, and then after reading them:

Can't you *hear* that? There's a key for you in the rhythms of what you write, John. *Listen* to them. Da-dum, da-dum, da-dum. Da-dum, da-dum, da-dum. Subject–verb, subject–verb, subject–verb. Sounds like a parade of circus elephants lumbering down a street, tail in trunk and trunk on tail. You've got to *hear* your sentences more to get a clearer connection between things, to see that this goes with this and not with that, this because of this and in spite of that. That's what writing is, working out the right relationship between things. Read your stuff out loud and *listen* to yourself more; then you won't have to take three sentences to say what you can say in one.

He'd nodded and smiled and said yes, he could hear it, he could see, and he'd left the Gorgon's office feeling encouraged. Rather vaguely encouraged, but his smile hadn't been completely phony. At least he could understand the Gorgon's changes as he'd made them, his pen flying across the paper. And, yes, they'd helped the writing. He'd had to give the Gorgon that.

But doing for himself and on his own what he'd watched the Gorgon do for him, he was discovering, was another thing again.

He looked at the opening of his paper for Assignment 4. He read it aloud.

The women look at the picture and see the man and woman on the trapeze as an inseparable unit. For the women, this particular view represents what they perceive as the ultimate male-female relationship. This relationship is based on fulfillment that stems from mutual effort toward a single goal.

  The first story is built around a marital conflict between the trapeze artists. Their problems are symbolized by their inability to reach out for each other during their act. There is an emphasis on cooperation in the story as the phrases "they" and "each other" appear often as the couple attempts to work their problems out. As they achieve their symbolic grasp at the end, becoming "man and wife again" is equated with learning "to communicate and to enjoy one another."

Oh my God, he thought. Sure it was only a draft he'd written. But oh my God.

He imagined reading it aloud to his study group—right after explaining, courtesy of Sandy, that the major criticism the Gorgon had been making of his prose was that it was too "loose," that it "sprawled," and that he needed to "tighten" things more. And then he imagined Sandy going to work with malicious pleasure on his first paragraph. "The women look . . . and see . . ." "For the women this . . . represents . . ." "This relationship is based . . ." Da-dum, da-dum, da-dum. Da-dum, da-dum, da-dum. Subject–verb, subject–verb, subject–verb. Three sentences instead of one. The elephant parade. Oh boy.

O.K. Let's try cutting then, just cutting, the way the girl in the Examining Room paper had:

  The women look at ~~the picture and see~~ the man and woman on the trapeze as an inseparable unit. ~~For the women, this particular view represents what they perceive~~ as the ultimate male-female

> relationship. ~~This relationship~~ based on
> fulfillment that stems from mutual effort towards
> a single goal.

No. It's all run together for one thing; it's just a jumble now, and it was run together in a way that screwed up what he'd meant. Which was? Well, simply that the women see something a certain way and this means they believe certain things, or seem to. . . . Maybe it's "because" that he meant then: the women believe certain things *because* they see things a certain way. Let's see if that's what you mean. Get "because" in there. And "believe."

> Because the women look at the man and woman on the
> trapeze as an inseparable unit they believe the
> ultimate male-female relationship is based on
> fulfillment that stems from mutual effort towards
> a single goal.

Not bad. Better anyway. It's better. Because of this, then this.
Was it *true* though, as a rendering of the women's stories, that is? It sounded awfully absolute. So soften it. Keep the connection but soften it a bit: because the women see this they *seem* to believe that. . . . That sounded more reasonable. What the women see, at least to judge from the stories, *suggested that* they believed something about relationships. How about that?

> Because the women look at the man and woman on the
> trapeze as an inseparable unit this seems to
> suggest that they believe . . .

But you don't need "because" and "this seems to suggest" both, do you? Let's try just:

> The women look at the man and woman on the trapeze
> as an inseparable unit suggesting that they
> believe . . .

That's it. That'll do it:

> The women look at the man and woman on the trapeze
> as an inseparable unit, suggesting that they
> believe the ultimate male-female relationship is
> based on fulfillment that stems from mutual effort
> toward a single goal.

Not bad. The elephants were gone; the connections reasonably clean. Not bad at all for 15 minutes work, he thought as he gathered up his books for class.

He knew he wasn't finished, not even with what he'd take to his study group. Indeed, that second paragraph he could see from his work with the first was not only full of elephants, but elephants who in the last couple of sentences had gone rogue and run amok. My God but the end of that paragraph was all over the place.

Right now it was.

The point was, he could see that now. And if he could see it, he could do something about it.

He was ready for Sandy anyway. An elephant hunter extraordinaire.

Assignment 5

H ere is still another way of talking about the "programs" or "preformed symbolic complexes" of the brain or mind, those structures that seem to influence not only what we say we see, but what we say that means:

Don't Let Stereotypes Warp Your Judgments

Is a girl called Gloria apt to be better-looking than one called Bertha? Are criminals more likely to be dark than blond? Can you tell a good deal about someone's personality from hearing his voice briefly over the phone? Can a person's nationality be pretty accurately guessed from his photograph? Does the fact that someone wears glasses imply that he is intelligent?

The answer to all these questions is obviously, "No."

Yet, from all the evidence at hand, most of us believe these things. Ask any college boy if he'd rather take his chances with a Gloria or a Bertha, or ask a college girl if she'd rather blind-date a Richard or a Cuthbert. In fact, you don't have to ask: college students in questionnaires have revealed that names conjure up the same images in their minds as they do in yours—and for as little reason.

Look into the favorite suspects of persons who report "suspicious characters" and you will find a large percentage of them to be "swarthy" or "dark and foreign-looking"—despite the testimony of criminologists that criminals do *not* tend to be dark, foreign or "wild-eyed." Delve into the main asset of a telephone stock swindler and you will find it to be a marvelously confidence-inspiring telephone "personality." And whereas we all think we know what an Italian or a Swede looks like, it is the sad fact that when a group of Nebraska students sought to match faces and nationalities of 15 European countries, they were scored wrong in 93 percent of their identifications. Finally, for all the fact that horn-rimmed glasses have now become the standard television sign of an "intellectual," optometrists know that the main thing that distinguishes people with glasses is just bad eyes.

Stereotypes are a kind of gossip about the world, a gossip that makes us prejudge people before we ever lay eyes on them. Hence it is not surprising that stereotypes have something to do with the dark world of prejudice. Explore most prejudices (note that the word means prejudgment) and you will find a cruel stereotype at the core of each one.

For it is the extraordinary fact that once we have typecast the world, we tend to see people in terms of our standardized pictures. In another demonstration of the power of stereotypes to affect our vision, a number of Columbia and Barnard students were shown 30 photographs of pretty but unidentified girls, and asked to rate each in terms of "general liking," "intelligence," "beauty" and so on. Two months later, the same group were shown the same photographs, this time with fictitious Irish, Italian, Jewish and "American" names attached to the pictures. Right away the ratings changed. Faces which were now seen as representing a national group went down in looks and still farther down in likability, while the "American" girls suddenly looked decidedly prettier and nicer.

Why is it that we stereotype the world in such irrational and harmful fashion? In part, we begin to type-cast people in our childhood years. Early in life, as every parent whose child has watched a TV Western knows, we learn to spot the Good Guys from the Bad Guys. Some years ago, a social psychologist showed very clearly how powerful these stereotypes of childhood vision are. He secretly asked the most popular youngsters in an elementary school to make errors in their morning gym exercises. Afterwards, he asked the class if anyone had noticed any mistakes during gym period. Oh, yes, said the children. But it was the *unpopular* members of the class—the "bad guys"—they remembered as being out of step.

We not only grow up with standardized pictures forming inside of us, but as grown-ups we are constantly having them thrust upon us. Some of them, like the half-joking, half-serious stereotypes of mothers-in-law, or country yokels, or psychiatrists, are dinned into us by the stock jokes we hear and repeat. In fact, without such stereotypes, there would be a lot fewer jokes. Still other stereotypes are perpetuated by the advertisements we read, the movies we see, the books we read.

And finally, we tend to stereotype because it helps us make sense out of a highly confusing world, a world which William James once described as "one great, blooming, buzzing confusion." It is a curious fact that if we don't *know* what we're looking at, we are often quite literally unable to *see* what we're looking at. People who recover their sight after a lifetime of blindness actually cannot at first tell a triangle from a square. A visitor to a factory sees only noisy chaos where the superintendent sees a perfectly synchronized flow of work. As Walter Lippmann has said, "For the most part we do not first see, and then define; we define first, and then we see."

Stereotypes are one way in which we "define" the world in order to see it. They classify the infinite variety of human beings into a convenient handful of "types" towards whom we learn to act in stereotyped fashion. Life would be a wearing process if we had to start from scratch with each and every human contact. Stereotypes economize on our mental effort by covering up the blooming, buzzing confusion with big recognizable cut-outs. They save us the "trouble" of finding out what the world is like—they give it its accustomed look.

Thus the trouble is that stereotypes make us mentally lazy. As S. I. Hayakawa, the authority on semantics, has written: "The danger of stereotypes lies not in their existence, but in the fact that they become for all people some of the time, and for some people all the time, *substitutes for observation.*" Worse yet, stereotypes get in the way of our judgment, even when we do observe the world. Someone who has formed rigid preconceptions of all Latins as "excitable," or all teenagers as "wild," doesn't alter his point of view when he meets a calm and deliberate Genoese, or a serious-minded high school student. He brushes them aside as "exceptions that prove the rule." And, of course, if he meets someone true to type, he stands triumphantly vindicated. "They're all like that," he proclaims, having encountered an excited Latin, an ill-behaved adolescent.

Hence, quite aside from the injustice which stereotypes do to others, they impoverish ourselves. A person who lumps the world into simple categories, who type-casts all labor leaders as "racketeers," all businessmen as "reactionaries," all Harvard men as "snobs," and all Frenchmen as "sexy," is in danger of becoming a stereotype himself. He loses his capacity to be himself—which is to say, to see the world in his own absolutely unique, inimitable and independent fashion.

Instead, he votes for the man who fits his standardized picture of what a candidate "should" look like or sound like, buys the goods that someone in his "situation" in life "should" own, lives the life that others define for him. The mark of the stereotype person is that he never surprises us, that we do indeed have him "typed." And no one fits this strait-jacket so perfectly as someone whose opinions about *other people* are fixed and inflexible.

Impoverishing as they are, stereotypes are not easy to get rid of. The world we type-cast may be no better than a Grade B movie, but at least we know what to expect of our stock characters. When we let them act for themselves in the strangely unpredictable way that people do act, who knows but that many of our fondest convictions will be proved wrong?

Nor do we suddenly drop our standardized pictures for a blinding vision of the Truth. Sharp swings of ideas about people often just substitute one stereotype for another. The true process of change is a slow one that adds bits and pieces of reality to the pictures in our heads, until gradually they take on some of the blurriness of life itself. Little by little, we learn not that Jews and Negroes and Catholics and Puerto Ricans are "just like everybody else"—for that, too, is a stereotype—but that each and every one of them is unique, special, different and individual. Often we do not even know that we have let a stereotype lapse until we hear someone saying, "all so-and-so's are like such-and-such," and we hear ourselves saying, "Well—maybe. . . ."*

Robert Heilbroner in the preceding essay makes clear why he believes seeing with, thinking with, stereotypes is in some senses natural to all of us. Also, he argues, it is a way of dealing with the world that has certain payoffs, to which there are certain advantages. Stereotypes help us make sense of the world's confusion, for instance—and with a minimum of mental effort. And perhaps there are other ways in which they help us get by as well.

But as what does stereotyping get us by?

For as Heilbroner also asserts, to see and to think with stereotypes is a habit of mind that also has certain disadvantages, for which we pay a price. Stereotypes "impoverish ourselves," he says. "A person who

---

*Robert Heilbroner, "Don't Let Stereotypes Warp Your Judgments." Reprinted by permission of Robert L. Heilbroner.

lumps the world into simple categories . . . loses his capacity to be himself—which is to say, to see the world in his own absolutely unique, inimitable and independent fashion."

In this assignment, you are going to be focussing on some writing in which a student in a composition course, asked to describe her experience with college, makes use of stereotypes. The purpose of the assignment is to enable you to use the writing *you* will be doing to help you develop a clearer understanding of the advantages and disadvantages of seeing, of thinking, with stereotypes.

The writing you are going to be working with in this assignment is a paper with a history.

Toward the end of a composition course a student turned in a paper to her teacher with a note that read as follows:

This is my fourth or fifth try at this paper. My in-class paper is garbage. I tried to rewrite it a couple of times over the term but they were garbage too. I finally got everything in place. So a lot of work went into this paper. A lot of learning resulted from it. Thank you.

P.S. I'm sorry I threw away all the other tries at this paper except the first. I know we're supposed to turn them in. But they were garbage anyway. Thanks again.

Here is the paper the student turned in with her note:

COLLEGE LIFE

I've never really been away from home before, so coming to the University of Pittsburgh, located in the center of a massive city, from a small town in northwest Pennsylvania certainly created a great deal of apprehension about college in general. I'm sorry to have to say that very little of the past two months I have spent here have helped me to adjust comfortably. New situations are bound to be threatening. This threat can be increased or decreased, however, depending upon a variety of factors.

My troubles began at registration. Somehow, thanks to my messed up advisor, I find myself the proud possessor of 19 credits plus marching band. You may gasp if you wish. Six of these credits involve three hours of laboratory work a week. And then of course there is the time involved in settling roommate problems, getting the work done outside of class that is necessary to comprehend what is going on in it, and in general becoming acclimatized to urban rather than country life. "Catch up ball" is the name of the game I've been playing for an entire semester. And being never caught up in my work due to lack of time doesn't add much to my concentration ability.

Being a statistic rather than a person hasn't helped me much either. My name is known in only two of my courses, the only two, not surprisingly, in which my work is up to standard. A lecture course given to three hundred people in which the need to "cover" material comes before anything else is hardly conducive to the creation of a learning environment, and how do you ask questions when they are never asked for, or when you don't even know the names of the people around you?

I'm not just complaining. I don't feel that to work out why the University of Pittsburgh may have been an ill-advised choice for me educationally is a "gripe-session." For many, Pitt may be an ideal school. It is important to understand, however, that the ability to concentrate in an environment conducive to learning is a highly individual matter, and that what may serve one student well may prove disastrous for another. Time in my case will provide the answer.

Here is the *first* version of the student's paper, the one she alludes to as having written in class (it was done in the first week of the course):

"COLLEGE LIFE SO FAR"

I've never really been away from home before, so there certainly was a great deal of apprehension about coming out here. Very little of the two weeks I've spent here have helped me to adjust comfortably.

Somehow, thanks to my messed up advisor, I am the proud possessor of 19 credits plus marching band. You may gasp, if you wish. The pressure of this much work is unbelievable. Band takes up at least nine hours a week, and I'm never caught up in my work due to lack of time. That doesn't add much to my concentration ability. *

Your assignment is to make the kind of sense of the information given you about this writer's writing that will enable you to explain to her how and why to improve it.

Prepare yourself to write this paper by developing a set of notes that will enable you both to identify the various stereotypes this writer uses (Being away from home always means what? Advisers are always what? Etc.) and what it might mean that the writer uses the sorts of stereotypes that she does. Make sure you refer to *all* the examples of this writer's writing that you have to work with. (These notes, like those

---

*This student paper was received and originally published by Kenneth Dowst of Trinity College. Kenneth Dowst, "The Epistemic Approach: Writing, Knowing, and Learning," in *Eight Approaches to Teaching Composition*, T. R. Donovan and B. W. McClelland, NCTE, 1980, p. 65.

you developed to write your paper for Assignment 4, you must turn in with your paper.)

Once you have written and studied your notes, use them to write at least a paragraph in which you explain in what senses the stereotypes this writer uses can be said to represent a way of seeing that has certain advantages for her, that can be said to help her get by.

Next, write at least a paragraph explaining in what senses the stereotypes this writer uses can be said to represent a way of seeing that has certain disadvantages, a way of seeing for which the writer may well pay a price.

Now, use what you have read and written to write a paper in which you imagine yourself talking to this writer about how and why to improve her writing. Speak as though you were speaking to the writer directly; you may construct a dialog if you choose. You may assume you have been asked by the writer herself to help her (she did not do well in her composition course), and that she knows you have read all of her writing that appears in this assignment. Your problem here, you will notice, is one of teaching strategy among other things. Just how are you going to enable the writer of "College Life" (and its antecedents) as you imagine her, to understand what you understand about her writing in such a way as to be able to do something about it?

N.B.   You're not expected to be an expert, of course, and probably won't get very far if you try to pose as one. On the other hand, you're a writer yourself. You've been doing some thinking about some of the problems this paper, and its history, might be said to pose. And you've had a chance to see this writer's work from a perspective she has not. Do the best you can to speak, one writer to another, in a way you hope will help her.

Seeing Assignment 5

PAT AND LOU

"Hi Pat," he said, banging his knees against the booth table as he slid into the seat across from her. And then, looking at the loaded ashtray, "Man. You smoke even more than I do, and that's a piece down the road. You ever try to stop?"

She just looked at him a moment, then shook her head, barely, her eyes never leaving his, and smiled. A small shaving of a smile.

"No need. There's fresh evidence, haven't you heard? Some guy in Louisiana has just discovered it keeps you young and desirable forever."

She seemed smaller than she was. She was very thin, all bone and ropy tendons, yet faded-looking somehow, unfocused, like an old photograph. Her eyes did not seem to belong with the rest of her. They were full and liquid, and looked irisless in the half light of the tavern.

"Yeah," he said. "I bet some guy in Louisiana."

"Truth. Straight from the canebrake," she said, and then, gesturing at her glass, "want a beer?"

She'd been the one who suggested they meet at Miller's, but of course he'd said O.K. He was the one asking for help, after all. At least that's what he'd told her he wanted.

82

"Coffee please," he said.

"I tried to stop smoking a couple of times," he went on. "Sort of tried. I made 23 hours once a couple of years ago. Well, a year ago." He lighted a Marlboro. "That was a long time for me," he said smiling at her.

"I went over your paragraph," she said tapping some sheets of paper lying in front of her. "I think I see some things you can do. What did the Gorgon say you needed when he gave you the Sale passage? Bridges?"

"Better bridges, yeah. Better relationships between my sentences. He said on my paper for 4 that I was 'and thening my life to death.' He gave me that Sale thing because he said he thought it was better than yelling at me to tighten my transitions."

"I see," she said, picking up the Sale. "This isn't bad."

[A writer] is asked a question, and he seeks to give an honest answer. It wasn't his question and probably isn't his subject, but perhaps he sees a way to make his answer his own, an expression of something he knows. What he knows is almost always a matter of the relationships he establishes, between example and generalization, between one part of a narrative and the next, between the idea and the counteridea that the writer sees is also relevant, between his experience and what he knows of the experience of others—in short, between any two parts of his knowledge. On the one hand this, on the other hand that; not this, but that; not just this, but also that; if this, then that; because this, that; that as an example of this; not this until that; yet, moreover, since, so, and: the list is potentially endless, and by inquiring into the exact relationship between things, a writer discovers what he knows, the words he wants.

"...a writer discovers what he knows, the words he wants." The matter of relating can extend down to the smallest matters and still be interesting. A tiny change, "a writer discovers what he knows, and then the words he wants," changes the relationships between the two clauses. To add "and then" is to say that the act of discovering is distinct from the act of finding the wanted words, as though knowledge preceded language in this instance. But regardless of whether it is ever possible to know something without knowing the words that express the knowledge, here the act of discovering is the act of finding words; for the writer there is no other way. To add "and then," in this case, would be to blur the sense of the entire preceding paragraph, and even to add "and" is to imply, however faintly, that the clauses describe separate actions. It is very important in this sentence that there be no relating words, because "what he knows" and "the words he wants" can only be properly related by modifying "discovers" equally and simultaneously. Relating words would only make the activities have some other relationship to each other than that of simultaneous action.

In this example a comma is the right relating "word." In others the semicolon can help because it can create a close but not quite clear relationship between two sentences.*

"O. K.," she went on, putting the Sale to one side and picking up another page. "Now here's the paragraph you did for 5 that you asked me to look at." She pushed it toward him.

```
     This person has the illusion, or "sees," her
advisor as someone who is supposed to know
everything; and when she finds herself smothered
with an overload of classes and band she blames it
all on her advisor. And she feels that her advisor
is "messed up," not her. As far as she can see, she
had nothing to do with her heavy class schedule,
and in reality, she probably didn't. Most likely,
she didn't take the time to sit with her advisor
and discuss how many credits she would be taking;
and if she did, she probably didn't take the time
to look into these classes and find out what they
involved, including band, before she met with her
advisor. Thus, her stereotyped image of her
advisor, as being "all knowing," got her by in many
ways. First, she didn't have to accept the
responsibility of doing some research on the
classes that she would be taking. And she didn't
have to talk to new people about classes they had
taken. And she didn't have to take the time to plan
her schedule. Moreover, by switching her
stereotyped image of her advisor to "messed up,"
```

---

*Roger Sale, *On Writing*. New York: Random House, 1970, pp. 71–72. Reprinted by permission of Random House.

she avoided having to take the blame for her hectic
life.

He nodded.

"And here," she said pushing another page toward him, "is all I did
with it. Read it and see what you think."

She placed the page so that both of them could see it. The dim light
of the bar brought their heads close, her hair almost against his cheek.
He read aloud, haltingly, keeping his place with his finger; she from time
to time corrected his rhythms.

Given how she writes

∧ This person has the illusion, or "sees," her
  t
advisor as someone who is supposed to know
everything; ~~and~~ *so* when she finds herself smothered
                          is able to
with an overload of classes and band she blames it
      ~~time someone else.~~ *It's*
all on ~~her advisor. And she feels that~~ her advisor
that's   *she can tell herself,*
~~is~~ "messed up," ∧ not her. As far as she can see, she
had nothing to do with her heavy class schedule,
                                  But   *m*
and in reality, she probably didn't. ~~M~~ost likely,
she didn't take the time to sit with her advisor
                                          either, or
and discuss how many credits she would be taking,
~~and~~ if she did, she probably didn't take the time
to look into these classes and find out what they
involved, including band, before she met with her
advisor. Thus, her stereotyped image of her
                                        gets
advisor, as being "all knowing," ~~got~~ her by in many
ways. ~~First,~~ She didn't have to accept the
responsibility of doing some research on the
classes that she would be taking; ~~And~~ she didn't
have to talk to new people about classes they had
taken; ~~And~~ she didn't have to take the time to plan
                  And the payoff is that by
her schedule. ~~Moreover,~~ ~~by~~ switching her
                                      another stereotype,
stereotyped image of her advisor to "messed up," ∧
she avoided having to take the blame for ~~her hectic~~
             s
~~life.~~ *any of it.*

"Well, what do you think?" she asked him, leaning back. "Do you think it reads better?"

He really was impressed.

"Hell, yes, Pat. It reads a hell of a lot better. It's a lot tighter. Thanks. Really, thank you. I thought you'd change a lot more in the paragraph, that you'd have to, I mean. You didn't even change what I said."

"Well," she said, "I did a little. A qualification here and there. 'Pay-off' is from the assignment. Little things. But Sale is good on the difference tiny changes make. I think what you say here is fine, as far as you go, incidentally. You don't deal with enough of the kid's papers yet, but what else you need to bring in from them you can bring in. Your argument makes sense, in other words."

"Oh I know," he said. "I mean I know I don't deal with enough in the papers yet. This isn't what I'm going to write for 5. I just wanted to get some things straight for myself, the way the assignment says. This is just the notes part, see? Like a draft?"

He stopped, bit his lip, and then plunged.

"Besides," he said grinning at her. "I had to knock out something to get to talk to you."

Her expression didn't change, but something had.

"Charming little old me," she said finally. "After what I said to Karen White Gloves you just couldn't wait to have me look at your writing, is that the picture?"

He sipped his coffee and then said, "Look Pat, you're the smartest one in our group. I think so anyway. And I've had the bad side of a lot worse mouths than yours. The worst you could have told me was to fuck off, and I've been told that before."

He grinned again.

"I survived. I'm a survivor, you know."

"Sure," she said, watching him through the smoke of her cigarette. "What's that got to do with me?"

"I just wanted to talk to you, that's all."

She was very still, coiled.

"I get it," she said. "It's because the kid who did those papers in Assignment 5 is another version of Miss White Gloves. You just couldn't resist the temptation to see some more of my lovely personality."

It really did surprise him. "The girl who wrote 'College Life' is like Karen? That's what you think?"

"You're damned right that's what I think. Lazy. Whiney. Manipulative. Self-Pitying. Aren't they both that? You were the one who told Karen to stop feeling sorry for herself, remember? And isn't that what you're saying in this paragraph about the writer of 'College Life,' that that's her trouble too? And you only touch the beginning of the paper.

It gets worse as it goes on. You're damned right I think they're the same. They're both losers."

At that moment he understood why she had attracted him, why he had wanted to talk to her. He thought of B-B Eyes in his handcuffs. He didn't respond to her right away.

"Well," he said finally, "she came back, Karen did. You said she wouldn't, remember? That took starch, you know? That took guts."

She hissed derisively, and stabbed out her cigarette, not looking at him, her mouth twisted and angry.

Neither of them said anything for a while.

"You know, Pat, I was a loser. I used to be king of the losers. Seriously. A real bum and a half. One point five. I don't think you have to stay a loser."

"Yes, I know," she flashed. "That's why you took back what you said to Karen at the second session, right? You wanted to make her a winner." And then she added nastily, "She's very pretty, isn't she?"

"You really think that's why I apologized to her, because I was coming on to her? You think that's the way I've acted since?"

"Well, why did you apologize to her? I'm damned if I would have." She barked a short unpleasant laugh. "I didn't. Maybe you noticed. I thought it was insulting what she did. And that piece of crap she gave us to read, that was worse. 'Do *you* see any boo-boos, Pat?' Jesus. I'll bet she tosses her head when she sings."

She ordered more beer. He got more coffee.

"Yeah. O.K. She was insulting. I didn't tell her I thought she wasn't, *or* that she was a good kid, *or* that she's pretty. In fact I told her I still thought her paper was sloppy, remember? All I told her I was sorry about was that I'd laughed at her. Actually, I was laughing at you laying into her. But that was wrong. I mean I was wrong. And that's what I apologized to her for."

"No, what you meant was that you thought I was wrong. I should have been more sweet and forgiving, I suppose."

"Look, all I'm talking about is me, what I did, O.K.?"

"You apologized because of a program you're trying to live your life by, right?" Her tone was still mocking.

"Damned right."

"What program?"

He considered it. And then decided.

"AA. Alcoholics Anonymous. I'm an alcoholic. I'm sober almost 3 years, but I'm an alcoholic. I was hooked on drugs too. I used anything I could get."

It stopped her. She pretended it was just information, but he'd seen the minnow flash at the back of her eyes and her quick glance at the beer.

He pointed at the beer and smiled.

"It's O.K., by the way. It's O.K. for you, just not for me. I mean it's O.K. for you if you're 21. You 21?"

"I've got a card that says so. AA says you treat losers like winners, then?"

"AA says when you do something you think is wrong, you better fix it. 'Promptly admit it,' is what we say. It's not a theory. I treated Karen like she didn't matter. That was wrong."

"Because she's really a winner."

"You know what a guy I know says about talking that way, Pat? He says you can bet your life there's losers, and that one way you know them is they think there's such a thing as a winner. The point is, I treated Karen like a loser and that's no good for me. I used to do it with people all the time, and it's no good for me. See, I don't *know* Karen is a loser, not any more than I know the girl in Assignment 5 is. Neither do you. Where the hell would I be if nobody ever gave me a chance to be anything more than what I was? King of the losers. That really was how I saw myself. Cream of the scum. AA gave me a chance to be something else."

"Too bad Karen can't join AA. And the kid in Assignment 5."

"It really is you know. I think about that a lot. I don't know about Karen, but the girl who wrote those versions of 'College Life' sounds a lot like an alcoholic in a lot of ways. A lot of ways. I mean she sounds the way people who are addicted sound. It's why we're addicted to begin with."

"Come on, Lou. The kid in 5 has a drinking problem?"

"Oh, I don't mean she drinks or uses or anything like that. I mean . . ."

He stopped, running through what he knew had saved his life.

"Look at it this way. The real problem in the assignment is how to talk to the writer of the paper, right? How to get through to her? That's why they set it up the way they do, isn't it—with all that talk about the importance of teaching? O.K. Now, how are you going to get her a ball she won't just bounce back over the net?"

"What do you mean 'get her a ball'? I'd tell her just what I told Karen. She could take it or leave it."

"Yeah? Well, she'd leave it; believe me. Yell at her and she'll just pull the plug on you. She'll just switch you right off. You'll be just another part of the system that's out to get her, so far as she's concerned. You think nobody ever told me to straighten out and grow up and all that jazz *before* AA? I was told that a lot, honey, believe me. A lot. And it never meant a thing to me. Not a thing. I just went right on using. See, the problem is how to get *her* to hear she's whiney and self-pitying."

"Karen heard me, didn't she? She hasn't pulled that batted eyelash stuff any more since that first session, has she?"

"No, she hasn't. But you told me yourself you thought she was going to drop the course, that we'd never see her again. Besides all you were telling her was what she couldn't do. We all were. Well, not Betty and Charlie maybe, but you and me. Anyway, the problem here in 5 is a lot more complicated. In 5 . . ." He fumbled in his notebook. "Here it is. . . . In 5 we're supposed to . . ."

"What the hell, Lou. More complicated. Karen knew better. This kid knows better too."

"Listen now, listen to what they say. We're supposed to talk to her 'about how and why to improve her writing.' Now *maybe* this girl knows better. Maybe. But she didn't write the paper just once and then drop it, you know. That's important, I think. Anyway, all I can tell you is that *I* didn't know better. I saw myself as a victim the same way this writer does. I *made* myself a victim the same way too, though of course I didn't realize that that's what I was doing at all. See, I talked about things this same way," he tapped his open notebook, "because that's how I thought things really were. And nothing got through because I had all the bases covered. I burned all the bridges. I flushed all the evidence the same way this girl does. I made *sure* nothing got through, see? And until AA, nothing ever did."

She leaned back and looked at him. Skeptically. But not just skeptically.

"I think you're making an awful lot, Lou, out of a crappy little set of papers. This kid's no addict."

"No?" he said, and drew heavily on his cigarette. "Well, I'll tell you, Pat. I didn't know I was an addict either."

BETTY AND SANDY

"This is nice of you, Betty. It really is. Look, I want you to know I didn't just cut those classes on Assignment 4. I really did have flu."

Sandy had a queer habit of twisting one side of her mouth down and to the side abruptly, like a reflex, in a way that suggested both urgency and tentativeness at the same time. It bared some of her lower teeth, which were very crooked and gaped, pickety looking.

"Anyway," she continued, "it's awfully nice of you to help me."

Betty laughed.

"Nobody's helped anybody yet. I just got here."

They were at the edge of the library study area with a table to themselves. Sandy had some dittoed pages spread in front of her.

"See, I can't take this to my study group. They're all on Assignment 5 now. And the Gorgon . . ." She twisted her mouth again. "Well, I don't think the Gorgon likes me very much. He thinks. . . . I don't think he thinks I'm serious."

"Oh I don't think the Gorgon dislikes people, really. He's scary, but it's just his way of making sure we *get* serious. That's what he's after, I think."

"See, Betty, what I wanted to go over was what Pat did. I mean the stuff she did on 4 that the Gorgon dittoed for the class to work on. Amy told me it was Pat's stuff. She's the one who picked up my paper on 4, Amy I mean, when I was sick. See, she lives in my dorm. I *guess* I could talk to Pat, but . . ."

She made a face.

"See, Karen lives in my dorm too," Sandy went on. "She told me she'd have dropped the course if it wasn't for you."

Betty smiled. She might have guessed. Michael had told her she was going to become a resident mother hen if she wasn't careful.

"You heard the Gorgon really liked what Pat did for Assignment 4, and he wasn't crazy about what you did? Incidentally, he wasn't crazy about what I did either. But that's what you want to talk about, Sandy?"

"Well, I . . . yes, I mean I sort of see why the Gorgon might have liked what Pat did, but what I want. . . . See, Amy said he liked the way Pat quoted. And he liked her notes. She didn't explain very much, Amy I mean, because she didn't want to catch flu. She just stood at the door of my room and sort of whooshed all this stuff across the floor to me and that was all she said. I was in bed."

The dittoed sheets Sandy had in front of her were those the class had worked on for Assignment 4. The paper she herself had written for 4 was not with them.

"I'm all over my flu now, though," Sandy added quickly. "I'm fine."

"Good," Betty said, nodding, amused. "That's good, Sandy."

"Anyway, that's what Amy said the Gorgon talked about in class, the way Pat quoted. See, this whole trip the Gorgon's into about quoting with *authority,* I never heard before. I can quote all right. I mean I know where to put the quotes and how to use brackets and the little dots when you leave things out and all that stuff. But I never heard about quoting with *authority* before. And, see, in our study group I'm going to have to show everybody . . ."

Sandy trailed off, gesturing vaguely.

"The Gorgon says you *don't* quote with authority, is that it?"

"He says the texts I work with control me. That's exactly what he said on my paper about the rhinoceroses. Then he said it again on the paper I wrote for 4 that Amy brought me."

"Well, he did talk in class about how the key to quoting well was to have what you write say 'I'm in charge of this material,' not the other way around."

"Actually, he wrote on my 4 that my prose is lumpy with quotations, like bad gravy."

"Like what?"

"Oh, he didn't say gravy. I said that. He said my prose was too full of lumps of quotation. 'Gouts,' he said. It reminded me of bad gravy. And then he said that he hoped class would help me to see how to quote with more authority and those of course were the classes I had to miss because I got flu."

"Sure," Betty said, nodding. "Of course. He wrote that on your paper because he knew he was going to go over Pat's stuff in class the day after you got your paper back and he wanted you to learn from what we did. He's big on that."

"O. K., so what did the Gorgon mean when he said Pat's paper was good because of her notes? Amy said he said that."

Again Betty laughed.

"Sandy, look. I'm no expert, you know. I'm not sure. . . . Let me get my copies of those papers. I took some notes on them in class."

She bent to get her notebook out of an attache case, which opened with an audible snap. It was a relic from her law firm days. She could feel Sandy watching her, and was suddenly self-conscious in her new Jordache jeans. She'd damn well drawn the line at buying a knapsack bookbag, however.

They both read through their copies of what the Gorgon had dittoed to work with in class.

Notes

| Men |

Pattern

Story I
violent physical sensation
(viol. slips surge / bulg. sinews)
Control?
no "because" (accident? / murder?
self-punish?
self-hatred?

love, love, love,
no couple / his vs her / no intimacy
loss?

Meaning of Patterns

control
power / possessive
passion rather than
caring

event centered
(contextless)

man controls // woman a
thing

avoidance of intimacy
out of fear?

what are men
afraid of?

Story II
"fell in love"
no "because" (universe tragic?)
he trains
emphasis on his loss. (punishment?)
his - her again — no intimacy

Story III
"he'd drop her" (no "because" control? murder)
woman just a body, a thing (punishment?)
"he had to get rid of her"/"she was so possessive". (ego)
loss? ("crumpled body;" "gold lamé"?
love passion to - - - what? be free?
his - her No Intimacy!

PARAGRAPH WRITTEN FROM NOTES ABOVE:

. . . The men's responses also seem
(depressingly) similar in pattern. There is
little concept of couple in their stories; rather,
what receives emphasis is the pivotal role played
by the man who quickly establishes a power
relationship with the woman. The first and third
stories, for example, glorify the man's raw
physical power (*he* thrills to the showing of the
"strength which surged from *his* arms into hers";
how would you like to have to *"constantly* catch
your wife" [italics mine]), and in the second it is
the power of the male as mentor we are to admire
(*"he* trained *her* to fly" [my italics]) . . .

"O. K.," Betty said finally. "Now this isn't Pat's whole paper remember, or all the notes she turned in either. It's just one section of her notes
and one paragraph, I don't know if it's even a *whole* paragraph, from
her paper."

"Right," Sandy said. "Amy said the Gorgon was just cutting out a section of things for us to look at and that he thought the writing was good because the notes are good. Amy said he thought the writing had authority."

"Well, yeah, but what I remember is that he said the *strength* of the paragraph *begins* with the notes. He liked Pat's notes because he said they showed a mind working. He said the paragraph showed that too. But he said he didn't want us to think that this was the only way to take notes and he didn't let us talk about whether we thought Pat was right or wrong about the stories either. He wanted us to see what made her argument effective. That's what he had the class on. What made Pat's argument strong. And yes, he did say she used the material from the assignment with authority. I wrote that down."

"What does he mean that Pat's notes show a mind working? They look sloppy to me. Some of the things she puts quotes around aren't quotes, like "because," and she doesn't put quotes around stuff that is a quote, like "bulging sinews." And she doesn't use *all* the quotes she has in her list when she writes her paragraph. See, my list was all quotes, but they were all correct, and I had a lot more things in my list than Pat does, and the Gorgon writes on my notes: 'Your trouble starts here.'"

"Is that all he wrote on your notes?"

"He said I didn't 'mediate' enough. Something like that. I never even heard the word before."

It was clear to Betty that Sandy did not want to show her her paper.

"O.K. That I do understand, because he used the word in class when he went over Pat's notes. See, what he liked in Pat's stuff is the way you can see her interpreting things, thinking about what something means. He liked the way you can see that *starting* in the notes, and then the way you can see it show up in her writing. I think that's what he means by 'mediate.' See, if you look at Pat's notes on the first man's story where she says 'no "because," ' it's like seeing her say to herself, 'there isn't any reason given in the story why the man drops the woman. There's no "because" for it.' She's only talking to her*self* there, you see. That's how she's using her notes, to have a dialog with herself the Gorgon said, so she doesn't have to use quotes right, or good grammar or anything. The important thing, the Gorgon said, is that the *writer* knows what she means, which he said Pat seems to—only he didn't use her name of course—because you can see her going on to think about the 'because' inside the parentheses. She asks herself if it was an accident maybe, or whether it was murder. And then she wonders, if it *was* murder, whether it was because the man hated the woman some way, or maybe hated himself and had to punish himself somehow. She's *thinking,* see, about what she's reading. That's what the Gorgon liked. That's all he means by 'mediate.' "

"And," Betty went on, taking up her ballpoint, "he showed how Pat does it in other places too, like down here, see, in her notes on story 2 and on 3 too. See these underlines in how she talks about story 3, *'he'd'* and *'her'?* The Gorgon said that that showed thinking, that it was like being inside somebody's head who's saying 'well, if *he'd* drop *her,* and there's no reason for it given in the story'—see how she does the 'because' thing again there?—'then maybe that means the man wants so much to control the woman that he's willing to murder her to do it!"

Betty stopped, her focus all of a sudden entirely on what she was reading. "I just noticed the way Pat brings up this idea of the men maybe punishing *themselves* in the stories they tell, because they're . . . it's a little hard to tell what she thinks the reason is . . . that they're afraid, I guess . . . afraid of intimacy in some way?"

She stopped. "Humm," she said shortly, and stopped again.

"I didn't see that when we went over this in class. I wonder what Pat did with that idea in her paper. I'll have to ask her."

"I wouldn't ask Pat about anything," Sandy said, looking to one side.

"Oh, Pat's not all that bad, you know, Sandy, if you don't take her head on. She's just as nervous about school as everybody else. And she really knows an awful lot. She looked up what Gorgon means and typed it out for us."

"She what?"

"She looked up what the name means. For study group. Charles said he'd always wondered where he got the nickname, and that he'd heard the Gorgon was supposed to be more than a monster that turned people to stone, and so Pat said she'd look it up. Here." She took a loose page from the front of her notebook and handed it to Sandy. "Here's what she gave us. You can have it if you want; I've got another copy."

ON THE GORGON

What was that snaky-headed Gorgon shield
That wise Minerva wore, unconquer'd Virgin,
Wherewith she freez'd her foes to congeal'd
    stone
But rigid looks of Chaste austerity,
And noble grace that dash't brute violence
With sudden adoration and blank awe?

Comus, lines 447—452

The lines in Milton are footnoted by Merritt
Hughes in his edition of *Comus* as follows:

> The traditional figure of Minerva, carrying
> the Gorgon's head as she is described in the
> Iliad V 738-41, is explained by Conti
> (*Mythologiae*, IV, v) as symbolizing the dread
> she strikes into her lustful enemies, "not one
> of whom dare arise when she wears the frightful
> Gorgon's head with its serpent-hair on her
> breast."

What this means, gang, is that we've had the Gorgon
all wrong! He's really no more than an instrument
of *Wisdom* (Minerva being the goddess of the same).
His only function is to petrify our *brutish*
natures so that our finer qualities can shine!
It's all in a good cause, in other words, and for
our own good.

Sandy read it through and said, "Well, I guess so. But I'm still glad I'm talking to you." She gestured at the dittoed pages. "O.K. If this is the way we're supposed to take notes, I haven't been doing it."

Betty leaned across the library table, pressed Sandy's wrist firmly, and said, "Look, Sandy, you have to be careful how you see all this. The Gorgon spent quite a while in the classes you missed on how you couldn't really say that one way of taking notes was right and another wrong. He told us this was important because we were going to have to work with notes a couple of times in the course, notes and drafts of papers. The point of it, he said, was to give us a chance to go at writing different ways. If we don't experiment, see, we can't learn. That's the idea. What he liked about Pat's notes was what they *look* like they helped her to do. He said he couldn't say for sure, that he was working back from her paper, I mean from that section of the paper he dittoed up."

"Where Pat quotes with authority, supposedly."

"Well, yes. She does too. See the way she underlines *'his'* and *'constantly'* and *'yours'* in her paragraph and says 'italics mine'? That shows she's stressing certain things in her reading, that it's *her* ideas she's concerned with. And the Gorgon liked the way Pat picked only the *best* details, rather what she seemed to think were the best details, to make her point. She has the stuff about 'bulging sinews' from the first man's story in her notes too, see, and the flipping. But she doesn't put all that stuff in her paper just because she took notes on it. She'd be beating a dead horse to put in *everything* she took notes on just because she took notes on it.''

"She'd be making lumpy gravy," Sandy said smiling.

"Right. She wouldn't be thinking about what the whole thing means to *her,* the way she shows she is when she puts 'depressingly' in parentheses. That's what shows her 'mediating.' She's saying, 'I'm in control of this material. It's not controlling me.' And she uses all three of the men's stories; she covers all the bases. The Gorgon liked how she did that too.''

"And that's what he means saying she quotes with authority?''

"I think that's what he means. Authority is like saying 'I've got *evidence* for why I believe something and here it is, but *what* I believe is what's really important and I'm going to make sure you don't forget it.' But the point is there's no one way of saying that. The only way you can be sure you *won't* say it, the Gorgon said, is *not* to do what Pat does here *somewhere, sometime,* when you have to write about something you're reading. He even said, Sandy, that some writers take notes that are just quotations, nothing else, just the way you did. Then they do the mediating in their heads. That's O.K., he said, if the *paper* shows a mind working the way Pat's does. But if your paper *doesn't* show a mind working, he said, then you might want to try taking notes a different way. You might want to add a step. Go ahead and list your quotations first, for instance, but then make a section like Pat's 'Meaning of Pattern' to help you see what all your quotes add up to. The Gorgon said Pat's notes were right on the borderline of being a draft of her paper because of the way she thinks with them.''

Sandy nodded and sighed, her mind on the notes she'd already written for Assignment 5, lying on her desk like, well, not even like John's elephants. At least John's elephants had been moving. Like a lot of dead lumps her quotations were. Like a pile of dead snakes.

But, she got to thinking on her way back to her dorm, if John got rid of his elephants, maybe she could goose some life into her snakes.

Make 'em sit up and sway even, she thought smiling to herself, maybe even mediate 'em into a song and dance.

Assignment 6

Robert May, the psychologist who conducted the experiment referred to in Assignment 4, says that in spite of the range of content and tone in the stories one gets when one asks people to say what they think is happening in the picture of the trapeze artists, there is a surprising unanimity in the *kinds* of stories told about the picture by men and in the *kinds* of stories told about the picture by women. "In general," he says, the "stories told by men tend to move from enhancement to deprivation . . . and stories told by women tend to move from deprivation to enhancement" (p. 20). ("Enhancement" May defines as a state of being characterized by "physical satisfaction, ability and success, growth or ascension, good feelings, being handled by others, insight and the like." May defines "deprivation" as a state of being characterized by "physical need or tension, failure, injury, painful effort, falling, unpleasant feelings, and so forth" [p. 18].)

But that the "programs" or "preformed symbolic complexes" we carry around in our heads *influence* what we say we see is not to say that they *determine* it—as May also makes clear he believes. He makes very pointed reference to a group of women working with the picture of the trapeze that included a number of "organizationally and politically active feminists." The pattern May found in these feminists' stories was quite different from those in both the stories told by other women *and by men*. The feminists' stories *begin* as do those May says are ordinarily told by men, with "enhancement," but "pride and self-confidence," rather than being "punished" (this is May's word, "punished") in the feminists' stories with "the catastrophic end," are rather celebrated and enjoyed. These changes May speaks of approvingly and says are to be expected from women doing something "to separate themselves from traditional sex roles" (pp. 27–28).

Similarly, Walker Percy, a part of whose essay you read for Assignment 3, is clear that the difficulties he believes there are in seeing the Grand Canyon do not make seeing it impossible.

> How can the sightseer recover the Grand Canyon? He can recover it in any number of ways, all sharing in common the strategem of avoiding the approved confrontation of the tour and the Park service. (p. 48)

And finally, Robert Heilbroner, part of whose essay on stereotyping you read for Assignment 4, not only asserts it is possible to change the habit of seeing and thinking with stereotypes; he concludes his essay with some advice about how we can help the change come about:

> Can we speed the process along? Of course we can.
> First, we can become aware of the standardized pictures in our heads, in other peoples' heads, in the world around us.
> Second, we can become suspicious of all judgments that we allow exceptions to "prove." There is no more chastening thought than that in the vast intellectual adventure of science, it takes but one tiny exception to topple a whole edifice of ideas.
> Third, we can learn to be chary of generalizations about people. As F. Scott Fitzgerald once wrote: "Begin with an individual, and before you know it you have created a type; begin with a type, and you find you have created—nothing."
> Most of the time, when we type-cast the world, we are not in fact generalizing about people at all. We are only revealing the embarrassing facts about the pictures that hang in the gallery of stereotypes in our own heads.

To say that the mind seems to have a *tendency* to move in certain ways, then, is not to say that a given mind has to work by formula. That we may be culturally or even biologically *influenced* in how we look at the world is not to say that how we grow up or whether we are male or female *predetermines* what we must become.

The question, of course (think back to some of the problems you may have had talking to the writer of the paper reproduced in Assignment 5), is one of exactly what to do to develop a way of seeing, of thinking, that is other than what Heilbroner calls "stereotypical." What exactly is one to do instead of confronting the Grand Canyon through the agency of "the tour and the Park service"?

And even more important is the question of how we know that what we may call an *un*stereotypical way of seeing or thinking is that at all. How do we know that in rejecting one "program," one set of "preformed symbolic complexes," one stereotype, we have done any more than replace it with another?

It is easy enough to say, as Heilbroner does, that to change the habit of seeing and thinking with stereotypes we must "become aware of the standardized pictures in our heads," become "suspicious" of certain of our "judgments," "learn to be chary of generalizations about people." But just how we are to "become aware," and just what the process is to result in are more problematic than Heilbroner's language would seem to suggest.

This assignment is to help us develop some alternatives to talking stereotypically about what one can do to develop a way of seeing, of thinking, that is other than stereotypical.

Describe a time in your life when you experienced someone's moving from what you would call a stereotypical way of seeing or thinking about something to a way of seeing or thinking that you would say was other than stereotypical. Again, as was the case with the paper you wrote for Assignment 3, this may but does not have to be something you went through yourself. You are a reader. You've seen plays and movies. You move in a world with other people.

Again also, describe the occurrence as though it were a scene in a novel or a short story, that is as a particular happening in which particular people move and speak. Include all relevant detail as to who was there and what was said and done. Be sure your account makes clear what the stereotypical way of seeing or thinking seems to have been a matter of in this instance, what the *un*stereotypical way of seeing or thinking seems to have been a matter of, and what seems to have caused the change.

In writing a narrative account of your experience for the first part of this assignment you have created what may be seen as a work of fiction. But you have also done what may be seen as a piece of research. Beginning on a separate sheet of paper, draw what conclusions you can from the scene you have created about what might be helpful to you in learning to see or to think in other than a stereotypical way.

Seeing
Assignment
6

AMY

To find in her life an example of "what you would call a stereotypical way of seeing or thinking" was no problem whatever. In fact, she thought wryly, she was beginning to wonder whether anybody ever thought in any other way. She remembered Julie's saying in class fairly early on in the term about the selection from Percy that it seemed to her you had to look at the Grand Canyon through *something*. And Frank had raised the whole thing again the same way he was always asking questions in study group. "Well, what's a way of thinking that *isn't* stereotypical, then?" he'd demanded of the Gorgon, who had fielded it by turning the question immediately on all the rest of them of course, who of course hadn't come up with anything. Alonzo tried. Maybe there are stereotypes and then there are stereotypes, he'd offered. But nobody had done anything with it and that had been that.

And what, she snorted to herself, made thinking with stereotypes such an evil thing anyway? Even Heilbroner admitted they were useful, and she could remember a time in her life when for her they'd been a lot more than that. She thought back to Robbie, whom she'd known before she'd met Tom, and to the night on which she'd concluded, to the night on which she'd been unable to do anything *other* than conclude, that all his athletic attentions to her had been only to get her to help him with his physics. The "man of her dreams" who finally knows "value" when he sees it had become in an instant "the school stud" dating "the school grind" in preparation for his college boards—while having Linda on the side. Well, what was she supposed to have concluded? That he'd really been honest and loving with her under all those lies? That he'd really cared about her? That he really *wasn't* like the men who wrote those stories about the trapeze artists? And that her mother had been wonderful about it all, considering? Just wonderful? Was that what an unstereotypical way of seeing was supposed to amount to? No thank you if it was. There was no way she was going to buy another way of seeing that time, or him, or her mother. Thanks but no thanks. Thanks very much, but no thank you, sir. He'd been a bastard, she'd been a fool, and her mother was the I-told-you-so nag. Stereotypes or not, that had been the way it had been.

So the problem was not to find what she "would call a stereotypical way of seeing or thinking in her life." The problem was to find an example of such a way of seeing or thinking becoming something else—and, she thought, slapping her open notebook, without one damned thing in the course to help her. There was nothing in this assignment anyway, except the claims of three people that seeing without stereotypes seemed to be possible. Unless you wanted to count the stories May mentioned that had been written by the feminists, and of course the Gorgon hadn't given them any of those to look at. Or unless you wanted to count Walker Percy, and the Gorgon hadn't given them the rest of what *he'd* said either. Maybe she should just become a feminist and see for herself. Or trot over to the library like a good little student and look up Percy's essay.

She began flipping irritably back through her notebook. Fat chance of there being anything to help her there. There was nothing in 5 . . . nothing in 4 . . . nothing in. . . .

What stopped her at Assignment 3 was neither the assignment nor the paper she had written for it. What stopped her was the dittoed *copy* of her paper, one of those that the Gorgon had passed out to everybody the day he'd used her paper as an example in class. Minus her name, of course. "To protect anonymity," the word was. Her original paper was there in her notebook too, the one she'd turned in to the Gorgon and on which he'd written only: "I hope the class we have on this can give you some ideas about how to rewrite it—though I'd suggest you wait a bit to do that. You don't *have* to rewrite understand, but I think to try might be valuable to you—for several reasons."

It was the dittoed copy of her paper that had stopped her, or more exactly the notes she'd taken in the margins of it, that day, that ghastly day, on which for about half the period the class had worked over what she had written—she pretending all the while, and with every resource she could command, that it was just a lesson in writing she was receiving, that its point was to help her get *better,* to help all of them get *better,* and that in any case no one in class could know who had written the paper, or would ever *have* to know who had written the paper. She'd made it to the end of the period somehow, but she had cut her anthropology class. Back in her room alone, she had cried—she (she had to smile at the connection in spite of herself) who just five minutes ago had been wondering whether thinking in stereotypes was all that bad.

Because stereotypes—the notes she had taken on the dittoed sheets brought the whole period back to her—had been what the class had landed on hardest in what she'd written, first in the sketch she had done and then in what she had concluded from it. No one had then used the term *stereotypes,* of course. The going terms then had been "pre-existing mental structures" or "pre-existing programs" from Assignment 2. "Preformed symbolic complex" came from the Percy quotation in 3. "PSC→PSC ab. PSC" she'd written at the end of her paper. That, she could remember, had been her rendering of Charles' comment in class, made toward the end of the period, a comment that had been the worse for her to hear because he had made it so impersonally, so summationally, and worst of all because she knew it was right. "It looks then," Charles had said, "as though what this writer has done in the scene part of her paper is to create the sort of preformed symbolic complexes that then lead her to come up with a lot of preformed symbolic complexes about preformed symbolic complexes." And the Gorgon had nodded and nodded, and even she could see that that was indeed exactly what she had done. She'd seen it then and she could see it now.

But when she'd *done* it, when she was writing her paper, she'd had no awareness at all of doing that.

And now here was Assignment 6, which also asked her to open her paper with what Charles had called a "scene part," to describe an event "as though it were a scene in a novel or short story."

She'd better see as much as she could see about just where and how things had gone wrong in what she'd written for 3 then?

She supposed she better had.

She was at least, by God, as capable as John was.

She set her jaw and read over both her paper and the notes she'd taken on it that day in class. She read them both over carefully, remembering, recreating:

PART 1

(handwritten: Like Senator)

The bazaar was in full swing when Thomas, my best friend and boyfriend, and I arrived. We tried our luck at several games of chance, and then we sauntered across the church lot to my mother's pick-a-ticket stand. When she saw me approaching, *(handwritten: beach / supermarket)* *(handwritten: comic book!)* she flashed me a brilliant smile, but at the sight of Thomas the smile quickly disappeared. She *(handwritten: water spaniel)* glared at him pure hatred, animosity, and rage on her face. She totally ignored him in the rudest manner that I have ever witnessed. The unbelievable coldness and malevolence that radiated from her became unbearable and Thomas walked away.

(handwritten: Group T.)

My mother turned on me as soon as Thomas had departed. She ranted and raved about our relationship especially how close it had become. *(handwritten: A lump! A lump! A lump!)* I tried to explain to my mother that Tom and I are best friends who share an extremely open and honest relationship. I told her that I am closer to him than any other person and that I can talk to him about anything and everything. She retorted by saying that it is impossible for him to be my best friend because of his sex. She believed that he couldn't possibly understand me the way that another female could. I replied that he *(handwritten: Sticks!)* understands me far better than anyone else and that he is the most trustworthy person that I have ever met. At that she turned and walked away, unwilling to try to comprehend how Thomas and I can possibly be such close friends while being of opposite sexes.

(handwritten: indirect discourse)

(handwritten: do dialogue but change likes)

PART 2

In my short sketch, the "preformed symbolic
complex" is my mother's attitude that a woman's
closest friend must also be a woman, even though
one of her closest friends is a man. This complex
is made up of old-fashioned notions concerning
what it is permissible for males and females to
discuss. For example, my mother doesn't believe
that a female and a male friend can discuss topics
like menstruation, gynecological problems,
pregnancy, and sex. She feels that these can only
be discussed with other females. I, however, can
only discuss these things with Thomas because of
our closeness. I'm not quite sure where these
complexes come from or how they develop. I believe
that in this case this pre-existing idea stems
from long-standing social concepts of male-female
sex roles and interactions. Women are never
supposed to broach subjects such as those
mentioned above. For a woman to discuss such
things with a man is . . . unthinkable. I do feel
that this complex is slowly vanishing as the roles
of men and women in society change.

Because no "souverign discovery"

Picture postcards
Tourist folders

A set up!

PART 3

Many difficulties between parents and children
could be resolved if the parents would only equate
their children's experiences and difficulties
with their own childhood experiences and
problems. Most parents had many of the same

Rigged!

disagreements with their parents as their
children have with them. If only they could see
that this is the case, then perhaps they would not
handle the situation in the same obsolete manner
as their own parents did. Parents must also
realize that their children are individuals with
the duty to lead their own lives and make their own
decisions as soon as they mature enough to be able
to do so. If the children were allowed to make
their own mistakes and learn from them, then
perhaps many of the difficulties could be avoided.

PSC → PSC @ PSC !
Redo // do day after bazaer w/ mother. dialogue.
// Like w/ Robbie, but more. I know this!

She was surprised at how much came back to her of what had led
her to make the notes on her paper that she had. She'd thought of
herself as bludgeoned numb by the classroom conversation, but as she
read over the notes she had made on her paper, she found she could
even recall, for the most part, exactly who in the class had said what.

It was her sketch, Part 1 of the assignment, that the class had spent
most time on and been roughest with. Alonzo had started things by
pointing out that her paper "represents a poor reading of the assignment. We're clearly told," she could remember his saying, "that we're
not to waste our time writing about monsters and saints." He also
pointed out that her paper was written "in indirect discourse—another
direct violation of the directions in the assignment," he'd said. "All you
hear in what this writer has is *that* the mother 'ranted and raved.' You
never hear *her* ranting and raving. You never hear what anybody here
actually said." The Gorgon, bless his inventive soul, had then raised the
question of whether it would be possible for the indirect discourse to
be made direct and had had the class try it. Amy recalled the effect
vividly:

"I am closer to Thomas than to any other person. I can talk to him
about anything and everything," I said.
"It is impossible for Thomas to be your best friend because of
his sex. He can't possibly understand you the way that another
female can," my mother retorted.
"He understands me far better than anyone else," I replied.
"He is the most trustworthy person that I have ever met."

Avery, or somebody, had said that that sounded awful, that the characters were like a couple of sticks, and that's when Julie had breezed in to say that that was the real way her paper had paid no attention to the assignment, that all we had here was a monster mom and a Christ-like child. The whole situation in fact was right out of a TV sitcom, a bad one, right out of a comic book. "The mother isn't a person. The daughter isn't a person. Thomas is just a lump." Mark had disagreed of course, and so had a couple of others, Frank, Steve maybe, Sandy, probably Karen—not exactly the heavy hitters of the class—which is what had led Pat to get her knife out in support of Julie by noting what she called "the *Woman's Day* group therapy talk" of "an extremely open and honest relationship," by wondering whether anyone really called a *boyfriend* "Thomas" ("he sounds like a senator"), and most humiliatingly of all, to point out that you wouldn't have to change much in the sketch to have what was written about Thomas apply to "a water spaniel." "I mean it," Pat had said through the laughter. "Listen:

> My mother turned on me as soon as Thomas had departed. She ranted and raved about me and my water spaniel, about our relationship, especially how close it had become. I tried to explain to my mother that my dog Tom and I are best friends . . . ."

And then she had added, "and so on." Everybody had found that very funny. Alonzo commented that the exchange could as easily have been one between a brother and a sister as a mother and a daughter. Karen—*Karen* for heaven's sake—had beat the poor dead horse some more by saying that things might as well be said to have taken place on a beach or in a drugstore as at a bazaar.

Parts 2 and 3 the class hadn't needed much time with. Both were, given the sketch, called predictable and both were called cliches. Because there was nothing in the sketch that anyone was willing to call, in Percy's language (the Gorgon of course had hauled in Percy) "the sovereign discovery of the thing" she'd written about, because her "people" had been on about the same level as Percy's "picture postcards," then *of course,* the class said, it was going to be the *mother* ("mums" had been Julie's term) who in Part 2 she could seem to get away with calling blind. And since *mums* was blind, why then it was reasonable to assume, wasn't it, as she'd done in Part 3, that it was *parents* who had to be asked to make allowances, who needed to learn how to adjust. Hence Charles' summation, and her having spent the rest of that morning in tears.

The thing she had written that day on the dittoed copy of her paper that intrigued her most now, however, was her final comment, a note to herself really, rather than a rendering of some element of the class conversation, and a note to herself that until now she had forgotten she'd written.

Redo. Do day after Bazaar with mother. Dialogue. Like with Robbie, but more. *I know this.*

It was not a note that would have made sense to anyone else. I *must* rewrite this paper was what she'd said to herself that day, even before the Gorgon had given her back what she'd turned in.

And I want to focus not on the scene at the bazaar, but on a conversation I had the next day with mother—about what had happened at the bazaar, yes, it was an important conversation in part for that reason, but it was more important for another reason, because it proved she didn't *always* see her mother as a monster at all. The conversation may have *started* that way, but it hadn't *ended* that way. Her mother had come to her room simply to put her down again, just the way she had over Robbie: what else could you expect, Amy? I told you so, Amy. But they'd ended up with an understanding. She'd been able to make her mother understand that there were different ways of defining relationships. In fact, she and her mother had been able to cry together that day. They'd shared that much.

Something important had happened in that conversation, and that note written on her paper, written to herself, written in anger and in defiance over what she had heard the class saying about how she saw life, had been her way of saying that she knew what it was. Her paper for Assignment 3, maybe even what she *said* had happened at the bazaar, that was one thing. But her note was a way of saying that she had a lot more than just a stereotypical way of seeing her mother and herself too, and that what had happened in the conversation she'd had the day after the bazaar proved it, proved it to her anyway, and could prove it to the class and the Gorgon as well.

She'd never written the paper. After all, it was the Gorgon himself who'd suggested she wait. But she was ready now and spent the afternoon working out "a stereotypical way of seeing or thinking" becoming something other than that.

She was lying on her bed, dry-eyed, not even listening to the Willie Nelson tape, not even thinking.

The knock on her door was tentative. There was a wait. Then her mother came in.

"You have a hell of a nerve not talking
to me this way. You walked away from me, remember?"

She didn't say anything. She hadn't looked at
her mother. She didn't even bother to turn her head
away.

"Amy, for God's sake. I spent all last week
picking you up and putting you back together again
after what he did to you. Don't you remember that?
Don't you remember Robbie? Now Tom comes waltzing
back into the picture and you expect me to welcome
him back with open arms, and when I don't you quit
talking to me. Is that fair? You've got some nerve,
Amy."

Her daughter's voice was cold, bitter, "I
didn't expect you to welcome him back with open
arms, no. But I did expect some politeness. He has
the right to some common courtesy, don't you
think?"

"Amy, my God, try to remember, won't you please.
Just try to remember just last week. Do you
remember saying you were going to kill yourself?
You didn't sleep. You wouldn't eat. He shattered
you. You expect me to be polite? You expect *me* to
forget all that? Tell me, why should I be polite to
him?"

"Because he's my *friend*."

"And yet just last week he said he needed more
than a sister, more than a friend, just the way
Robbie needed Linda, remember?"

"He's still my *friend*."

"Amy, do you know what you mean by friend? And do
you know what he seems to mean by it? Did you know

what you meant by it with Robbie, and what he
meant?"

"I know."

Her mother was silent for a moment.

"Can't you see, Amy, it's you I care about, not
him."

"But *he's* what I care about. What I cared about,
I mean. You took care of that yesterday."

"What? What are you saying?"

"That we won't be going out any more, mother.
Just that. You got your way."

Her mother sat down on the bed next to her and
tried to smooth her daughter's hair. Amy
stiffened. Her mother withdrew her hand and just
sat. Then she rose and looked out the window.

"You mean," her mother said finally, "that my
telling him I wanted him to come to the door for you
instead of blowing the horn was too much for
him the way Robbie needed Linda just because I
wouldn't let you go camping with him for the
weekend?"

"He said he feels uncomfortable here and
unwelcome. That's why he blows the horn. He
doesn't like the rude treatment."

"It only takes someone ten seconds to come up to
the door. You're not a carhop, Amy. You can't let
him treat you like that. You can't keep letting *men*
treat you the way you do."

"It's my life, mother. When are you going to see
that? He's what I wanted. He was my *friend*. And now
he's gone."

Her mother had stood by the window just watching
her, and then began to cry softly.

```
          "Oh, Amy," she said. "Your friend, yes. Oh yes.
      It's your life. I see, Amy, believe me. I see."
```

All afternoon it took her to do no more than that. She was drained and disappointed. She knew that the sketch wasn't finished, but had no clear sense of where to go with it, what to do with it, what it meant any more. Something was going wrong. She'd missed something somewhere, she had a feeling. She'd known well enough what she'd *wanted* the sketch to express when she sat down to write it. The thing that had made that conversation that day with her mother so different from any of the others she had had with her about her boyfriends had been her recognition of her mother's concern for her, her honest concern, and how she had been able to use that recognition to really talk to her mother, like a person, and to help her understand. That her mother, product of another generation, conditioned by a different set of values, a particular person with a particular history, should act out of single parent frustration at a pattern in her daughter's life that *she* could understand *only* as demeaning and ultimately self-destructive, was something to sympathize with, not to condemn, and Amy had been eager to show she could write generously about it. Her sketch was to have been a compassionate revelation of how she and her mother had reached a shared understanding. She'd even used the third person to be sure to stay objective. And she was certain she'd not made up anything about what had happened.

But what she'd written was . . . it just didn't feel right somehow.

What had gone wrong, anyway? Had she, as Assignment 6 suggested could happen, substituted one set of stereotypes for another somehow?

No. That didn't seem to be it.

Had her mother understood all that she . . . ?

What had her mother understood?

She'd missed something, all right.

What, though? And where?

Assignment

7

Part I

But when it comes to seeing, the mind can work in more than just one way—as your ability to cope with the following problem will demonstrate:

Assume that a steel pipe is embedded in the concrete floor of a bare room as shown below. The inside diameter is .06" larger than the diameter of a Ping-Pong ball (1.50") which is resting gently at the bottom of the pipe. You are one of a group of six people in the room, along with the following objects:

100' of clothesline

A wooden handled carpenter's hammer

A chisel

A box of Wheaties

A file

A wire coat hanger

A monkey wrench

A light bulb

Assuming also that your life depends on it, list as many ways as you can think of (in ten minutes) to get the ball out of the pipe without damaging the ball, tube, or floor.*

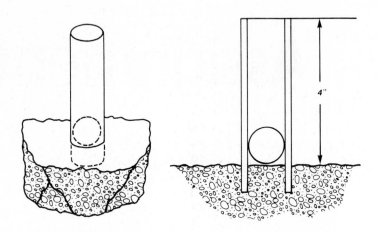

After spending ten minutes on the problem above, move to Part II of the assignment.

Part II

Here is an anecdote told about Robert Frost that can be seen as relevant to what you did in working with Part I of this Assignment:

> Frost had already made up his mind that he would hate algebra. But, here again, his dread of appearing to be stupid in class helped him overcome an initial distaste. Before long the little problems acquired the charm of puzzles. It was a new game for him, and at one phase of it he became so absorbed that his sheer concentration brought him through a public performance before he had time to grow self-conscious.

---

*From *Conceptual Blockbusting: A Guide to Better Ideas* by J. L. Adams. Copyright © 1974, p. 32. Reprinted with the permission of W.H. Freeman and Co.

The incident occurred on a day when the superintendent of schools visited the algebra class and pleasantly challenged the students to take one step beyond what they had learned. The visitor wrote on the blackboard an algebra problem that required a new process. He assured the students they knew enough about algebra to solve the problem, and to recognize the new process, if they would only try. Troubled and uncertain, the entire class stared in silence until Rob impulsively exclaimed, "I can do it."

The boy was so intent on describing each of the separate steps that, for the moment, he was not bothered by shyness. Even the superintendent's interruptions, for the purpose of leading him on, seemed like stimulating countermoves in a game of wits. When he finished and was praised for his ability to make mental rearrangements of algebraic facts already learned, Rob was proud of his accomplishment. More than that, it dawned on him that he had suddenly discovered something about the process of original thinking. It was always a matter of putting together known quantities in fresh ways . . . . , a process of putting this and that together, with enough originality, to solve a problem.*

This, the second part of Assignment 7, is to enable you to see what you, as a writer, can discover for yourself about "the process of original thinking" by examining the "mental rearrangements" you made in order to see a way of getting the Ping-Pong ball out of the pipe under the conditions stipulated.

Prepare yourself to write this paper by considering first your own solutions for getting the ball out of the pipe in the context of some other solutions to the problem that have been offered. Did you think of crushing the Wheaties to a powder and stirring the ball to the top of this powder with one end of the unraveled coat hanger, for example? Did you think of having all six people urinate in the pipe? Did you think of smashing the light bulb and cutting a small vein in each person's arm with the broken glass in order to draw enough blood to float the ball to the top of the pipe? How about smashing the handle of the hammer with the monkey wrench and digging the Ping-Pong ball out of the pipe with two splinters of wood—did you think to do that?

And then ask yourself, if you got any of these solutions, how it was exactly that you got them? What did you do to come up with a way of getting the ball out of the pipe? Ask yourself also, if you didn't think of

---

*Thompson and Winnick, *Robert Frost: A Biography.* New York: Holt, Rinehart and Winston, 1981, pp. 43–45. Reprinted by permission of Henry Holt and Company, Inc.

all of the solutions listed above, if most people wouldn't, *why* that seems to be the case. We all know that broken glass can cut, and that cut people bleed, and that blood is a liquid, and that Ping-Pong balls float on liquid, don't we? Maybe we didn't visualize the various items clearly enough? Maybe we'd forgotten that a Wheaties' flake—mentally right before our very eyes—will powder if crushed on concrete? That a hammer (or in a pinch, even a monkey wrench) has what it takes to perform such an operation?

Once you have located yourself with what all ways of getting the Ping-Pong ball out of the pipe seem to have in common, no matter how many of them you may have come up with yourself, write a paper in which you address the following questions.

Exactly what sorts of "mental rearrangements" seem necessary for people to come up with solutions to the problem stated in Part I of this assignment? What exactly is being rearranged? That the mind is capable of making such "rearrangements" means it has what ability? Think carefully about your phrasing of things here. You put together "known quantities in fresh ways," to be sure, and "with . . . originality." One can come to think other than stereotypically by "learn[ing] to be chary of generalizations about people," too. Or become a better writer by thinking clearly. For all the good that kind of talk ever did anybody.

Since you're a student at a college interested, among other things, in developing your ability to use "the process of original thinking," what suggestions do you have about what teachers might do in their courses to help you develop this ability of the mind? Be specific here. Draw on your own experience to describe *particular* processes to be implemented with *particular* materials in a *particular* course that you think might have a chance of forcing students to be "original" in the way that the problem of the Ping-Pong ball in the pipe does.

Finally, how do you explain that this ability of the mind, normal to all normal people, is worth working to develop—and is valuable for more than solving algebra problems and getting Ping-Pong balls out of pipes in sealed rooms? Address this question on a separate page.

Seeing Assignment 7

MARK

As usual, it was Julie's remarks in study group that had meant the most to him, even though (as usual) he wasn't quite sure he'd completely understood her, let alone how to use what she'd said. Again, she'd thrown him off, and right from the start, with what his grandfather would have called her brass—the way this time she'd asked him, and first thing in group, she without one thing on under her Yale sweatshirt, whether *he'd* thought to pee in the pipe in front of those five other people, and then had giggled at his embarrassment. They all let Julie get away with more than they should have in study group probably, even Steve. But she'd have been a lot harder to do without than she was to tolerate and all of them knew it. Alonzo once had referred to her as a catalyst, to which Steve had added, "yeah, twice removed." There was no question that she made things happen. She made things happen that made things happen.

Just once, though, he'd like to have left a study session with a little more than that. Just once he'd like to have left feeling other than dumb, with some clear sense of what the whole thing had amounted to, with some clear sense of how the stuff they talked about connected with the paper he had to write. He'd never, not ever, come away from a study session with an idea of what to write about.

Over his Micky-D coffee—he always stopped in McDonald's after study group—he tried once again to work back to where his confusion started. Alonzo had been saying that the whole assignment had to do with creative thinking, obviously—things were always obvious to Alonzo—and then Julie had said sure, but that the assignment used the end of Heilbroner's essay to make fun of that kind of talk, and the point was you had to *un*create to be creative, you had to be able to smash what you saw into pieces you could then put together some other way, that the hammer in this problem, for example, wasn't going to do you any good at all as a hammer; nothing in the list of objects was going to help you as what it was.

"So that's how you break a stereotype, then?" Avery had asked her, intense: "You break it up and then use the pieces to make something else?" And Steve had said no, because the light bulb is still a goddamn light bulb, no matter what you do with it, and then Julie had said no by God it *isn't*, not in this situation, not if you bust it up and make a razor out of it, and if you *don't* do something like that with the stuff you have to work with here you're going to die. "Stevie babycakes," she'd added.

"Yes," Alonzo had said, " 'your life depends on it,' the assignment says, so that's one of the parameters of the problem. But how does the anecdote about Frost factor in?"

Parameters of the problem. Factor in. God.

And then Alonzo and Julie had got into it about what uncreating was and Steve kept saying no, no, no to everything and Avery had just clammed up and listened and of course so had he. Then Julie had quoted some Frost and that jerk Alonzo had asked whether anyone knew the Frost poem about the crow shaking snow out of a tree and of course no one did and here he was again with his stupid coffee feeling no, no, no, dumb, dumb, dumb.

But for some reason what stayed with him was what Julie had said. You had to *un*create to be creative. So then you see creatively, un-stereotypically, as Avery said, when you break up what you see into something different from what it is, so you can then turn it into something else? Was that it? It sounded crazy. It reminded him of that old joke his grandfather had told him: When is a door not a door? Why, when it's ajar, of course.

But that was all a trick with words. Doors *weren't* jars and that was the point and Steve was right. You break a light bulb and what you got is a broken light bulb, or still a light bulb anyway. A rose is a rose is a rose, isn't it? A rose by any name is still a rose? He'd gotten *that* much from Miss Matthews' English class. You didn't turn the world into something else just because you wanted to, or even because you needed to.

So how *did* you think originally then, and what could teachers do to force students to do it, and what was the value of it and how was all *that* connected with getting some damned Ping-Pong ball out of a pipe when he hadn't even thought to pee in it or bleed in it or spit in it, when all he'd been able to think of, in fact, was using the ends of the coat hanger like a pair of giant tweezers. He hadn't thought of any of the other solutions. None of then. Not one. None, none—

Nun.

He remembered the nuns.

Another trick with words, of course. None, nun. Just anunther trick with words.

But he remembered the nuns in Atlantic City and how he'd seen them first and what they were, and then how he'd seen them again, the same group of nuns, but not the same, because the difference they'd made had . . . .

He'd never really worked that part of it out, why they'd made such a difference to him that bright, cold day in Atlantic City.

It was in early June, an unseasonably cold day in early June in the middle of the last week they'd ever spend in high school, a week of un-school really, with their graduation certain, exams done, college for all four of them a gold-plated guarantee, a magic time. They were the rat pack, hanging tight together all through high school, one for all and all for you know what. They worked out how they'd bus down, just for the day, just for the hell of it they said to each other, from Philadelphia. Harv had been to Atlantic City before, once, but with his folks; he hadn't played. Outside the movies, none of the rest of them had ever seen a gambling casino.

They set rules for themselves of course. Nobody was to know, first of all, not before they went anyway, because they were supposed to be in school even if there wasn't anything for them to do besides sign yearbooks. There was to be no beer. And nobody was to take any more than they could afford to lose.

For the rest of his life he'd remember walking into the enchanted kingdom of the Tropicana. He'd heard his grandfather say once that the most wonderful thing about the race track for him was the smell of the program he'd buy to study the night before, and the casino took him that way, fell on him in a raw, red rush like a promise he'd wanted made the whole of his life. It raised him, lifted him like a wave, carrying the four of them into invulnerability it seemed, past themselves, beyond the laws of chance, outside time, into an innocent pornography of signs and symbols: sweet cherries, plums and oranges, and even more sweetly singing bells—hieroglyphs to the universe even so, fundament, the stuff that dreams are made on.

They split, of course. They agreed to meet in an hour. By the escalator. The slots held him on bright wings, long enough to complete the alchemy anyway, to turn his money into both more and less than that. He bought $5.00 worth of quarters from a booth, a tiny tight roll of quarters, which he added to from a change girl who passed while he pulled the silver arm and pulled again and his mind flamed and danced. Oh, he won you bet. He hit and hit again, and all riiii! One more time! And he cashed his counted quarters back into bills which he also counted.

He strode the casino like an inheritor. This was Action. This was him, looking for Action. And then, abruptly, he turned some of the bills back into silver again and again the uncounted silver into uncounted paper, back to metal, to paper, to money finally. To money again.

He counted his money, all of it, all of what he had left. And then in disbelief he recounted it. He laughed shortly and shook his head, blushing, obscurely ashamed.

They headed for the boardwalk, sounding a bit hollow even then, even to themselves, with their jaunty losers' infield chatter.

Pick a number! God, I couldn't pick my nose in that place.

Let's eat. Then we'll work our way down to Caesar's Palace.

You got it. I don't mind my plow cleaned, but I'd just as soon they didn't try to sharpen and polish it at the same time.

The nuns were in a close group on the boardwalk headed in the opposite direction, 15 or 20 of them maybe, in traditional dress, heads slightly bowed, silent, walking quickly though, intent.

"A knot of nuns," Jimmy murmured as they swept by. "I wonder what they're doing here."

People made way for them, staring, as though they were a pack of cyclists.

"They're like a flock of crows," Pete said, who was Catholic. "You don't see them much in full habit any more. Jeez. What a life."

"Nonlife you mean," he heard himself say, sorry as soon as he had, though Pete just smiled.

They went to Resorts, Harrahs, the Sands, but it was Caesar's Palace that finished them, first driving them together, they played in a group there, and then passing them from the slots to blackjack, which threw them on to craps, that tossed them to roulette, that scissored the life out of them, the four of them. He fed his last six quarters like tribute into the system while Harv and Pete and Jimmy watched. And then while they paid, he watched.

They were together but he wasn't with them, and he felt more miserable than he had any way of accounting for.

"Well, I guess that's called getting what you asked for, right guys?"

Jimmy said, and Harv muttered, "Next time, mothers. Next time," sarcastically, in his Jimmy Cagney voice.

He bantered too, of course. He pretended.

Why did he feel so awful, as though he'd violated something? It wasn't just the money. Even then he'd known that.

What then?

All he knew was that he made no sense to himself all of a sudden. He felt vulnerable and frightened. And for some reason he felt even worse at the thought of going home.

They groped into the glare of the boardwalk again, short with each other, irritable. Pigeons and gulls swarmed around empty benches, fighting each other for spilled popcorn. He felt dwarfed by everything. The gaping skeletons of two more unfinished casinos, high as hills already. The souvenir shops. A place that sold footlong hotdogs, and blowing on a wire, a set of colored T-shirts reading "Atlantic City" with women's breasts stenciled on the front. The beach was filthy, covered with what looked like the leavings of a storm: wads of clothing, or weeds maybe, bright bits of twisted plastic, newspapers, enormous lengths of rusted pipe. The stumps of an old jetty green with sea slime rose and fell through the water.

"Let's walk out to the end of the pier," Pete said and they did that, went all the way out Ocean I, past the Foods From All Nations, the miniature golf course, all the way to the end, and leaned over the rail at the end, and hung there shivering in the cold spring wind, looking down, spitting down through the circling gulls to the great swells of water heaving through the pilings. They looked back to the waves breaking soundlessly on a brown stretch of beach, deserted except for a couple of surf fishermen bundled in jackets. They looked back to the boardwalk tiny in the distance, crawling with people.

Then all of a sudden there were the nuns again.

Like a line of ants they threaded themselves down from the boardwalk and then two by two wound a way across the littered sand. Heads down, arms cradled, they headed for the surf, flowing as easily around the shoals of trash as though they were rolled on wheels.

"Look at that, for Christ's sake!" Jimmy said. "Will you look at that!"

Evenly down they came, steady, in spite of the wind billowing their robes, catching their wimples like kites.

And then, almost at the edge of the water, one of them broke from the rest and raced for the surf, just one at first, bare feet white and flying, but then another, and another quickly, and then a pair, robes held up slightly, elbows wide. They stood in the shallow backwash of the yellow surf, very still, bare to the knees, watching the water ebb around their ankles. And those they had left raised their heads, and saw, and then gathered in a half-circle just above the wet sand, faces shining in the late afternoon sun, watching, waiting. And then two of these moved from the rim down, and at the fresh coming of the sea, robes awash, lifted one of the waders, raising her at the hips, high and then higher, higher than their shoulders, while she, stretching up, reaching up, found it seemed, and for a moment, just for a moment—

"Oh," he said softly, and suddenly out of nowhere it had flashed back to him, something his grandmother had told him about a long time before. She had heard it in Siberia, she said, where she'd lived as a child. In the winter she'd heard it, where on deep, clear nights of unbelievable cold, 50 degrees below zero, 60 below, if you stood very still, and blew a breath, and listened, you could hear the tiny crystals of ice falling musically, mystically to the snow. She said it was called the whisper of stars.

But it made no sense to him. There was no connection. It made no sense that the scene had meant anything to him at all. He wasn't Catholic. And the nuns had moved on, just a tiny black line again, and nothing was really changed. Harv hadn't even seen the lifting and Jimmy said they'd have to hurry or they'd miss the bus. The casinos winked and gibbered in the distance still. Mindlessly, the ocean heaved and sighed through the pilings on its way to the snuff-colored beach, empty again, except for the fishermen, serious as wood. And they were busted, the four of them, broke and whipped, and nothing would change that.

But they were going home and he'd been ready to then, he remembered, and he hadn't been.

So something *had* changed. Something was different. Something had been *made* different.

And in that then, in that then as he remembered it now, sipping coffee, was a key, he had a feeling, to the ball in the pipe, maybe to Frost working on algebra—and, as he was to see later, a lot later, the key also to himself in the middle of the rest of the world.

Assignment 8

The ability to see in other than a culturally or biologically determined way, the ability to see in a way that might be described as other than stereotypical, is connected, it would seem, with one's ability with language: with the various ways one has of being able to name what makes up the world, and with the various ways one has of being able to connect those various names with one another. Blood, for example, can be named as a fluid on which objects of a certain buoyancy will float, as well as being called a substance that can flow and change shape without separating when under pressure, usually red, circulating in the heart, arteries, and veins of vertebrates. And naming it one way as opposed to naming it some other way can make a difference.

Here is a writing teacher talking on the subject of naming, of defining, with his students:

> It's a real question, when you define what you see, what it is you're defining. I stand on a grassy knoll, for example, and look north to the horizon. "Those are hills like white elephants," I say, "just the way Hemingway described them." Someone at my elbow, how-

ever, with a geologist's hammer, says, "Nonsense. Those are drum-
lins, and what's more they're plastered over with triassic age ar-
kose." A third person, potbellied, in a flowered shirt, picking his
teeth, comes up behind us. "That," he says, pointing at what we're
looking at, "is why I can't get Channel 4 to come in right." We're
all looking at the same thing, but what are we defining? We're
defining what we're seeing of course. But at the same time, *through*
defining what we're seeing, we're also defining what it is, *who* it is,
we're representing ourselves as at a particular moment.*

And to *develop* our ability with language, to *develop* our ability to
represent ourselves as different things for particular moments on the
basis of how we use the names or definitions we have for the world, two
processes, those of reading or hearing, and of writing or reflecting
would seem essential. We need to learn different names, different definitions for phenomena, that by challenging us to re-examine our already
familiar names, can be the means of our developing a new way of
seeing. And we need the opportunity to test the effectiveness of different names by making use of them. Indeed, one way of describing your
situation as a student in college is to say that you are having as a reader
and writer to learn and to demonstrate your command of a number of
names or terminologies or languages with which to interpret
phenomena that you may have understood differently before you came
here.

There are difficulties to using reading and writing to develop a new
way of seeing, a number of which you have had occasion to examine
in this course already, in the work of others, perhaps even in your own.
Our culture is filled with what Walker Percy has called preformed symbolic complexes, and for a good deal more than the Grand Canyon—
complexes that can get between readers and what they read. And new
terminology for describing phenomena, particularly when it is new to
the person making use of it, does not automatically result in a way of
seeing that is very new after all.

On the other hand, that group of feminists mentioned by Robert
May, a group he specifies as both "organizationally and politically active" remember, did much more, he claims, than just break or reverse
what could be called a culturally, perhaps even a biologically conditioned way of seeing. And Henri Nouwen says this of the process of
articulation:

---

*Adapted from: William E. Coles, Jr., *The Plural I*. New York: Holt, Rinehart and Winston,
1978, p. 46.

It is not hard to see how real a change takes place in our daily life when we find the courage to keep our thoughts to ourselves no longer, but to speak out, confess them, share them, bring them into conversation. As soon as an embarrassing or exhilarating idea is taken out of its isolation and brought into a relationship with someone, something totally new happens. This obviously requires much courage and trust, . . . but as soon as we have taken the risk, our thoughts themselves receive a new quality.*

This assignment is an opportunity for you to examine some of the ways in which there are both advantages and disadvantages to using the processes of reading and writing to develop a new way of seeing.

Here are two papers written several years ago by the same student in a freshman composition course. Paper I was an in-class essay written at the beginning of the course in response to the question of what it was the students hoped to get out of attending college. Paper II—you will notice it is unfinished—was written toward the end of the term as an evaluation of Paper I. The student writer gave both papers to her teacher with a note that read as follows:

I know I'm not finished yet, but I don't know how to go on from where I am. Do you have any suggestions?

I

For years I was a working mother of four. We needed money for our daily expenses. Also, we were trying to repair our house so that the roof wouldn't fall on our heads. It takes a lot of extra cash to keep two cars running and food on the table. Anyone who has stopped at a gas station recently or stood in line at a supermarket knows this. Four children can keep you hopping when it

---

*Henri J. M. Nouwen, *Clowning in Rome.* Garden City, NY: Doubleday, 1979, p. 71.

comes to clothes as well as food too. And we had to think about their education as well.

Our children have all left home now, or, are finishing school or will soon, so at last there's time for me to study political science as I've always wanted to. Everybody in the home is all for this because they are sure as I am sure that to know what I'm talking about in political discussions will make me happier.

I think that happiness is worth shooting for by everybody. It's one of the things that makes living in America so great. You can wait until the right time and then do exactly what you want if you plan things right. And doing what you want is what life is all about. It's worth it to reach a goal.

II

I look back on that first paper I wrote for this course this term with a mixture of amusement and embarrassment. I could say I was pushed for time when I wrote it, which I was, but that isn't the whole story. What I said in the paper was pretty much what I'd been telling friends, and myself, for a lot of years, and that's what bothers me. That's me on the paper there, some of me anyway. And what kind of number is this gal trying to do on herself?

I was never worried that the roof was going to fall on our heads. A lot of the money I made working we used to make over a game room and to build a patio, not to "repair" the house. We never had to worry about clothes or going hungry. And it was

because I worked that we needed two cars in the
first place. That talk about food and the price of
gasoline and the kids' education is mainly gas
itself. "Four children can keep you hopping." So
can two. So can one. So can the garden or the front
lawn.

The sentence that bothers me most though is the
last one of the second paragraph. "Everybody" was
not "all for" my going back to school to begin
with. I can still remember the questions I got when
I first raised it. "Will it take a lot of time?"
"Will you expect me to do the washing and
cleaning?" They weren't sure I was going to be
"happy" going back to school at all. Even if they
had been, I don't think that that would have made
them "all for" it. And of course I wasn't sure
either. I was scared to death. Mrs. Pepper goes to
college. Most of all I'm not so sure that knowing
"what I'm talking about in political discussions"
will automatically make anybody in my family
happy. When I blasted my husband's generalization
about "Reaganomics" the other night with some
facts that made him look pretty silly we ended up
not talking to each other for the rest of the
evening. This is what makes living in America so
great? If this is what life is all about, then
where do we go from here? Do I just keep reaching
for my goal? Maybe I couldn't have seen all of what
college was going to mean in my life, but I could
have prepared myself better if I hadn't told
myself just what I'd told everybody else. "Oh yes,
I'm going to start college in the fall and I'm very
excited." "Oh yes, Rich thinks it's great." "Oh

```
yes, it's good we can finally afford it." "Oh yes,
I've always liked to read." Clichés, all of them. I
set myself up with them . . . [paper unfinished]
```

Of these two papers and the student's note her writing teacher said to a colleague:

This paper seems to involve some important things in this student's life, things I think she has to work out for herself. I will talk with her about her *paper* of course, but before I do, I'm thinking of having her read this essay by Alice Walker. I'm going to tell the student that I want this essay to say two things to her.

First of all, I want to praise what she's done in writing that second paper. Even though it isn't finished, she's taken an important step in what she's written so far, and I'm hoping the Alice Walker essay can put her in touch with her accomplishment.

But at the same time there are liabilities to what she's doing in that second paper. Alice Walker won't help her with those exactly, but this student shows she has more than enough ability as a reader and writer to see and address them for herself once she begins working on how to finish her essay. This is the second thing I'm going to tell her that I think Alice Walker's essay can help her with. There are a lot of things in that essay that I think this writer might pick up on and use to take still another step—as a writer, and perhaps as more than a writer too.

Here is the Alice Walker essay being referred to by this teacher:

I come out of a black community where it was all right to have hips and to be heavy. You didn't feel that people didn't like you. The values that [imply] you must be skinny come from another culture . . . Those are not the values that I was given by the women who served as my models. I refuse to be judged by the values of another culture. I am a black woman, and I will stand as best I can in that imagery.

— Bernice Reagon,
BLACK WOMEN AND LIBERATION MOVEMENTS

Saving the Life That is Your Own:
The Importance of Models
in the Artist's Life

There is a letter Vincent Van Gogh wrote to Emile Bernard that is very meaningful to me. A year before he wrote the letter, Van

Gogh had had a fight with his domineering friend Gauguin, left his company, and cut off, in desperation and anguish, his own ear. The letter was written in Saint-Remy, in the South of France, from a mental institution to which Van Gogh had voluntarily committed himself.

I imagine Van Gogh sitting at a rough desk too small for him, looking out at the lovely Southern light, and occasionally glancing critically next to him at his own paintings of the landscape he loved so much. The date of the letter is December 1889. Van Gogh wrote:

> However hateful painting may be, and however cumbersome in the times we are living in, if anyone who has chosen this handicraft pursues it zealously, he is a man of duty, sound and faithful.
>
> Society makes our existence wretchedly difficult at times, hence our impotence and the imperfection of our work. . . . I myself am suffering under an absolute lack of models.
>
> But on the other hand, there are beautiful spots here. I have just done five size 30 canvasses, olive trees. And the reason I am staying on here is that my health is improving a great deal.
>
> What I am doing is hard, dry, but that is because I am trying to gather new strength by doing some rough work, and I'm afraid abstractions would make me soft.

Six months later, Van Gogh—whose health was "improving a great deal"—committed suicide. He had sold one painting during his lifetime. Three times was his work noticed in the press. But these are just details.

The real Vincent Van Gogh is the man who has "just done five size 30 canvasses, olive trees." To me, in context, one of the most moving and revealing descriptions of how a real artist thinks. And the knowledge that when he spoke of "suffering under an absolute lack of models" he spoke of that lack in terms of both the intensity of his commitment and the quality and singularity of his work, which was frequently ridiculed in his day.

The absence of models, in literature as in life, to say nothing of painting, is an occupational hazard for the artist, simply because models in art, in behavior, in growth of spirit and intellect—even if rejected—enrich and enlarge one's view of existence. Deadlier still, to the artist who lacks models, is the curse of ridicule, the bringing to bear on an artist's best work, especially his or her most original, most strikingly deviant, only a fund of ignorance and the presumption that, as an artist's critic, one's judgment is free of the restrictions imposed by prejudice, and is well informed, indeed, about all the art in the world that really matters.

What is always needed in the appreciation of art, or life, is the larger perspective. Connections made, or at least attempted, where none existed before, the straining to encompass in one's glance at the varied world the common thread, the unifying theme through immense diversity, a fearlessness of growth, of search, of looking, that enlarges the private and the public world. And yet, in our particular society, it is the narrowed and narrowing view of life that often wins.

Recently, I read at a college and was asked by one of the audience what I considered the major difference between the literature written by black and by white Americans. I had not spent a lot of time considering this question, since it is not the difference between them that interests me, but, rather, the way black writers and white writers seem to me to be writing one immense story— the same story, for the most part—with different parts of this immense story coming from a multitude of different perspectives. Until this is generally recognized, literature will always be broken into bits, black and white, and there will always be questions, wanting neat answers, such as this.

Still, I answered that I thought, for the most part, white American writers tended to end their books and their characters' lives as if there were no better existence for which to struggle. The gloom of defeat is thick.

By comparison, black writers seem always involved in a moral and/or physical struggle, the result of which is expected to be some kind of larger freedom. Perhaps this is because our literary tradition is based on the slave narratives, where escape from the body and freedom for the soul went together, or perhaps this is because black people have never felt themselves guilty of global, cosmic sins.

This comparison does not hold up in every case, of course, and perhaps does not really hold up at all. I am not a gatherer of statistics, only a curious reader, and this has been my impression from reading many books by black and white writers.

There are, however, two books by American women that illustrate what I am talking about: *The Awakening,* by Kate Chopin, and *Their Eyes Were Watching God,* by Zora Neale Hurston.

The plight of Mme Pontellier is quite similar to that of Janie Crawford. Each woman is married to a dull, society-conscious husband and living in a dull, propriety-conscious community. Each woman desires a life of her own and a man who loves her and makes her feel alive. Each woman finds such a man.

Mme Pontellier, overcome by the strictures of society and the existence of her children (along with the cowardice of her lover), kills herself rather than defy the one and abandon the other. Janie Crawford, on the other hand, refuses to allow society to dictate behavior to her, enjoys the love of a much younger, freedom-loving man, and lives to tell others of her experience.

When I mentioned these two books to my audience, I was not surprised to learn that only one person, a young black poet in the first row, had ever heard of *Their Eyes Were Watching God* (*The Awakening* they had fortunately read in their "Women in Literature" class), primarily because it was written by a black woman, whose experience—in love and life—was apparently assumed to be unimportant to the students (and the teachers) of a predominantly white school.

Certainly, as a student, I was not directed toward this book, which would have urged me more toward freedom and experience than toward comfort and security, but was directed instead toward a plethora of books by mainly white male writers who thought most women worthless if they didn't enjoy bullfighting or hadn't volunteered for the trenches in World War I.

Loving both these books, knowing each to be indispensable to my own growth, my own life, I choose the model, the example, of Janie Crawford. And yet this book, as necessary to me and to other women as air and water, is again out of print.* But I have distilled as much as I could of its wisdom in this poem about its heroine, Janie Crawford:

I love the way Janie Crawford
left her husbands
the one who wanted to change her
into a mule
and the other who tried to interest her
in being a queen.
A woman, unless she submits,
is neither a mule
nor a queen
though like a mule she may suffer
and like a queen pace the floor.

It has been said that someone asked Toni Morrison why she writes the kind of books she writes, and that she replied: Because they are the kind of books I want to read.

---

*Reissued by the University of Illinois Press, 1979.

This remains my favorite reply to that kind of question. As if anyone reading the magnificent, mysterious *Sula* or the grim, poetic *The Bluest Eye* would require more of a reason for their existence than for the brooding, haunting *Wuthering Heights,* for example, or the melancholy, triumphant *Jane Eyre.* (I am not speaking here of the most famous short line of that book, "Reader, I married him," as the triumph, but, rather, of the triumph of Jane Eyre's control over her own sense of morality and her own stout will, which are but reflections of her creator's, Charlotte Brontë, who no doubt wished to write the sort of book *she* wished to read.)

Flannery O'Connor has written that more and more the serious novelist will write, not what other people want, and certainly not what other people expect, but whatever interests her or him. And that the direction taken, therefore, will be away from sociology, away from the "writing of explanation," of statistics, and further into mystery, into poetry, and into prophecy. I believe this is true, *fortunately true*; especially for "Third World Writers"; Morrison, Marquez, Ahmadi, Camara Laye make good examples. And not only do I believe it is true for serious writers in general, but I believe, as firmly as did O'Connor, that this is our only hope—in a culture so in love with flash, with trendiness, with superficiality, as ours—of acquiring a sense of essence, of timelessness, and of vision. Therefore, to write the books one wants to read is both to point the direction of vision and, at the same time, to follow it.

When Toni Morrison said she writes the kind of books she wants to read, she was acknowledging the fact that in a society in which "accepted literature" is so often sexist and racist and otherwise irrelevant or offensive to so many lives, she must do the work of two. She must be her own model as well as the artist attending, creating, learning from, realizing the model, which is to say, herself.

(It should be remembered that, as a black person, one cannot completely identify with a Jane Eyre, or with her creator, no matter how much one admires them. And certainly, if one allows history to impinge on one's reading pleasure, one must cringe at the thought of how Heathcliff, in the New World far from Wuthering Heights, amassed his Cathy-dazzling fortune.)

I have often been asked why, in my own life and work, I have felt such a desperate need to know and assimilate the experiences of earlier black women writers, most of them unheard of by you and by me, until quite recently; why I felt a need to study them and to teach them.

I don't recall the exact moment I set out to explore the works of black women, mainly those in the past, and certainly, in the beginning, I had no desire to teach them. Teaching being for me, at that time, less rewarding than star-gazing on a frigid night. My discovery of them—most of them out of print, abandoned, discredited, maligned, nearly lost—came about, as many things of value do, almost by accident. As it turned out—and this should not have surprised me—I found I was in need of something that only one of them could provide.

Mindful that throughout my four years at a prestigious black and then a prestigious white college I had heard not one word about early black women writers, one of my first tasks was simply to determine whether they had existed. After this, I could breathe easier, with more assurance about the profession I myself had chosen.

But the incident that started my search began several years ago: I sat down at my desk one day, in a room of my own, with key and lock, and began preparations for a story about voodoo, a subject that had always fascinated me. Many of the elements of this story I had gathered from a story my mother several times told me. She had gone, during the Depression, into town to apply for some government surplus food at the local commissary, and had been turned down, in a particularly humiliating way, by the white woman in charge.

My mother always told this story with a most curious expression on her face. She automatically raised her head higher than ever—it was always high—and there was a look of righteousness, a kind of holy *heat* coming from her eyes. She said she had lived to see this same white woman grow old and senile and so badly crippled she had to get about on *two* sticks.

To her, this was clearly the working of God, who, as in the old spiritual, ". . . may not come when you want him, but he's right on time!" To me, hearing the story for about the fiftieth time, something else was discernible: the possibilities of the story, for fiction.

What, I asked myself, would have happened if, after the crippled old lady died, it was discovered that someone, my mother perhaps (who would have been mortified at the thought, Christian that she is), had voodooed her?

Then, my thoughts sweeping me away into the world of hexes and conjurings of centuries past, I wondered how a larger story could be created out of my mother's story; one that would be true to the magnitude of her humiliation and grief, and to the white woman's lack of sensitivity and compassion.

My third quandary was: How could I find out all I needed to know in order to write a story that used *authentic* black witchcraft?

Which brings me back, almost, to the day I became really

interested in black women writers. I say "almost" because one other thing, from my childhood, made the choice of black magic a logical and irresistible one for my story. Aside from my mother's several stories about root doctors she had heard of or known, there was the story I had often heard about my "crazy" Walker aunt.

Many years ago, when my aunt was a meek and obedient girl growing up in a strict, conventionally religious house in the rural South, she had suddenly thrown off her meekness and had run away from home, escorted by a rogue of a man permanently attached elsewhere.

When she was returned home by her father, she was declared quite mad. In the backwoods South at the turn of the century, "madness" of this sort was cured not by psychiatry but by powders and by spells. (One can see Scott Joplin's *Treemonisha* to understand the role voodoo played among black people of that period.) My aunt's madness was treated by the community conjurer, who promised, and delivered, the desired results. His treatment was a bag of white powder, bought for fifty cents, and sprinkled on the ground around her house, with some of it sewed, I believe, into the bodice of her nightgown.

So when I sat down to write my story about voodoo, my crazy Walker aunt was definitely on my mind.

But she had experienced her temporary craziness so long ago that her story had all the excitement of a might-have-been. I needed, instead of family memories, some hard facts about the *craft* of voodoo, as practiced by Southern blacks in the nineteenth century. (It never once, fortunately, occurred to me that voodoo was not worthy of the interest I had in it, or was too ridiculous to study seriously.)

I began reading all I could find on the subject of "The Negro and His Folkways and Superstitions." There were Botkin and Puckett and others, all white, most racist. How was I to believe anything they wrote, since at least one of them, Puckett, was capable of wondering, in his book, if "The Negro" had a large enough brain?

Well, I thought, where are the *black* collectors of folklore? Where is the *black* anthropologist? Where is the *black* person who took the time to travel the back roads of the South and collect the information I need: how to cure heart trouble, treat dropsy, hex somebody to death, lock bowels, cause joints to swell, eyes to fall out, and so on. Where was this black person?

And that is when I first saw, in a *footnote* to the white voices of authority, the name Zora Neale Hurston.

Folklorist, novelist, anthropologist, serious student of voodoo, also all-around black woman, with guts enough to take a slide rule and measure random black heads in Harlem; not to prove their inferiority, but to prove that whatever their size, shape, or present condition of servitude, those heads contained all the intelligence anyone could use to get through this world.

Zora Hurston, who went to Barnard to learn how to study what she really wanted to learn: the ways of her own people, and what ancient rituals, customs, and beliefs had made them unique.

Zora, of the sandy-colored hair and the daredevil eyes, a girl who escaped poverty and parental neglect by hard work and a sharp eye for the main chance.

Zora, who left the South only to return to look at it again. Who went to root doctors from Florida to Louisiana and said, "Here I am. I want to learn your trade."

Zora, who had collected all the black folklore I could ever use. *That Zora.*

And having found *that Zora* (like a golden key to a storehouse of varied treasure), I was hooked.

What I had discovered, of course, was a model. A model, who, as it happened, provided more than voodoo for my story, more than one of the greatest novels America had produced—though, being America, it did not realize this. She had provided, as if she knew someday I would come along wandering in the wilderness, a nearly complete record of her life. And though her life sprouted an occasional wart, I am eternally grateful for that life, warts and all.

It is not irrelevant, nor is it bragging (except perhaps to gloat a little on the happy relatedness of Zora, my mother, and me), to mention here that the story I wrote, called "The Revenge of Hannah Kemhuff," based on my mother's experiences during the Depression, and on Zora Hurston's folklore collection of the 1920s, and on my own response to both out of a contemporary existence, was immediately published and was later selected, by a reputable collector of short stories, as one of the *Best Short Stories of 1974.*

I mention it because this story might never have been written, because the very bases of its structure, authentic black folklore, viewed from a black perspective, might have been lost.

Had it been lost, my mother's story would have had no historical underpinning, none I could trust, anyway. I would not have written the story, which I enjoyed writing as much as I've enjoyed writing anything in my life, had I not known that Zora had already done a thorough job of preparing the ground over which I was then moving.

In that story I gathered up the historical and psychological threads of the life my ancestors lived, and in the writing of it I felt joy and strength and my own continuity. I had that wonderful feeling writers get sometimes, not very often, of being *with* a great many people, ancient spirits, all very happy to see me consulting and acknowledging them, and eager to let me know, through the joy of their presence, that, indeed, I am not alone.

To take Toni Morrison's statement further, if that is possible, in my own work I write not only what I want to read—understanding fully and indelibly that if I don't do it no one else is so vitally interested, or capable of doing it to my satisfaction—I write all the things *I should have been able to read.* Consulting, as belatedly discovered models, those writers—most of whom, not surprisingly, are women—who understood that their experience as ordinary human beings was also valuable, and in danger of being misrepresented, distorted, or lost.

Zora Hurston—novelist, essayist, anthropologist, autobiographer;

Jean Toomer—novelist, poet, philosopher, visionary, a man who cared what women felt;

Colette—whose crinkly hair enhances her French, part-black face; novelist, playwright, dancer, essayist, newspaperwoman, lover of women, men, small dogs; fortunate not to have been born in America;

Anaïs Nin—recorder of everything, no matter how minute;

Tillie Olson—a writer of such generosity and honesty, she literally saves lives;

Virginia Woolf—who has saved so many of us.

It is, in the end, the saving of lives that we writers are about. Whether we are "minority" writers or "majority." It is simply in our power to do this.

We do it because we care. We care that Vincent Van Gogh mutilated his ear. We care that behind a pile of manure in the yard he destroyed his life. We care that Scott Joplin's music *lives!* We care because we know this: *the life we save is our own.**

What might a writing teacher find important and praiseworthy in this student's evaluating her second paper as she has? How might the Alice Walker essay "put her in touch with her accomplishment"?

What liabilities are there in what this student is doing in her second paper? How might it be argued that the writer of the paper "shows she

---

*Alice Walker, "Saving the Life That Is Your Own: The Importance of Models in the Artist's Life" from *In Search of Our Mother's Gardens.* Copyright © 1976 by Alice Walker. Reprinted by permission of Harcourt Brace Jovanovich, Inc.

has more than enough ability as a reader and writer to see and address them for herself"?

What "things" are there in the Alice Walker essay that this student might "pick up on"? How might she use them to take another step "as a writer, and perhaps as more than a writer too"?

Finally, draw back a bit to examine some of the implications of what you have said so far. Speculate on the possible advantages and disadvantages of this teacher's offering her student what she does to help her develop a new way of seeing.

A good way of developing a point of view from which to write this paper is to take some notes on the evidence you are given to work with much as you did on the material you were presented with in Assignments 4 and 5. You will notice, however, that what you are being asked to do with the information you have to work with in this assignment will necessitate a different note taking plan. Again, as you did for Assignments 4 and 5, be sure to turn in your notes with your paper.

Seeing
Assignment

8

STEVE

He didn't always read the things she'd developed a habit of enclosing with her letters as carefully as he knew she would have liked him to—the photocopies of poems, of pages from books she was reading, of sections from magazines. More and more they'd come to bear on a single theme, it seemed to him, on "the meaning of what they had together" as she kept putting it, and her obsession with it made him extremely uncomfortable. Those other voices made it clear how important the subject was to her at the same time they made it harder and harder for him to know exactly what she was trying to say about it. Was something changing for her in some way? Was she saying that something had to change for them? Was something going to have to change about *him?* He was anxious about her, bewildered, annoyed. What did she want to fuss things so for, anyway? They had a good thing going. He knew that he loved her, that their plans for marriage were real to them both—real enough in fact to have enabled him, to have enabled the two of them, though not without a lot of initial protest, to accept their parents' request that they attend different universities. So what was all this? Why couldn't she leave well enough alone?

What she said this time in her letter about what she was sending with it, however—it had arrived Wednesday, and just after he'd finished reading through Assignment 8—focused him hard on the photocopied pages that had cost her two extra stamps to enclose. Toward the end of her letter she had used the word "stereotype" and also the word "models," the same terms he'd just been making his way through in Alice Walker, and she used both words in relation to a piece of student writing and to some pages about love, all of which (of course) had to do with him and with her, with them.

"Dear Stevie Wonder," she began (as she always did):

Do you groan at the enclosures, more from your madwoman at Ohio State? Do you say, she is at it again, pretending to write a long letter while she lets others do her talking for her? And after ten days of nothing?

Not so, chum. Not this time. It's not just junk mail I'm unloading on you here. I want you to read what I'm sending you here because it's about you and me, dear heart, and if that's boring to you, well, I can't help it if we're the most important thing in my life right now.

The two papers about the boat came out of the book we're using in my English class. The boy who wrote them, whoever he is, reminds me of you and me that night last August when we walked in the oatfield behind your house and had that fight. I thought about that night the whole time we discussed those papers in class, about what the boy might have discovered from doing the second one, and about what I couldn't explain to you very well that night when we talked.

The following two papers were written several years ago by a freshman at a university in circumstances similar to those in which you find yourself in this course. The writing assignment to which they were addressed reads:

Write an account of a moment when you changed your mind about an event in the past. You saw things one way. Then something happened. Now you see them another way—differently.

Make clear in your writing about this moment the difference that the difference makes, what you now see that your seeing differently amounts to or means.

The student turned in both versions of the paper included here with a note attached to them that read as follows:

I thought you might want to see the result of some advice I gave myself. The first paper I know is a mish-mash. But it's almost as though it told me to write the second. I don't know whether the second paper deals with all the assignment, I think it does. But even if it doesn't, I'm still glad I rewrote the paper. I discovered something doing it that I didn't know before.

Here are the two versions of the student's paper:

I

I was about ten years old when we bought it. It was an old gaff-rigged sloop which had been built some twenty years ago by my great-uncle. He was 92 then and a little too old to go sailing, but he was still building boats as he had been his whole life. As my father was his favorite nephew he sold it to him for a bargain price. The old boat having been used as a rental for some 20 years had gotten a little worn. Its varnish was peeled, paint chipped, caulking pulled and wood cracked. It sank until the wood swelled up enough, and its cotton sails smelled of mildew.

But my father loved it. He spent weeks getting her back into working condition. He talked about her smooth lines and the grace with which she moved

through the water. I thought she was a
broken down old tub that wasn't worth
the firewood she contained.

The time came when we had enough
money to move up to bigger and better
things. Our new boat had nylon sails,
orlon lines, was rigged for racing and
was eight feet longer. It's more of a
racing machine than a boat. I liked this
new boat and I still do, although I must
admit I wouldn't mind something bigger
and newer. In recent years I've sailed
in just about every kind of boat from 12
to 40 feet long, mostly in races.

Then some time ago a friend made a
crack about "my old tub" while we were
examining some new boats at a boat show.
I immediately took the same defensive
position that my father had taken a few
years earlier. I realized that some of
my most pleasurable sailing experiences
had been aboard that boat. My father too
must have recalled his childhood
experiences with my great-uncle when he
defended his position.

My great-uncle didn't reach 93, and
the boat is now firewood I believe.

II

We were looking at the new boats at
the boat show the way a pro-football

coach looks over the newest crop of rookies. They shone like cars in a showroom, right through the finger smudges. I couldn't keep my hands off that sleek plastic any more than anyone else could. It was like touching something alive.

And then my friend said: "A little different from that old tub you used to whack around the bay in, aren't they?"

He meant the *Ellen,* which is also my mother's name. It was an old gaff-rigged, wooden sloop built by my great-uncle who had been building boats his whole life. For twenty years he used the boat as a rental. And then my father bought it. I remembered the blisters I'd raised sanding back that old mahogany, grumbling, and rolling strip after strip of caulking for my father to jam into the keel. I remembered the first sail. The wood had come up as dark as shoe polish when we'd stained it, but the sails still smelled of mildew. My father's hands were white on the tiller and his face was bright with sun. I lay on the deck watching the water slice at the prow, not looking at him because I couldn't stand it. Afterwards he wiped the spray rails with chamois, and he bought me soda pop. On the bay we sang.

We'd moved up to bigger boats.

Plastic, just like the ones I was
looking at, with orlon ropes and nylon
sails, all of them rigged for racing. I
like racing. But as I ran my hand down
the sides of a thirty-five footer, the
whole hull poured in one piece by a gang
of workmen who probably couldn't wait to
get home to watch television, I thought
of the *Ellen*, long since chopped up for
firewood. My friend was right. The boats
were different all right.*

It was just that afternoon that you'd finished making over your shed into the studio for your mother, remember? And you took me in it to show me, and you laughed when the first thing I said was how good it *smelled,* all that nice clean wood. And then when I said, "what a gift, Steve, what a gift," you got nervous and shooed me out and we went walking in the oats.

I had to *pull* it out of you what your mother had said, and you were embarrassed when you told me how she'd come into the new studio that afternoon and had just kept clapping her hands like a little girl and had started singing. And do you remember I kissed you and said "that's what I love about you; that's what I love about you" and you said, "what, a damn studio?" and I said, "no, the embarrassment," or something like that. You didn't say anything for a while and then you said that that was silly, that women were silly. Then I got mad and said that that was just the trouble with you and with all men, that you didn't understand anything and then we had the fight.

Well, I see some things now about all that that I didn't then. The first paper the boy does is you the way you first talked about the studio and your mother. The second paper is what I pulled out of you in the oatfield, because the second paper is really about the boy and how he loves his father. (Incidentally, do you see that the boy can't stand to look at his father's happiness any more than you

*William E. Coles, Jr., *Composing II*. Rochelle Park, NJ: Hayden Book Company, Inc., 1981, pp. 71–73. Copyright © William E. Coles, Jr.

could watch your mother clapping her hands?) What I loved in you that night wasn't your embarrassment. It was the way you could say you loved your mother through your work on the shed. And I got mad when you couldn't *see* that, or when you couldn't say so the way the boy who wrote about the boat did.

Do you see now? What I love about you is that you have different kinds of love in you, and Stevie my wonder, that's important for us.

The second thing I'm sending is from a book by M. Scott Peck called *The Road Less Traveled,* and, as you can see it's on "love" (remember I said *don't* groan):

In some respects (but certainly not in all) the act of falling in love is an act of regression. The experience of merging with the loved one has in it echoes from the time when we were merged with our mothers in infancy. Along with the merging we also reexperience the sense of omnipotence which we had to give up in our journey out of childhood. All things seem possible! United with our beloved we feel we can conquer all obstacles. We believe that the strength of our love will cause the forces of opposition to bow down in submission and melt away into the darkness. All problems will be overcome. The future will be all light. The unreality of these feelings when we have fallen in love is essentially the same as the unreality of the two-year-old who feels itself to be king of the family and the world with power unlimited.

Just as reality intrudes upon the two-year-old's fantasy of omnipotence so does reality intrude upon the fantastic unity of the couple who have fallen in love. Sooner or later, in response to the problems of daily living, individual will reasserts itself. He wants to have sex; she doesn't. She wants to go to the movies; he doesn't. He wants to put money in the bank; she wants a dishwasher. She wants to talk about her job; he wants to talk about his. She doesn't like his friends; he doesn't like hers. So both of them, in the privacy of their hearts, begin to come to the sickening realization that they are not one with the beloved, that the beloved has and will continue to have his or her own desires, tastes, prejudices and timing different from the other's. One by one, gradually or suddenly, the ego boundaries snap back into place; gradually or suddenly, they fall out of love. Once again they are two separate individuals. At this point they begin either to dissolve the ties of their relationship or to initiate the work of real loving.

By my use of the word "real" I am implying that the perception that we are loving when we fall in love is a false perception—that our subjective sense of lovingness is an illusion. Full elaboration of real love will be deferred until later in this section. However, by stating that it is when a couple falls out of love they may begin to really love I am also implying that real love does not have its roots in a feeling of love. To the contrary, real love often occurs in a context in which the feeling of love is lacking, when we act lovingly despite the fact that we don't feel loving. Assuming the reality of the definition of love with which we started, the experience of "falling in love" is not real love for the several reasons that follow.

Falling in love is not an act of will. It is not a conscious choice. No matter how open to or eager for it we may be, the experience may still elude us. Contrarily, the experience may capture us at times when we are definitely not seeking it, when it is inconvenient and undesirable. We are as likely to fall in love with someone with whom we are obviously ill matched as with someone more suitable. Indeed, we may not even like or admire the object of our passion, yet, try as we might, we may not be able to fall in love with a person whom we deeply respect and with whom a deep relationship would be in all ways desirable. This is not to say that the experience of falling in love is immune to discipline. Psychiatrists, for instance, frequently fall in love with their patients, just as their patients fall in love with them, yet out of duty to the patient and their role they are usually able to abort the collapse of their ego boundaries and give up the patient as a romantic object. The struggle and suffering of the discipline involved may be enormous. But discipline and will can only control the experience; they cannot create it. We can choose how to respond to the experience of falling in love, but we cannot choose the experience itself.

Falling in love is not an extension of one's limits or boundaries; it is a partial and temporary collapse of them. The extension of one's limits requires effort; falling in love is effortless. Lazy and undisciplined individuals are as likely to fall in love as energetic and dedicated ones. Once the precious moment of falling in love has passed and the boundaries have snapped back into place, the individual may be disillusioned, but is usually none the larger for the experience. When limits are extended or stretched, however, they tend to stay stretched. Real love is a permanently self-enlarging experience. Falling in love is not.

Falling in love has little to do with purposively nurturing one's spiritual development. If we have any purpose in mind when we fall in love it is to terminate our own loneliness and perhaps insure this result through marriage. Certainly we are not thinking of spiritual development. Indeed, after we have fallen in love and before we have fallen out of love again we feel that we have arrived, that the heights have been attained, that there is both no need and no possibility of going higher. We do not feel ourselves to be in any need of development; we are totally content to be where we are. Our spirit is at peace. Nor do we perceive our beloved as being in need of spiritual development. To the contrary, we perceive him or her as perfect, as having been perfected. If we see any faults in our beloved, we perceive them as insignificant—little quirks or darling eccentricities that only add color and charm.

If falling in love is not love, then what is it other than a temporary and partial collapse of ego boundaries? I do not know. But the sexual specificity of the phenomenon leads me to suspect that it is a genetically determined instinctual component of mating behavior. In other words, the temporary collapse of ego boundaries that constitutes falling in love is a stereotypic response of human beings to a configuration of internal sexual drives and external sexual stimuli, which serves to increase the probability of sexual pairing and bonding so as to enhance the survival of the species. Or to put it in another, rather crass way, falling in love is a trick that our genes pull on our otherwise perceptive mind to hoodwink or trap us into marriage. Frequently the trick goes awry one way or another, as when the sexual drives and stimuli are homosexual or when other forces—parental interference, mental illness, conflicting responsibilities or mature self-discipline—supervene to prevent the bonding. On the other hand, without this trick, this illusory and inevitably temporary (it would not be practical were it not temporary) regression to infantile merging and omnipotence, many of us who are happily or unhappily married today would have retreated in wholehearted terror from the realism of the marriage vows.*

I *order* you not to misunderstand me about the Peck. It is *not* my way of my saying that I think the only attraction between us is sexual, or my way of trying to play shrink with you. I want you to read the Peck because I want you to see how important it was to me what I sensed that night in the oatfield, and how important it is you not see it as "women being silly."

I believe what I saw in you that night was what Peck calls "real love." I know it sounds stupid put that way, sort of like a stereotype of Christian love or something, but I know Peck is trying to talk about something real because I felt it in you and feel it in you and I know it's in me too because I can feel it.

I know how hard you worked to make that studio for your mother last summer (and a "mamma's boy" you aren't!), how you had to do it at night and on weekends because of your job (and me). I know the love that came out of, and why her singing embarrassed you, and why *I* embarrassed you. But I think it's important, my Stevie, that *you* know you have this ability to really love. You must know that and not be embarrassed by it because we are going to need it, I think, particularly when we marry.

---

*M. Scott Peck, *The Road Less Traveled*. New York: Simon & Schuster, 1978, pp. 87–90. Reprinted by permission of Simon & Schuster, Inc.

I know I sound like I think I have some big psychological insight here, but I really don't. And if I sound like I think I know all about marriage, well, that *is* silly, because what I'm trying to say is I know I don't. I think that's why I've been sending you all this stuff that I say is about you and me and that I know you don't know what to do with. You see, I want very much to be married to you, but it scares me too, I mean all I don't know about it, all we may not really know about each other. I know we'll change, but I don't know into what or how to get ready for it. We're always talking in psychology about models and how important they are for determining a sound procedure for dealing with something. I'm sending you this stuff in this letter as models, to show you what I think we *can* have, not to complain about what we don't. I want us to have the best life together we can have, Stevie Wonder. And there's so much junk out there about what love is, and what a good relationship is, and who men and women *really* are. We're going to need all the models we can find.

I love you,

Sarah

Assignment 9

Professor Kenneth Dowst of Trinity College, in an article entitled "The Epistemic Approach: Writing, Knowing and Learning" ("Epistemic" means having to do with knowledge or knowing), takes the position that of all forms of language using—thinking, speaking, gesturing, etc.—writing is the one from which the language user "stands to learn the most." The language *user*, notice. The *writer*. He develops this position by speaking first of his understanding of the nature and function of language generally:

> Language in a sense comes between the writer's self and objective reality, modifying the former as it gives shape to the latter. . . . One knows, then, not what is "out there" so much as what one tells one's self is out there, tells one's self by means of symbol systems paramount among which is natural language. Primarily (though not exclusively) by means of language—thought, spoken, or written— one represents the world to one's self: one translates raw percepts into a coherent experience and transmutes discrete experiences into more abstract sorts of knowledge. By seriously experimenting in manipulating language (on a page, for instance), one experiments in knowing, in understanding the world in different ways.

A corollary is that a way of knowing the world involves a way of conceiving of one's self. . . . The way we use language, then, seems not only to reflect but in part to determine what we know, what we can do, and in a sense who we are. To say this is not to deny that phenomena really exist, and not to assert that powerful natural and social forces may be abolished with the sweep of a pen. It is rather to say that our manipulation of language shapes our *conceptions* of the world and of our selves.

Professor Dowst then goes on to explain how, given his view of the relation of language to knowledge, "writing can be an activity of great importance to the writer":

While one in effect composes his or her world by engaging in any sort of language-using, it is by means of writing that one stands to learn the most, for writing is the form of language-using that is the slowest, most deliberate, most accessible, most conveniently manipulable, and most permanent. While a person's short-term memory can hold at any time only six or seven "bits" of information, a written paragraph can hold thousands. It can fix them while a writer experiments in connecting them in various ways, in replacing some with others, in supplementing them with others, in rearranging them, in abstracting and generalizing from them. A writer can tinker with a paragraph for minutes or hours, until it expresses to the writer's satisfaction patterns of cause and effect, evidence and conclusions, interrelationships of data, relevance and irrelevance, denotation and connotation—patterns that establish the "world" in which the writer knows and acts, patterns far too complex and coherent to be created by mere thinking or mere speaking.*

While not always stated so directly, such a way of seeing writing and its connection with interpreting is by no means the concern of English teachers in composition classrooms only. Here for example, in this description of a required course called Psychology of Personal Growth, taught at a community college in Illinois, a teacher is explaining to her students why and how reading and writing are important to their learning in the course.

---

*Kenneth Dowst, "The Epistemic Approach: Writing, Knowing, and Learning," in *Eight Approaches to Teaching Composition,* ed. by T. R. Donovan and B. W. McClelland, pp. 68–70. Copyright © 1980 by the National Council of Teachers of English. Reprinted by permission of NCTE.

To help you better understand the process of human growth, you will regularly be asked in this course to analyze *written* accounts of experience. For how people use words directly affects what they know, and therefore what they believe they can do, what kinds of choices they believe they have in their lives. In fact, learning, whether conscious or unconscious, may be seen as the result of a composing process. We compose when we order events, thoughts, feelings. We compose when we make connections and distinctions, when we see relationships. We compose when we bring things together into new combinations, when we form new ways of seeing the world and ourselves. The reason we will regularly focus on *written* accounts of experience is that writing, because it is a slower and less natural composing process than speaking, and so a good deal more difficult to do, can result in a learning process that is deeper and more far-reaching and more permanent than what results from talk. Writing and reading and rewriting, because they give individuals a chance to examine closely the implications of the exact words they use, to clarify thoughts, to edit thinking, and so to create an interpretation to which they have more of a commitment, can result in learning that is far more than a matter of insight at a moment in time.

When a writer shares her writing with another, she can get other visions of her ideas and their relationships to one another; she can be helped to see more forcefully and clearly the implications of her having arrived at the meanings she did in the ways she did; can, that is, be helped to become a better reader of her own work. Thus sharing writing with others can give a writer an opportunity to adjust or refine what she has said in order to see better what she sees. And viewed this way, the activities of reading and writing can be understood as ways of *growing* as well as ways of learning.

You will get most from your own papers for this course if you see the writing of them not just as an opportunity for you to report what you've concluded but as an opportunity for you to grow as an interpreter of the psychology of human growth. I, of course, will expect your papers to be of acceptable quality for a college course. I won't endorse your presenting yourself in a sloppy, haphazard manner—punctuation random, paragraphs disorganized or unfocused, because it is a version of *yourself* you are going to be presenting and you are better than that. And, of course, you will have the opportunity to expand and revise what you say as many times as you wish until we are both satisfied that the learning experience of your papers is a learning experience you will be able to use. Though I will keep a record of your work and its revision, in order to encourage honest exploring and risk-taking, I will not assign a letter grade to your papers.*

When asked by a teaching assistant to provide an example of a student's writing, reading, and then rewriting that she would say showed someone's adjusting or refining what they said in order to see better what they see, the psychology teacher offered three versions of a single student paper about which she said this:

Here's a young woman writing about a time in her life when she gave herself some good advice that she *didn't* follow. She was dealing with the question of how she'd explain *now* what she'd experienced then. I think the three versions of this paper are a good example of what you're asking to see. She turned them all in together and said she'd written them over the space of a couple of weeks without the intervention of any reader other than herself. I don't know whether this young woman becomes a better reader because she tries to write better or the other way around, but even though she could probably profitably revise her paper further, I'd say the three versions of it here show somebody learning. In fact I'd go further than that. I'd say the three versions of this paper show somebody in the act of growing up. What this student does helped clarify for me a comment made about revision by Adrienne Rich. "Revision," she says, "the act of looking back, of seeing with fresh eyes, of entering an old text from a new critical direction—is for us [women] more than a chapter in cultural history; it is an act of survival. Until we can understand the assumptions in which we are drenched we cannot know ourselves."

I

    The situation that caused so many conflicting
feelings within me still brings havoc to my pride
when I discuss it. In discussing it, I have to
admit that I was normal. I was not the pillar of
strength I had envisioned myself as, nor was I

---

*From a course description used by Professor Mary Olson of Oakton Community College, Des Plaines, Illinois. Used by permission.

immune to certain weaknesses I had even denied possession of.

In my Senior year of High School, I led a very carefree existence. My biggest worries revolved around making it to all my activity meetings, making my speech for the office of class Secretary, and the most common preoccupation--the opposite sex. I wanted what all my friends wanted. To be part of a we, an us, a me and my boyfriend. But in the process of forming such a liason, I wanted to be the one in control; to have things end up as planned, planned by me. This would not be the case.

It was in April that I found out I was being pursued. I need not say his name, and I'd rather not. For some reason it feels better if I don't. . . . Naturally, I let my friends in on what was happening, and the looks of surprise were very amusing. My "suitor" as one may call him, had a very interesting trait--he had as many ex-girlfriends as I had fingers. Maybe even toes. I didn't plan to be made another one of his conquests, and I informed my friends of this, much to their great relief. I informed myself also. I didn't find myself very convincing, though. I couldn't help feeling mischevously flattered. After all, his past girlfriends were always considered the best looking. When I came down to earth, I started looking for alterior motives for him asking me out. I couldn't envision me measuring up in the "looks" department, and I hoped I had alot more character than those I was comparing myself to. But maybe I really didn't?

I remained indignant to the idea, and to him,

until one night. That's all it took. A nice dinner,
perfect manners, a boost of ego, and I was smitten.
Why didn't I listen? It was good advice I had given
myself. But was it reasonable? It was like telling
myself not to cry at a sad movie. I had planned just
to go out with him once, but . . .

[The ellipses in this paper are the writer's. Nothing has been omitted
from the text.]

II

I was approaching the end of my senior year of
High School. "Things" were going very well--I was
having a good time. I had many friends, occasional
dates, and many activities. It was then that I
became involved with a young man named Kenny. He
was a year older than myself, just into the Coast
Guard, and very good looking. It was all three of
these characteristics that both perplexed and
intrigued me.

When he first asked me out, he did so in a very
shy, humble manner. This upset me. I "knew" he
could not be shy; after all, he had dated half the
female population in my home town. I was very
indignant towards him, keeping my guard up at all
times. But he persisted in his pursuit, very
humbly of course. I gave in and went out with him. I
really don't think I had ever planned not to.

My advice to myself up to that point had been
aimed at the idea of not becoming another one of
his conquests. However, it seemed a rather forced
kind of advice, an oblidged warning to myself. And
while I continued to tell myself that he was not
what I wanted, he was exactly what I wanted at the

time, or very, very close to it. And everything
that was not supposed to happen according to my
advice, did, except the ending. That was seemingly
predictable, and in the voice of my own advice, one
might say that I did become another one of Kenny's
conquests. After he had returned to his station,
we had continued writing and calling for four long
months, until he abruptly had a change of heart.
This "change of heart" left no room for caring
about how I received the news. It was delivered,
and I was left with a vicious attack of "I told you
so" phrases coming from my advisory self. But why
should I have done any differently? How long could
I have "played it cool" with someone who was
treating me so well, and made me feel very good
about myself?

I'll never know how long his sincerity lasted,
or if it had ever existed, at all. But I no longer
condemn myself, or think myself foolish. There was
much more to the entire situation than I being
right or wrong in getting involved. Yes, I would
have been safe from the kind of hurt and utter
confusion I experienced had I listened to my
advice. But would I have been right in doing so?
What would I have gained in doing so? I would not
say that I learned from my mistake, because I no
longer consider that situation to be a mistake.
But I will say I learned. Isn't that what the past
is for--to laugh at, to cry at, to treasure, and to
learn from? And not only did I learn how to be part
of that kind of "we" situation, but also how
important it is to remain an "I" in the process. I
had to learn to cope with myself when it was all

over, and in doing so, I discovered that I had not lost a part of me to Kenny. I had discovered a new dimension to the "I" who was not defeated after all.

III

When he first asked me out, he seemed shy, humble even. This upset me. I knew he could not be shy; hadn't he dated half the women in my home town? I was indignant, keeping my guard up. And I was interested. He persisted. When I went out with him, I told myself I'd given in. I don't think I had ever planned not to.

My advice to myself up to that point had been aimed at the idea of not becoming another of his conquests. The obligatory warning maybe? Because while I continued to tell myself that he was not what I wanted, another part of me must have known that he was exactly what I wanted. Or close to it.

For a while, everything, according to my advice, that was not supposed to happen did, and *vice versa*.

Except the ending.

My advice would say I became another one of Kenny's conquests. After he returned to his Coast Guard station, we continued writing, calling. For four months. He then had what he called a Change of Heart. I was left with a vicious attack of "I told you so phrases" coming from my advisory self.

But should I have done differently? How long could I have played it cool with someone who was treating me so well, who made me feel so very good about myself?

A Change of Heart.

I'll never know how long his sincerity lasted.
Or if it had ever existed. Worst of all, I'll never
know that he *wasn't* sincere, that he isn't still.

A Change of Heart.

On good days I no longer think myself foolish.
There was much more to the entire situation than my
being right or wrong about getting involved. Yes,
I'd have been safe from the kind of hurt and utter
confusion I experienced had I listened to my
advice. But would I have been right in doing so?
What would I have gained in doing so? Might I not
have lost something too? On good days I tell myself
I'd have lost a lot.

I will not say that I've learned from my
mistake, because I'm no longer sure the situation
was a mistake. And I know I've learned. I learned
how to be part of a we situation. I learned to cope
with myself when it was all over, I had to. So I
discovered a new dimension of myself. On good
days, these days, I can almost believe it was worth
it.

This community college teacher is, as we are not, a trained psychologist. We cannot know exactly what was in her mind in saying the three
versions of the student paper "show somebody learning" or "somebody
in the act of growing up." But as readers and writers we can say a great
deal about what happens from version to version of this student paper,
about what the paper moves toward and from what, and about what
this movement seems to suggest is happening to the writer.

Write a paper in which you say what you see happening in this
paper, version by version, from your perspective as a reader and a
writer. However you define the movement of this paper, version to
version, make clear both what *you* mean by the terminology you choose
and how your reading of the versions leads you to use such terminology.

Bearing in mind the complications that can attend someone's using the processes of reading and writing to develop a new way of seeing, conclude your paper by explaining how you would talk to this writer, as you imagine her, about what she has done as a writer in composing these three versions of her paper, and about what she could do to profitably revise the paper further if she wanted to. As you did in Assignment 5, speak in this section of your paper as though you were addressing the writer directly.

As you did for Assignments 4, 5 and 8 prepare yourself to write this paper first by taking some notes on the evidence you have to work with. This writer, for instance, has different ways of talking about the same events, version by version of her paper, different ways of explaining her motivations and Kenny's, different ways of understanding the meaning of her experience, and so forth.

Once you have developed a set of notes from which to begin writing your paper, compose a *draft* of your paper and then a revision of the draft. Be sure to turn in both your notes and your draft with your revision.

Seeing Assignment 9

KAREN

What puzzled her, for a change, was something other than the problem of the assignment.

"The three versions of the student paper 'show somebody learning' or 'somebody in the act of growing up.'"

For sure, and she had no trouble seeing a dozen ways she could talk about how to see it that way—no matter what the psychologist may have had in her head.

What exactly had happened to *make* it happen though, to get version II out of I and III out of II "without the intervention of any reader other than the writer herself." That was *her* question—or more exactly became her question the more conscious she became that version I of the three was the sort of writing that a year ago she wouldn't have seen that much wrong with.

"Or maybe even," a part of her cooed, "would have produced yourself?"

"O.K.," she admitted to herself with a grin, "or maybe even would have produced myself."

She still couldn't think back on that first meeting of their study group without a hot rush of angry shame—the day that Pat had told her she wrote like a teenybopper and called her a bubblehead. She'd have dropped the course that day she knew had she not heard Pat telling Lou that that's just what she would do, and had Betty not taken her for coffee.

And this kid had written version I of her paper and then all on her own had written version II without having had something like a building collapse on her?

Because as Karen had good reason to know, the kid probably wrote version I of her paper believing it was the truth *and* exactly what the psychology teacher was asking for, "honest exploring and risk-taking." The thing was an act, of course, a put-on—all that cutesy-poo flopping around about her "suitor"—but not an act that the kid necessarily would have known was an act when she went into it. Maybe something had happened in her psychology class the way the Gorgon had blasted Lou about sincerity? "So what that this is a *sincere* piece of writing," she could hear him bellowing, "an honest piece of writing, even supposing anybody could know a thing like that? You can be honest as a writer and completely wrong, or just plain dumb. Cockroaches are honest, right? Really sincere people—'I am a telephone'—are in institutions."

It wasn't very likely, though, that the psychology teacher had ever talked like that, not to judge from the way she talked in her course description—it's "a version of *yourself* that you are going to be present-ing" in your writing, and that kind of stuff. The class sounded like—what had Charlie's phrase been yesterday?—"your basic warm and support-ive environment." And even if the psychology teacher *had* said some-thing like what the Gorgon said to Lou, chances are this kid wouldn't have picked up on it as having anything to do with her. She didn't sound all that much different from the writer of "College Life," the one Alonzo described as "locked in a system" and that Lou called an addict. And the woman in 8 said she'd set herself up for years talking like an airhead. *For years* nothing had got through to her, she said.

O.K. So the kid here didn't have a Gorgon or somebody like Pat riding over her life on a power mower. What *had* happened to get her from version I to version III of her paper in just a couple of weeks? Something must have. Even the assignment didn't say *nothing* had happened, only that no other readers were involved.

The woman in 8 needed some models, her teacher said.

So maybe the girl in 9 had found a model of some sort? Somebody to imitate? Something to imitate? Maybe *after* some kind of Pat-like slap in the face, some kind of catastrophe or disaster like what had hap-pened to her in study group, or maybe like Mark telling about how first he'd gone broke in Atlantic City and then had really seen the nuns? Some catastrophe from some*where* if not from somebody?

Catastrophe.

Disaster.

The connection rang a bell of some sort.

Had one of the assignments mentioned "disaster" as a way to grow up?

Was it from a paper they'd read in class? Had somebody in study group said . . . ?

It was in study group, but it wasn't something somebody had said. It was out of that essay by Percy that the Gorgon had given them only part of, one piece back at Assignment 3 and another at Assignment 6. Charles had hunted up and photocopied the whole essay for the rest of them when they'd talked about an unstereotypical way of seeing. He said he'd had a feeling that Percy had gone on to talk in his essay about some things you could do to see unstereotypically—which in study group both he and Pat had seemed to think he had, though she hadn't been able to follow either Percy or the conversation Pat and Charles had had about what Percy was saying.

She did remember that Percy had said something about "disaster" though because both Pat and Charles had mentioned it, and that it was connected with . . . "reviving"? Was that what Percy had said? "Disaster" could bring a "reviving"? Something like that.

She flipped back to the copy of the Percy essay Charles had passed out and that she'd tucked in her notebook next to Assignment 6. She'd marked off the part the Gorgon had quoted in red:

> How can the sightseer recover the Grand Canyon? He can recover it in any number of ways, all sharing in common the stratagem of avoiding the approved confrontation of the tour and the Park Service.

Oh yeah. "Recover it." It was *recovering,* not *reviving.* O.K. The disaster stuff had come after that somewhere.

She read quickly, skimming through the first sentences of paragraphs:

> It may be recovered by leaving the beaten track. The tourist leaves the tour, camps in the back country. He arises before dawn and approaches the South Rim through a wild terrain where there are no trails and no railed-in lookout points. In other words, he sees the canyon by avoiding all the facilities for seeing the canyon. If the benevolent Park Service hears about this fellow and thinks he has a good idea and places the following notice in the Bright Angel Lodge: *Consult ranger for information on getting off the beaten*

track—the end result will only be the closing of another access to the canyon.

It may be recovered by a dialectical movement which brings one back to the beaten track but at a level above it. For example, after a lifetime of avoiding the beaten track and guided tours, a man may deliberately seek out the most beaten track of all, the most commonplace tour imaginable: he may visit the canyon by a Greyhound tour in the company of a party from Terre Haute—just as a man who has lived in New York all his life may visit the Statue of Liberty. (Such dialectical savorings of the familiar as the familiar are, of course, a favorite stratagem of *The New Yorker* magazine.) The thing is recovered from familiarity by means of an exercise in familiarity. Our complex friend stands behind the fellow tourists at the Bright Angel Lodge and sees the canyon through them and their predicament, their picture taking and busy disregard. In a sense, he exploits his fellow tourists; he stands on their shoulders to see the canyon.

Such a man is far more advanced in the dialectic than the sightseer who is trying to get off the beaten track—getting up at dawn and approaching the canyon through the mesquite. This strategem is, in fact, for our complex man the weariest, most beaten track of all.

It may be recovered as a consequence of a breakdown of the symbolic machinery by which the experts present the experience to the consumer. A family visits the canyon in the usual way. But shortly after their arrival, the park is closed by an outbreak of typhus in the south. They have the canyon to themselves. What do they mean when they tell the home folks of their good luck: "We had the whole place to ourselves"? How does one see the thing better when the others are absent? Is looking like sucking: the more look-ers, the less there is to see? They could hardly answer, but by saying this they testify to a state of affairs which is considerably more complex than the simple statement of the schoolbook about the Spaniard and the millions who followed him. It is a state in which there is a complex distribution of sovereignty, of zoning.

It may be recovered in a time of national disaster. The Bright Angel Lodge is converted into a rest home, a function that has nothing to do with the canyon a few yards away. A wounded man is brought in. He regains consciousness; there outside his window is the canyon.

The most extreme case of access by privilege conferred by disaster is the Huxleyan novel of the adventures of the surviving remnant after the great wars of the twentieth century. An expedition from Australia lands in Southern California and heads east.

They stumble across the Bright Angel Lodge, now fallen into ruins. The trails are grown over, the guard rails fallen away, the dime telescope at Battleship Point rusted. But there is the canyon, exposed at last. Exposed by what? By the decay of those facilities which were designed to help the sightseer.

This dialectic of sightseeing cannot be taken into account by planners, for the object of the dialectic is nothing other than the subversion of the efforts of the planners.

The dialectic is not known to objective theorists, psychologists, and the like. Yet it is quite well known in the fantasy-consciousness of the popular arts. The devices by which the museum exhibit, the Grand Canyon, the ordinary thing, is recovered have long since been stumbled upon. A movie shows a man visiting the Grand Canyon. But the moviemaker knows something the planner does not know. He knows that one cannot take the sight frontally. The canyon must be approached by the stratagems we have mentioned: the Inside Track, the Familiar Revisited, the Accidental Encounter. Who is the stranger at the Bright Angel Lodge? Is he the ordinary tourist from Terre Haute that he makes himself out to be? He is not. He has another objective in mind, to revenge his wronged brother, counter-espionage, etc. By virtue of the fact that he has other fish to fry, he may take a stroll along the rim after supper and then we can see the canyon through him. The movie accomplishes its purpose by concealing it. Overtly the characters (the American family marooned by typhus) and we the onlookers experience pity for the sufferers, and the family experience anxiety for themselves; covertly and in truth they are the happiest of people and we are happy through them, for we have the canyon to ourselves. The movie cashes in on the recovery of sovereignty through disaster. Not only is the canyon now accessible to the remnant: the members of the remnant are now accessible to each other; a whole new ensemble of relations becomes possible—friendship, love, hatred, clandestine sexual adventures. In a movie when a man sits next to a woman on a bus, it is necessary either that the bus break down or that the woman lose her memory. (The question occurs to one: Do you imagine there are sightseers who see sights just as they are supposed to? A family who live in Terre Haute, who decide to take the canyon tour, who go there, see it, enjoy it immensely, and go home content? A family who are entirely innocent of all the barriers, zones, losses of sovereignty I have been talking about? Wouldn't most people be sorry if Battleship Point fell into the canyon, carrying all one's fellow passengers to their death, leaving one alone on the South Rim? I cannot answer this. Perhaps there are such people. Certainly a great many American families would swear they had no such problems, that they came, saw, and went away happy. Yet it is just these families who would be happiest if they had gotten the Inside Track and been among the surviving remnant.)*

Let's see, "the beaten track," no not that one. "Dialectical movement," no. "Outbreak of typhus" from inside a paragraph caught her. There it was. And she read back.

Umm . . . , no. No, it wasn't either. The typhus was connected with the "breakdown of symbolic machinery," whatever that was.

Next paragraph.

Ah ha. Here it is, "disaster."

Wait a minute, though. It's *national* disaster Percy's talking about. *"Threads,"* she'd written in the margin. *"Brave New World."* Well, whatever the girl in Assignment 9 had experienced, it wasn't the aftermath of nuclear holocaust.

She went back to the paragraph on typhus, reading carefully:

It may be recovered as a consequence of a breakdown of the symbolic machinery by which the experts present the experience to the consumer. A family visits the canyon in the usual way. But shortly after their arrival, the park is closed by an outbreak of typhus in the south. They have the canyon to themselves. What do they mean when they tell the home folks of their good luck: "We had the whole place to ourselves"? How does one see the thing better when the others are absent? Is looking like sucking: the more lookers, the less there is to see? They could hardly answer, but by saying this they testify to a state of affairs which is considerably more complex than the simple statement of the schoolbook about the Spaniard and the millions who followed him. It is a state in which there is a complex distribution of sovereignty, of zoning.

The park is closed and a family has the whole of the Grand Canyon to themselves. And that somehow makes them see better. They really see the Grand Canyon. They have the whole of the Grand Canyon to themselves, and . . .

Well, with that part of things she *could* connect. It was like the way she and everybody else out there that day had had the whole of the Minneapolis airport just to themselves. For 36 hours they'd had the place to themselves, shut off from everything by the freak March snow, and it had been a lot more than *symbolic* machinery that had broken

---

*Walker Percy, "The Loss of the Creature," *op. cit.*, pp. 48–51. Reprinted by permission of Farrar, Straus and Giroux.

down that day. Nobody got into the airport and nobody got out. Not any way at all. No way. Not for 36 hours. The main highway out there had been jammed solid with abandoned cars. She saw it all later in a helicopter shot on the national news, the cars scattered like pick-up-sticks and then mounded into humps as the snow had gone on and on and on.

Maybe it *was* a national disaster she'd been in.

But no, it wasn't. Not for her it wasn't, not any more than Percy's family had suffered from the "outbreak of typhus in the south." But she'd seen things better out there in the airport in Minneapolis. She was clear on that, remembering.

Well, not seen. Heard. It had to do with what she'd heard in the airport that day. The night of that day.

It had been an O.K. trip out to her aunt and uncle's in Minnesota, though she'd done it more for her mother than anything else.

"Oh, Karen. They really want to see you. They're paying your plane fare. You'll only be away from Kevin a couple of days, you know."

She knew. But it was *three* days she was to be away. Three days of spring vacation, and he'd been working with her on her backhand.

The visit with them was O.K. though. They were really nice to her. And what Kevin called her "Type A personality" she kept pretty much in control.

At seven the morning she was to leave the snow was no more than an absent-minded sprinkling, but she was nervous anyway, prickly with impatience in the cozy kitchen, sitting around with those thick mugs of even thicker Norwegian coffee. She knew the storm wasn't supposed to hit until early evening, that her plane was to leave at noon, and that they were only about an hour's drive from the airport. She was nervous anyway.

Don't worry, her uncle had said several times, we're out of February, you know. And indeed, she'd seen the March buds herself, swollen like popcorn at the edge of the Northfield River. By eight the snow was full, downy, shawling the bayberry bushes, piling steadily into the black forks of trees.

They left Northfield for the airport in the pickup, she and her uncle and her niece, Jamie. She had trouble staying with the steady cheerfulness of his conversation, her niece's chatter. The wind had come up on the parkway, driving the snow at a steep slant, granuled now, clicking against the windshield. There were a good 4 inches of it by the time they got to Minneapolis International.

"You'll be O.K., though," her uncle said. "Snow is a way of life out here."

They posted the first delay of her flight about noon. Damn. She'd be O.K. all right. Sure she'd be O.K. Why had she come? Why had she come at all?

There were 6 inches of snow then, and counting.

At one they were all shunted over to TWA, she at a dead run with her backpack, marched into a plane the size of an auditorium, and told they'd be lifting out for Detroit in half an hour.

8 inches.

Three times trucks sprayed the wings, turning back the cover of snow like a blanket, and three times they were rolled back to wooly mammoth sleep. By five o'clock there were 11 inches of snow and not even the airlines were pretending any more. The loudspeakers were off, the computers down. It took her uncle and Jamie 3 hours to get back to Northfield, her aunt told her over the phone. "I don't know what to tell you to do, Karen" she said. "What are you going to do?"

The last ground transportation, a limo from Mankato with 4 wheel drive, left about six. By eight even the candy machines had run out. They cleared and closed the concourses. Small knots of people sprawled on the floor of the main terminal watching the snow whine and sniff and whirl at the eaves of the plate glass observation windows.

15 inches.

A group of college kids got up a bridge game over an arrangement of luggage. There were no more lines at the telephones. People started to notice each other.

About time for the St. Bernards, wouldn't you say?

Oh? Well, I was in Denver last summer. *Sort* of in Denver. Actually, I was on my way to Wyoming.

God, I hope her mother lets her stay. She's a good sitter, but her mother always wants her home by six.

18 inches, 19, 20, 21.

And then it started, way down at the other end. A short, low burst of sound, as though from a tunnel. Imploring, like a cry.

"What was that?" a man across from her asked no one in particular.

It had stopped.

"I thought I heard . . ."

It came again.

"There. That. Did you hear that?"

She had. It was sound, in a sort of rhythm. Then nothing. Then again, low and harmonic. Then silence.

But no. Not silence. A pause, maybe.

"What is that anyway? Music?"

The whole main level of the airport began to flow toward it, as though the axis of the earth had tipped.

"I don't know," she heard a woman say. "It sounds like singing, doesn't it? Is it people singing?"

Starting. Then stopping.

No, that was the *song* starting and stopping. It *was* singing, it sounded like . . .

"I don't believe it," a man said. "Is that *Dixie?*"

It was.

But it wasn't.

	Ah		
		~~way~~	
	wayyy.		ay
			ay
~~Ahhhh~~			

It was real slow and dignified, like a funeral.

	eee		
		~~laaand~~	
Dix			
~~In~~			

They sang it again for them, of course, for all of them, just standing around at first, but then sitting in rings on the floor, even the security guards, some Japanese flight attendants, students, old people, maybe 300 of them all together. The choir was from some place north of Duluth on their way to compete in a songfest in Germany, stuck like all the rest of them between one way of life and another. Nobody in it looked to be over 17, and most seemed younger. They looked like angels to her, white and serious, their voices pure as rain. A lot of what they sang she didn't know. They did a church thing, in Latin, like an anthem, only a lot fancier. They sang some spirituals. And then a snapping, rolling chunk of something that she heard a man behind her say was Fred Waring, by God. That's *Fred Waring!*

In '76 the sky was reeed—

Was it!

With Thunder rumbling overheeead—

You bet!

Making Old King Geor orge shake in his beeed—

But she felt the gift of it. And for the first time in her life, she was convinced, she really heard music. She wept without self-consciousness, without even knowing at first that she was weeping. It was all so beautiful to her. It was so beautiful.

After maybe half an hour a stranded TV crew piled up from the lower level with lights and cameras and great black loops of cable. Everybody had to get up and move back and that ended it all somehow.

Well, it did and didn't.

Because she wanted to be by herself for a change. She had no desire to flirt or even to talk to anybody and she stretched out alone alongside one of the cleaned out vending machines, not worrying whether she slept or not, hearing harmony still, hearing unison.

She woke to the smell of tobacco. He was a college student, headed for Bismarck, sitting crosslegged on the floor alongside her with two canvas bags. He stubbed out his cigarette awkwardly when he saw he'd awakened her, and apologized. She just smiled, feeling peaceful, lazy. It was four in the morning and still snowing.

She hiked herself up on her elbows to sit beside him. They talked about schools for a while, home. The boy—Sam?, Sandy?—was thin and intense and plucked at things nervously. He brought up the singing, calling it a concert. He said he'd seen her there. She nodded and said it had been super, really super, and that she'd liked "Dixie" best, she thought.

"You know," he said, after thinking about it for a moment, "What I can't figure out is how good they really are, those kids."

Kids. It made her smile. He was only a year older than she was.

"I mean I know they're *good*. They won that contest up north and all. A guy told me that. But do you think they're as good as they sounded?"

"I don't know," she said. "They sounded really good to me. I never heard anything like it. Some people were crying even. I thought they were beautiful."

"Yeah," he said, moving his index finger in squares on the indoor–outdoor carpet. "I guess." And then he said, "they sounded good to me too." And then, "maybe how good they are isn't the point though."

Neither of them said anything for a while. They just sat there watching the snow fall through the airfield ground lights.

"Do you think they knew what they did," he asked, "I mean the way they brought us there? They brought everybody in a group, the whole airport, did you see that? And those TV bastards, did you see them? We never even got a chance to thank those kids, I mean to applaud for them or anything. Not in a group the way they brought us there. They looked scared the whole way through too, did you notice that? They were nervous the whole way through."

"Oh, I think they knew what they did," she said. "There were a lot of us there. *Everybody* was there. I'm sure some of them knew."

"Well," he said, after a bit, "maybe that's not the point either."

And a little after that they drifted back to sleep.

He was gone when she woke up in the middle of the morning. Her plane left at five that afternoon.

What had touched her so with all of it?

The singing? Well, yeah, sure, but it was more than that.

Song then?

Or music?

Music. That was it. Music itself.

And why so? Why had she heard the way she'd heard?

Because of the snow. Because there'd been a disaster.

Yes, but no too, because it hadn't been a disaster for her finally. It had been fun. It had been bigger than fun.

O.K. It was what the disaster did then, what the snow had done. It had slowed her down. It had made her listen. It had made it possible for her to listen really hard.

It had slowed her down.

She flipped up to Assignment 9 again, to the quotation from Kenneth Dowst about writing's slowing you down:

Writing is the form of language-using that is the slowest, most deliberate, most accessible, most conveniently manipulable, and most permanent.

Yes. And later:

A writer can tinker with a paragraph for minutes or hours, until it expresses to the writer's satisfaction patterns of cause and effect, evidence and conclusions, interrelationships of data, relevance and irrelevance, denotation and connotation—patterns that establish the "world" in which the writer knows and acts, patterns far too complex and coherent to be created by mere thinking or mere speaking.

Maybe that's what the girl had done to get from version I to II to III. She'd written, which had slowed her down, which had slowed her down so that she could hear, so that she could—what was that Adrienne Rich thing?

She turned a page of the assignment.

Here—so that she could "understand the assumptions in which she was drenched," so she could then tinker, the way . . . the way the girl writing the examining room paper had, who had also written a disaster of a paper, but which wasn't that finally, not any more than the snow had been a disaster for her, or than what Pat had said to her in study group was either, not finally it wasn't, not after what Betty had said to her that same day and what Lou had said to her in front of everybody at their next meeting.

She'd been slowed down.

She'd been made to listen.

Writing could do that?

It had done it for Amy. She'd heard her say so in class. She hadn't seen the paper, but she'd heard Amy say that she'd written about herself and her mother believing one thing but that writing about it showed her something else.

So writing could do that.

Maybe it was writing then that had got the girl from version I to version II to version III of her paper. Maybe writing had been the slap and the model both, negative but not just negative because it was necessary. You wrote and read and listened and then wrote again so that you could *see* with what you wrote, so that you could begin to really see.

Assignment 10

We have seen the language-using process of writing, particularly when it involves the process of revising, referred to as a way of learning, as a way of growing. In the following excerpt it is referred to as that which can lead to a "discovery," to the seeing of "something new about ourselves and our topic."

In the process of writing, we begin with what is inchoate and end with something that is tangible. In order to do so, we both discover and construct what we mean. Yet the term "discovery" ought not lead us to think that meaning exists fully formed inside of us and that all we need do is dig deep enough to release it. In writing, meaning cannot be discovered the way we discover an object on an archeological dig. In writing, meaning is crafted and constructed. It involves us in a process of coming-into-being. Once we have worked at shaping, through language, what is there inchoately, we can look at what we have written to see if it adequately captures what we intended. Often at this moment discovery occurs. We see something new in our writing that comes upon us as a surprise. We see in our words a further structuring of the sense we began with and we recognize that in those words we have discovered something new about ourselves and our topic. Thus when we are successful at this process, we end up with a product that teaches us something, that clarifies what we know (or what we knew at one point only implicitly), and that lifts out or explicates or enlarges our experience. In this way, writing leads to discovery.*

But it is no news to any of us that as writers, we often fail for one reason or another to be "successful at this process." Sometimes the fault is a matter of inexperience or inability, to be sure, but other times what we do and do not do as writers may be said to be the result of choice, more or less acknowledged, more or less faced up to. And though sometimes we get by anyway, sometimes we don't—as the following narrative may be said to demonstrate.

Toward the end of the semester, the teacher of an introductory course for physics majors gave his students this writing assignment:

You are working to master the discipline of physics. This assignment is for the purpose of helping you to define for yourself what exactly it is that you are doing.

Choose some law or principle that is important to you as a physicist and imagine yourself in the position of wanting to explain to a nonphysicist, to someone indeed who does not even know mathematics, why this law or principle is important in your field. What do you say? (Speak in this part of your paper directly to the person you imagine you are addressing.)

In the second part of your paper look back at what you've said. What kind of a job do you think you've done? What do you think you explain well? What do you not explain so well?

Finally, and this is the most important part of your paper, on the basis of your experience in this assignment with both your explanation and your evaluation of your explanation, how do you define the discipline of physics?

The final paragraph of one student's paper addressing that assignment, done by a student who had earned an A in her work for the course up to that point, read as follows:

---

*Sondra Perl, "Understanding Composing," in *College Composition and Communication,* 31 (December 1980), pp. 367–368. Copyright © by National Council of Teachers of English. Reprinted by permission of the NCTE.

The discipline of physics is the science of dealing with the properties, changes, and interaction of matter and energy. I couldn't explain this very well using the Secnd Law of Thermodynamics, because I couldn't use any math. Still I think I did a rather good job because I believe the layment ought to know the importance of the idea of entropy. Also time is tid up with increasing disorganization. Which is important. All in all I hope the layman I'm speaking to can see how the Second Law of Thermodynamics is a cornerstone to the disciplene of physics.

The physics teacher bracketed that paragraph and at the end of the student's paper wrote:

This paragraph is typical of the writing here as a whole. As a draft, the paper might have been valuable. What's really annoying about your passing it off as finished work, however, is that you don't seem even to *care* that you display in it a very cheap understanding of physics as a subject, a discipline, a system. Don't waste your time "correcting" the paper. If you want to revise it, rewrite it, I'd be glad to hear what you have to say.

The student, who had not been earning an A for nothing, turned in a second paper with this as its final paragraph:

What I think I did well in my explanation of the Second Law of Thermodynamics was explaining *that* it has to do not only with the laboratory concept of heat transfer, but also with such universally important things as temperature, time, and the ultimate fate of the universe. Because I couldn't use math, and because my own knowledge is limited, what I don't think I did so well was to explain just *how* it is connected with these things. To do that, not only would I have to teach the nonphysicist math, I'd have to teach him everything I know about physics and probably a lot more besides. I'd define the discipline of physics then as a way of "dealing with the properties, changes, and interaction of matter and energy," but in a system in which any one thing is connected with all other things in such a way as to be completely understandable only to someone who knows his way around the system.

Again the teacher bracketed the student's final paragraph. At the end of the revised paper he wrote:

Now you're talking—and as somebody I can have a conversation with. This paragraph in particular is beautifully done. You've discovered some things that are very important to understand—about physics and beyond—as I hope the attached passage can help you see.

Here is what the physics teacher attached to his student's paper:

To break through toward a creative act, it is necessary to twist out of phase whatever conventional laws appear to hold. This does not mean that it is necessary to defy all the basic hypotheses of our phenomenology, but that it is necessary to defy them *apparently*. Then, through the cracks which appear when the laws are twisted out of phase (all this attained through conscious self-deceit), things can be seen in a new way. So long as the rules are accepted as immutable "laws of vision" the world always will appear to be the same and no novelties can be discovered or fabricated. Many highly trained people naturally tend to think in terms of the dogma of their own technology and it frightens them to twist their conventions out of phase. Their conventions sometimes constitute a background of knowledge upon which they rely for their emotional stability. Such experts do not want cracks to appear. They identify their psychic order with the cosmic order and any cracks are signs of their orderly cosmos breaking up. . . .

One classic example [of speculative play with logical systems] is Lobachevsky's invention of non-Euclidean geometry. . . . The new geometry . . . seemed at first mere wilful play, irresponsible in fact. The closed system of Euclidean geometry was judged to be true, not only logical in itself, but also descriptive of the nature of the space as experienced. This representative accuracy of Euclidean geometry is "true" of everyday spatial relationships in that it enables us to handle those relationships with "reasonable" accuracy. However, this "representative accuracy" is a function of traditional ways of perceiving and categorizing our experience of everyday space, traditional ways which are accepted but are neither true or untrue. Lobachevsky's invention has therefore two important consequences: 1) It questions the degree of "representative accuracy" which was traditionally attributed to the Euclidean system. Thus Lobachevsky's system tended to make the familiar strange. When we live with the familiar system without questioning it, we lose our awareness of the unfounded (even questionable) assumptions which underlie the system and our acceptance of it. We attribute a false concreteness to what in reality is only a symbolic representation, a conceptual tool. When the established system was questioned in a "strange" way by Lobachevsky, the system, its assumptions, and its implications became more clear for what it was. 2) Lobachevsky's invention also makes it possible at least to conceive (if not to see) other ways of interpreting the human experience of space. Contemporary concepts of the nature of the nuclear astro-physical world would be impossible if we were still locked into the assumption that Euclidean geometry provides the final symbolic language for the expression of spatial relationships.

Language itself—mathematical symbols or words and phrases—when combined into a logical self-consistent pattern threatens constantly to deceive us as being "concrete," as not only expressing ways of thinking, but also being the way things in themselves are. This threat to constructive imagination assumed two interrelated forms: 1) over-development of expertly elaborated systems of internal consistency; 2) over-development of "apparent" and everyday concreteness. Thus Euclidean geometry, over-developed as a self-consistent system, tends to atrophy in a meaningless closed circle of expertise. Over-developed as concrete and self-evidently valid, it atrophies by becoming confused with a representative description of actual space.*

---

*William J.J. Gordon, *Synectics: The Development of Creative Capacity,* pp. 95 and 125–126. Copyright © by William J.J. Gordon. Reprinted by permission of William J.J. Gordon 121 Brattle St., Cambridge, Mass.

Write a paper about the transaction described above in which you address the following questions:

What specifically does this teacher seem to be finding fault with in his criticism of the final paragraph of the first version of this student's paper? What in the student's writing might lead him to say that the student doesn't seem to *"care"* what she displays in the paper, and to call the student's representation of her understanding of physics "cheap"? What kind of distinction is the teacher making between "correcting" and "revis[ing]" the paper?

What is there about the second version of the student's final paragraph that you think might lead the teacher to praise it as he does? What might he mean by saying "this paragraph . . . is beautifully done," for instance? What might he mean, do you imagine, by saying "Now you're talking—and as somebody I can have a conversation with"?

What do you think the teacher might mean by saying that the student has "discovered some things that are very important to understand—about physics, and beyond"? How might the passage from W.J.J. Gordon help the student see the importance of her "discovery"?

Seeing Assignment 10

STUDY GROUP III

Their making presentations in study group had been Alonzo's idea, and he had proposed it just that way. Julie had grumbled at first, saying none of the other groups worked that formally, and that she didn't like the idea of turning theirs into a board meeting. But they'd ended the session agreeing at least to try it. "We'll just take turns being responsible for saying what we think is important to talk about in an assignment, that's all," was the way Alonzo had explained himself. "Ten minutes at the start of a session. Fifteen tops. We don't have to keep doing it if we don't get anything out of it." It had helped, as even Julie had had to admit. "Making a presentation" was the way they'd all come to refer to what Alonzo, pre-med and a science major, had volunteered to do for their session on Assignment 10.

"Now, I think the best way into the assignment," he began, handing each of them a couple of stapled photocopied pages with their names written neatly at the top, "is through what the teacher calls the student's discovery about science. Then we can move to look at some of the things the teacher might mean by giving the student the material on Lobachevsky."

Julie giggled. "What's this, Alonzo," she said gesturing at the sheets of paper, "personalized instruction, or what? And you sound just like the Gorgon."

"And remember, Alonzo," Mark said, "you said there wouldn't be any high-tech talk."

"Yes, well, could we read the anecdote first, please?" They read:

Some time ago I received a call from a colleague who asked if I would be the referee on the grading of an examination question. He was about to give a student a zero for his answer to a physics question, while the student claimed he should receive a perfect score and would if the system were not set up against the student. The instructor and the student agreed to submit this to an impartial arbiter, and I was selected.

I went to my colleague's office and read the examination question: "Show how it is possible to determine the height of a tall building with the aid of a barometer."

The student had answered: "Take a barometer to the top of the building, attach a long rope to it, lower the barometer to the street, and then bring it up, measuring the length of the rope. The length of the rope is the height of the building."

I pointed out that the student really had a strong case for full credit, since he had answered the question completely and correctly. On the other hand, if full credit was given, it could well contribute to a high grade for the student in his physics course. A high grade is supposed to certify competence in physics, but the answer did not confirm this. I suggested that the student have another try at answering the question. I was not surprised that my colleague agreed, but I was surprised that the student did.

I gave the student six minutes to answer the question with the warning that the answer should show some knowledge of physics. At the end of five minutes, he had not written anything. I asked if he wished to give up, but he said no. He had many answers to this problem; he was just thinking of the best one. I excused myself for interrupting him and asked him to please go on. In the next minute he dashed off his answer which read:

"Take the barometer to the top of the building and lean over the edge of the roof. Drop that barometer, timing its fall with a stopwatch. Then using the formula $S = \frac{1}{2} at^2$, calculate the height of the building."

At this point I asked my colleague if *he* would give up. He conceded, and I gave the student almost full credit.

In leaving my colleague's office, I recalled that the student had said he had many other answers to the problem, so I asked him what they were. "Oh yes," said the student. "There are a great many ways of getting the height of a tall building with a barometer. For example, you could take the barometer out on a sunny day and measure the height of the barometer, and the length of its shadow, and the length of the shadow of the building, and by the use of a simple proportion, determine the height of the building."

"Fine," I asked. "And the others?"

"Yes," said the student. "There is a very basic measurement method that you will like. In this method you take the barometer and begin to walk up the stairs. As you climb the stairs, you mark off the length of the barometer along the wall. You then count the number of marks, and this will give you the height of the building in barometer units. A very direct method.

"Of course, if you want a more sophisticated method, you can tie the barometer to the end of a string, swing it as a pendulum, and determine the value of 'g' at the street level and at the top of the building. From the difference of the two values of 'g' the height of the building can be calculated."

Finally, he concluded, there are many other ways of solving the problem. "Probably the best," he said, "is to take the barometer to the basement and knock on the superintendent's door. When the superintendent answers, you speak to him as follows: 'Mr. Superintendent, here I have a fine barometer. If you tell me the height of this building, I will give you this barometer.'"

At this point I asked the student if he really did know the conventional answer to this question. He admitted that he did, said that he was fed up with high school and college instructors trying to teach him how to think . . . in a pedantic way . . . rather than teaching him the structure of the subject.*

There were appreciative grins.

"I just love this guy," Steve said. "I love him. 'Mr. Superintendent.' He's just great."

"This is sort of like the Ping-Pong ball in the pipe, isn't it?" Avery said tentatively.

"Hey, it is like that assignment, you know?" Mark said. "You make the coat hanger into tweezers. This guy turns the barometer into a present."

"Yeah," Julie said, "and a yardstick, and a pendulum, etcetera, etcetera, but what exactly is the point, Alonzo m'dear?"

---

*Alexander, Calandra, "Angels on a Pin: A Modern Parable," *Saturday Review,* December 21, 1968. Copyright © 1968 *Saturday Review.* Reprinted by permission.

"Well obviously there's a connection between the story and the Ping-Pong ball in the pipe problem, but the point *here* is that what the student in the story is saying is the same thing the girl in Assignment 10 shows she's discovered about physics when she revises her paper."

Everyone stared at him.

"Could you, ah, trot that by one more time, Alonzo honey?" Julie said finally. "For us slower folk? And it's a *student* in the assignment, or a young woman. Not a *girl*. Just the way—" she tapped the pages he'd given them with her middle fingernail—"just the way it's a student here, O.K.?

Alonzo grimaced and bowed ironically in Julie's direction.

What a pain, Mark thought again, that the guy has to look like such a stud. At least he could wear horn-rimmed glasses or something. Alonzo was on the swimming team. He looked supple as a cat. It irritated Mark the way he always sat next to Julie in class.

"What I'm saying," Alonzo explained, "is that I think what this teacher wanted the students to see is what makes physics physics, do you see? See, for me to try to explain why the Second Law of Thermodynamics is important in physics, *without using math,* I mean really explain it, the 'how' and the 'why' of it rather than the 'that,' as the student says, is a kind of contradiction in terms. Either nothing like an explanation will have gone on, or at the end of the conversation the layman wouldn't be a layman any more. He'd be a physicist."

He looked at Julie.

"Lay*person,* I mean. The lay*person* wouldn't be a lay*person* anymore. *She'd* be a . . . physicette, O.K.?"

"Cut it out, Alonzo," said Steve, who was in engineering. He remembered very clearly a remark Alonzo had made in class early in the term: "Most scientists see engineers in about the same way medical doctors see chiropracters, you know." It was the "you know" that had galled him. "You don't have to patronize us. We're not stupid. O.K? So no physicist could explain the Second Law of Thermodynamics *fully* to a nonphysicist without using math. Are you saying this teacher in the assignment gave the students a problem that was impossible, then?"

"Wait a minute," Mark, who was a history major, said. "What do you guys mean you couldn't explain the law without using math?"

"Well, you couldn't," Alonzo said. "Not really. Look." He turned over his photocopied pages and took up his ballpoint. "Let me give you a very simple formula here and—"

"No fair, Alonzo," Julie cut in. "No formulas, no math. You made a deal."

Alonzo sighed and leaned back in his chair, looking at the ceiling.

"See, Mark," Steve said leaning toward him, "it would be like trying to explain to somebody *why* their checking account was overdrawn without using numbers. That's not an exact analogy, but you see the problem you'd have."

"Well, that's *part* of the problem you'd have," Alonzo added. "You couldn't explain the 'how' at all, but you'd probably have trouble with the 'that' too you see, because . . . well, you see something like heat transfer connects with a lot of other things in physics. So to explain the Second Law *fully* you'd have to explain all those other things as well. You'd find yourself going on forever."

"So everything is connected with everything else, sort of the way one thread can unravel a whole sweater?" Avery offered. "Is that what you're saying?"

"Or how about this, guys?" Julie asked them. "Are you saying that the system of physics is like a code that exists between people who have the same meaning for a particular phrase that may mean *something* to other people, but not what it does for the in-group? We were at dinner at my family's a couple of weeks ago, the whole pack of us, and my sister's boyfriend said about something that it was real. And then my youngest sister said, 'Yes, it's *only* real,' and we all burst out laughing, I mean all of my family, because with us that has a particular meaning, that phrase, that all of *us* understand, but my sister's boyfriend of course didn't. He thought we were crazy laughing the way we did."

"What's it mean 'it's only real'?" Mark asked her, fascinated, but Steve kept them on track.

"I still want to know, Alonzo, whether you think the teacher has given the class an impossible problem. Is that what you're saying?"

"No," Alonzo said. "I wouldn't say that. The parameters of the problem as the physics teacher has defined it allow—"

Then Julie broke in.

"Look, I was first, Steve. And *I* still want to know where the barometer story comes in, Alonzo."

Alonzo held up his hand, smiling. "Whoa. Whoa. One problem at a time people, O.K.? All right, Julie, female persons first. Let's take the barometer story. I think what the student is doing, the student in the anecdote I mean now, is reminding his teacher, the one who posed the problem with the barometer, that physics is a system, but that the teacher's question suggests it isn't."

"What is the right answer to the question, anyway," Avery asked him. "I mean what's the teacher want?"

Alonzo explained, and then continued. "But see, that's the point. That's only the right answer to a particular question. A barometer inside the system of physics has a specific function, sort of the way the phrase 'it's only real' means something special to Julie's family. Actually, that wasn't a bad analogy, Julie. Now, *inside* the system of physics a barometer is an instrument for measuring pressure. But what the student is saying is that *outside* the system of physics a barometer can be a lot of different things, a ruler, a pendulum weight, a bribe even, and so on. The teacher has asked a bad question, you see, or rather has asked a question badly. His question seems to assume that physics *is* the world, that a barometer is only one thing and has only one function and that isn't true. Physics *isn't* the world. It's just a way of making sense of the world. And his student is pointing that out to him. Lobachevsky's invention had the same function, of course."

"Just the way, Stevie Babycakes," Julie said, putting her arm around him, "a light bulb can be a lot of different things, remember?"

"Look, Julie," he said, shoving her, "I understood *that*. All I was getting at was—"

"Could we stay with this, please?" Avery asked, and then asked Alonzo, "So the student in the story is a kind of a purist, is that it?"

"Well, yes," Alonzo said, "I think that's what he means when he makes the distinction he does at the end, don't you—between being taught to think in a pedantic way as opposed to learning the structure of the subject? The world and formulas about the world are different. That's what he's saying. He's acting like a real scientist."

"Sort of a smart-assed real scientist though, isn't he?" Julie interjected. "Bet you've never acted like that, Alonzo."

"Look," Mark said, "I'm still not sure I get all this. You say physics and the world are different."

"They are, Mark," Alonzo said, "they are." His tone was condescending. "That is, they may be. You can't always tell, you know. Is light, that is, does light, consist of particles or waves? Nobody really knows. That's the essence of science, Mark. A lot of people think that science is a matter of facts, objectivity, that kind of thing. Even scientists can forget what science is. Well, pseudo-scientists, anyway. But science is just a set of systems for *dealing* with the world. It's not the world itself."

"By 'pseudo-scientists' I suppose you mean engineers, right Alonzo?" Steve said, his face flushed. "I suppose you think that when we work certain engineering problems we just aren't conscious that we're leaving out things like the curvature of the earth."

Alonzo looked at him, grinning. "Come on, Steve. Don't be so touchy."

"Look you two," Mark said, "I want to get this straight. I want to get *something* straight for once in one of these study groups. So I'll play the dope, O.K.? Now let me take something very simple in physics, like the earth goes around the sun. Is that true or not?"

"Interesting problem, Mark," Alonzo said pointing at him. "Does the earth go around the sun, or does the sun go around the earth? A very interesting problem. More complicated than you might think."

"Right," Julie snorted. "A very interesting problem. Ptolemy may have been right. We ought to have some T-shirts made up for our study group 'Ptolemy Was Right.'"

"Julie, stop it!" Steve said to her. "It really *is* an interesting problem. Alonzo is being a shit about it, but it is. I heard an astro-physicist—also an engineer, Alonzo, a pseudo-scientist—talk about it at our high school last year. What he said, Mark, was that the problem of whether the earth goes around the sun or whether the sun goes around the earth is one of such unbelievable magnitude that he couldn't begin to address it. He said that as a scientist his position was like that of someone asked to explain how the pool balls had gotten into the pockets of a pool table as the result of a game he'd never seen and didn't know existed as a game. 'As a scientist,' this man said, 'I'd take the simplest explanation I could find for the phenomenology that was confronting me. I'd say that someone put the balls in the pockets—when in fact they got to be where they are through the ridiculously complex procedure of a stick hitting a ball which then hits another ball which caroms off a cushion, and then maybe another, and then rolls into a pocket.' In the question and answer period somebody asked whether you could get a rocket to the moon in a . . . well, in a Ptolemaically conceived universe. The man said that of course you could. It would take a computer about the size of Australia, he said. But he said you could do it."

Alonzo listened carefully, his hands steepled, nodding as Steve talked.

"Yes," he said. "Of course."

"But see, Mark," Steve went on, "see the interesting thing about all that is. . . ." He put his glasses back on quickly and dug into his briefcase. "We just got this passage in my. . . . Here. Here it is. Now just listen to this about science and truth for a minute, O.K.? There aren't any numbers in it, by the way. *My* physics teacher, an engineer, gave us this. It's Niels Bohr, the physicist, talking to Einstein. . . ."

"That wouldn't be *Albert* Einstein by any chance, would it, Baby-cakes?" Julie put in.

"Shut up, Julie. Just listen to this now, you guys. I think this is really great." His eyes shone as he read:

In the Institute in Copenhagen, where through those years a num-ber of young physicists from various countries came together for discussions, we used, when in trouble, often to comfort ourselves with jokes, among them the old saying of the two kinds of truth. To the one kind belong statements so simple and clear that the oppo-site assertion obviously could not be defended. The other kind, the so-called "deep truths," are statements in which the opposite also contains deep truth.*

---

*Niels Bohr, "Discussion with Einstein on Epistemological Problems in Atomic Physics," in *Atomic Physics and Human Knowledge*. New York: John Wiley and Sons, 1958, p. 68.

"That's all I was getting at," Alonzo said airily, waving a hand. "Science won't get you to truth. The Heisenberg Uncertainty Principle, and all that. Physics is just one of the systems of science. That's what the physics teacher in our assignment wants the students to see."

"That's it then? The student in our assignment got the right answer the second time?" Avery asked him. "You're saying that's why the teacher praises him?"

"*Her,* Avery," Alonzo said, "as Julie will remind us. The student's a *her.* And sure that's why the teacher praises her, and gives her Lobachevsky too. I mean basically. What else?"

Julie hissed in exasperation.

"You know, Alonzo, you would think that—that the difference between this student's first paper and her second is that she got the right answer. That's exactly what you'd think. And it's just as cheap as the student was."

"Meaning?"

"Meaning mister," Julie said with real heat, "that 'cheap' is the difference between the way you talk about science and the way Steve just did. What *you* don't seem to understand, Alonzo, is. . . ."*

---

*I am grateful for the assistance of my colleagues Professors Alec Stewart, physicist and Dean of the Honors College of the University of Pittsburgh, and John Warnock of the University of Wyoming who aided me in my presentation of science in both *Assignment 10* and *Seeing Assignment 10.*

Assignment 11

We have been examining some of the complications that can attend someone's using the processes of reading and writing to develop a new way of seeing, but it is understandable that we do not ordinarily think of the ability to revise, to change what we see by changing the language with which we create patterns or shape events, as an ability which could involve us in conflicts. At least at one level we exercise the ability almost unconsciously, virtually automatically, and usually to solve an immediate problem. Though we will not find, for example, a definition for a word like "chair" in the dictionary that reads "may be thrown through locked windows in the event of a room's being filled with lethal gas," few of us in such a situation would have to work very long at what else a chair may be than something to sit on. And fewer of us still would see the revising process here as other than that which results in a clear gain. In changing our way of describing what we see, we've changed what it *is* that we see. And in doing *that,* we're then able to do, to be, at least momentarily, something we wouldn't be able to do or to be otherwise. Where's the conflict? What conflict could attend the process that makes it possible for us to use a nail file as a screwdriver in a pinch, or that enables us to roll up a newspaper to discipline a high-spirited puppy without seem-ing even to think about it?

Here is an account of what could be called a conflict with the revising process on which all new ways of seeing seem to depend. Annie Dillard, author of the following passage, is describing the findings of a writer named Morris von Senden as he reports them in a book entitled *Space and Sight:*

When Western surgeons discovered how to perform safe cataract operations, they ranged across Europe and America operating on dozens of men and women of all ages who had been blinded by cataracts since birth. Von Senden collected accounts of such cases; the histories are fascinating. Many doctors had tested their patients' sense perceptions and ideas of space both before and after the operations. The vast majority of patients, of both sexes and all ages, had, in von Senden's opinion, no idea of space whatso-ever. Form, distance, and size were so many meaningless syllables. A patient "had no idea of depth, confusing it with roundness." Before the operation a doctor would give a blind patient a cube and a sphere; the patient would tongue it or feel it with his hands, and name it correctly. After the operation the doctor would show the same objects to the patient without letting him touch them; now he had no clue whatsoever to what he was seeing. One patient called lemonade "square" because it pricked on his tongue as a square shape pricked on the touch of his hands. Of another postop-erative patient, the doctor writes, "I have found in her no notion of size, for example, not even within the narrow limits which she might have encompassed with the aid of touch. Thus when I asked her to show me how big her mother was, she did not stretch out her hands, but set her two index-fingers a few inches apart."

For the newly sighted, vision is pure sensation unencumbered by meaning: "The girl went through the experience that we all go through and forget, the moment we are born. She saw, but it did not mean anything but a lot of different kinds of brightness." Again, "I asked the patient what he could see; he answered that he saw an extensive field of light, in which everything appeared dull, con-fused, and in motion. He could not distinguish objects." Another patient saw "nothing but a confusion of forms and colours."

The mental effort involved in these reasonings proves over-whelming for many patients. It oppresses them to realize, if they ever do at all, the tremendous size of the world, which they had previously conceived of as something touchingly manageable. It oppresses them to realize that they have been visible to people all along, perhaps unattractively so, without their knowledge or consent. A disheartening number of them refuse to use their new vision, continuing to go over objects with their tongues, and lapsing into apathy and despair. "The child can see, but will not make use of his sight. Only when pressed can he with difficulty be brought to look at objects in his neighbourhood; but more than a foot away it is impossible to bestir him to the necessary effort." Of a twenty-one-year-old girl, the doctor relates, "Her unfortunate father, who had hoped for so much from this operation, wrote that his daughter carefully shuts her eyes whenever she wishes to go about the house, especially when she comes to a staircase, and that she is never happier or more at ease than when, by closing her eyelids, she relapses into her former state of total blindness." A fifteen-year-old boy, who was also in love with a girl at the asylum for the blind, finally blurted out, "No, really, I can't stand it any more; I want to be sent back to the asylum again. If things aren't altered, I'll tear my eyes out."

Some do learn to see, especially the young ones. But it changes their lives. One doctor comments on "the rapid and complete loss of that striking and wonderful serenity which is characteristic only of those who have never yet seen." A blind man who learns to see is ashamed of his old habits. He dresses up, grooms himself, and tries to make a good impression. While he was blind he was indifferent to objects unless they were edible; now, "a sifting of values sets in . . . his thoughts and wishes are mightily stirred and some few of the patients are thereby led into dissimulation, envy, theft and fraud."*

Though it is difficult if not impossible for those who have been able to see from birth to imagine what the experience of seeing for the first time must have been for the patients described above, it is quite possible for a college student, particularly a college student who is taking his or her education seriously, to know something of the conflicts that can attend the development of a new way of seeing. As a college student you may not yourself be in anything like the situation described by the student writer represented in Assignment 8, for example, but you certainly are in the situation of having as a reader and writer to learn a number of new names or terminologies or languages with which to interpret phenomena that you may have understood differently before you came here. And pressured, challenged from different quarters to use these languages to re-examine much that you knew another way,

---

*Annie Dillard, *Pilgrim at Tinker Creek*, pp. 25–29. Copyright © 1974 by Annie Dillard. Reprinted by permission of Harper & Row, Publishers, Inc.

it is no exaggeration to say that you may someday have to cope in your own terms with something like the conflicts the student writer represented in Assignment 8 experienced in hers—if indeed you are not doing so already.

Here is the way a former college president described his way of seeing and of dealing with the expression of these conflicts as he experienced it in undergraduates:

> And here I confess that I adopted a principle . . . in my treatment of young men which I sometimes almost believe to be theoretically true, viz.: that often . . . they are deranged, and therefore when grossly insulted personally, I did not feel it necessary to notice it. I mean, that in college they come under the influence of views, feelings, and prejudices, so different from those of men in common life, that charity should lead us to regard them as we would men under strong hallucination, if not partial insanity, assured that after they have left college, they will see the fallacy of many of the sentiments and prejudices that lead them while in college to abuse one another, oppose the Faculty, justify convivial excesses, and sympathize strongly with those disciplined for gross immoralities, so as to organize rebellion against lawful authority. I had found that if we could, by bearing and forbearing, get such men through college and away from the influence of false notions, they would generally rally and become respectable. Hence, I made every effort to get them over this Rubicon, and never suffered the grossest personal insults, if unknown to the world, to prevent my laboring in behalf of one whom I looked upon as infatuated. [p. 320]

That paragraph about undergraduates and their behavior was written by Edward Hitchcock in a book published toward the end of his life describing among other things his nine years as president of Amherst College (an all-male institution at the time): *Reminiscences of Amherst College, Historical, Scientific, Biographical, and Autobiographical: Also of Other and Wider Life Experiences* (Northampton, Massachusetts, 1863). Hitchcock was a Professor of Chemistry and Natural Science and also a Professor of Natural Theology and Geology. By many of his students he was remembered as an inspiring teacher.

What sort of educational stance is being taken here by this former college president? How does he seem to see students, the world of college, the world outside college? What does he seem to mean by speaking of students as "deranged," for example, as "infatuated"? What might he mean by seeing students in college as coming "under the influence of views, feelings, and prejudices . . . different from those of men in common life"? What might such "views" or "false notions" be, and who might they come from? Is it Bad Apples in the student body or in the faculty of a college community that Hitchcock is speaking of, do you think? And what sort of reasoning might lead this ex-president to conclude that in the world *outside* college, former students "will [come to] see the fallacy of" many of their earlier ideas, will "generally rally and become respectable"?

What would it be like to be a student in the world of a college run on the educational principles articulated by Edward Hitchcock? How, that is, do you think the adopted principles of this former president might be felt or experienced by students as an educational policy?

If you could design an ideal college for yourself, what sorts of educational principles would it be run on and how would you experience them as an educational policy?

Seeing Assignment 11

AVERY

She closed the door of her room and leaned back against it, eyes shut, trembling with excitement still, feeling more alive and yet stranger to herself than she could remember.

So this was seeing. This was what it was all about.

She felt as though she'd eaten something that was still alive inside her, zipping around in chunks, like a lot of shooting stars.

Revelation. It had been a revelation she'd experienced, one that had come unbidden but that had changed nothing less than her awareness of everything, and that had brought with it a whole new sense of herself. It was more than that she'd just been stirred, or moved, the way Karen had said she was by the singing in the Minneapolis airport, the way Mark had been by the nuns. And though it was *like* what Amy had said happened to her when she wrote out the conversation she thought she'd had with her mother, it was more than that too, because Amy said she'd had to write to see what she'd seen, and then think, and then rewrite, and then think again and write again—and it hadn't been that way for her at all. What she'd seen at the screening had come like a sunburst, and all at once, illuminating everything, enlarging her.

A sorting out there would have to be, she knew. Oh my, yes. But she'd always been good at that sort of thing. Her father was a career army officer whom all three of his daughters still jokingly called "sir" on occasion, and playing it by the numbers was natural to her. She'd always learned easily whatever she'd had to learn without thinking about it very much—and also, she noted bitterly, without ever having been encouraged to think very much about what that involved. Oh, she was good at details, all right.

The important thing was this sense of herself as more than that, this new sense of herself as someone who was capable of receiving what she'd just been given.

Looking back, she could see that it had been building up for a while. More and more, particularly in her study group where Julie and Alonzo and recently even Steve leaped like chamois from idea to idea, she'd started to see herself as, well, wimpy sort of. Colorless. Avery the Country Mouse. Just last week Julie had said to her: "You know Avery, if you had a draft card, you wouldn't burn it. You'd tear it in half." It hadn't been meant to hurt her. She knew that. But she could also remember sitting at her desk most of the rest of that night, her head cradled sideways on her arms, staring at the unrecognizable golden blur she'd become in the curves of the brass desk lamp that sat not six inches from her eyes. She was a good student and what else? Had she ever learned to trust herself more than just half way? What was the price of having learned to play it by the numbers?

"Sounds to me like you could use a shot in the arm—if I know my girl," her father had said to her Sunday on the telephone.

Well, his "girl" had had one and then some. She went back over what had happened, looking around her room as though it belonged to someone else.

She'd never really seriously considered cutting the screening, but only because going to class was a habit with her. There was no way she had expected to see anything in the film version of The Wizard of Oz that she hadn't seen already. She knew the movie as well as she did Monopoly, which she and her sisters had been able to play on car trips with no more than a pair of dice, the cards, and a stack of false money. She'd watched the movie every year of her life when it came on television, right through high school, most of the time with her family. Her father in fact had once taken a night flight back from California just to be with them for the showing. The Wizard of Oz was home for her. America. Ironically, the very morning of the screening a videocassette of the movie had arrived from her father. He'd wrapped it himself in gay paper and written a note: "For my Dorothy. May she dodge fireballs forever. You sounded glum chum on the phone Sunday. I hope this helps to cheer you up." It was a special message. For years, one section of the movie, the Witch's attempt to torch the Scarecrow, had driven her into a tight curl of terror against her father's chest.

She'd gone to the screening in spite of its having started to rain while she was in her economics lecture. She'd had to walk halfway across campus to get there.

A "screening" was what they called it in her film course when they showed one of the films the class was studying. And it was always "films" that were screened. Never movies. The screening of *Oz* was for a paper the class had to write: "*The Wizard of Oz* as a variant of the American Dream."

Even in that only slightly darkened, overheated classroom with the projector whirring and clicking distractingly through the soundtrack, everybody steaming from the cold November rain and smelling like blankets, things had started out for her in the movie much as they always had. Her consciousness of Auntie Em, Henry, and Miss Gulch as stereotypes hadn't really bothered her, and the twister was wonderfully done still. She'd had to make no allowances at all for its being a special effect, generated, she'd learned in her course, with a silk stocking. She felt herself smile the same smile she always had at Dorothy's comment when the movie shifted to Oz and to technicolor: "Toto, I've got a feeling we're not in Kansas anymore." But the four main characters for some reason began to make her uneasy. In a way they were the same figures she remembered from the time she could remember: one of tin, one of straw, that impossible lion with the New Yawk accent, and Dorothy of course. Judy Garland. She'd known for quite a while that most of them were dead, but it gave her a queer feeling at the screening to have to think of them that way, particularly Judy, though hadn't she been dead the longest? Everybody's Sweetheart, her film instructor had called her with a sneer. A high octane Shirley Temple. Miss American Pie—dead at 47, he'd said, of an overdose of just about everything.

The scene that had done it, however, dislocating her completely, was the one in which the four main characters escape from the poppy field to head for the Emerald City shimmering in the distance, all spires and light and jewels and promise, The Emerald City where they'd get a heart for the Tin Woodman, a brain for the Scarecrow, courage for the Lion, and for Judy, home. Because all Judy wants is to go home.

But why? it had suddenly, shockingly, occurred to her to ask. Why is that what Judy wants, *all* she wants?

Home to what?

Home to the pigs in Kansas? She wants to go back home from where troubles melt like lemon drops to a life of 14 hour workdays? Back from arching rainbows and singing flowers to the mute brown dust of a wretched farm, blown to nothing no doubt, like so many others in the Depression, like half the prairie states? Because that's what had happened. She knew. She was studying the Depression in her economics class, had read of the dust bowl and the plummeting stocks, of the bread lines and the strikes and the hired strike breakers. And the *Oz* film had been made in 1939. That was the Depression. That was the height of the Depression, wasn't it? Was *Oz* then the American Dream of The Depression?

Or was it the American Dream as packaged for *consumption* in 1939 at the height of the Depression? Did Judy *really* want to go back, or was she only *said* to want to go back because . . . because that's what the people . . . no . . . not the people, the man, the men, the male chauvinist power elite who made the film, because that's what the power structure *wanted* people to believe was the right thing for Judy to want, the right thing for women to want in particular, the right dream for America to subscribe to?

The question, which ceased to be one for her the moment she had articulated it, rocketed the film into a whole new dimension. Nothing she saw from that point on, as insight opened into insight, connection folded into connection, was as it had been.

She remembered a boy in her economics class telling her that the myth of Paul Bunyan wasn't really a myth at all, not a folk myth anyway, not a people's myth, but rather a Madison Avenue creation, really a Wall Street creation, invented to make the American public accept the ravaging of the forests in Michigan, Wisconsin, and Minnesota by Big Business. Ah ha. She suddenly saw that *Oz* was no more than this, a film of propaganda twisting the American Dream into the kind of vicious lie that would convince people they didn't really *need* things like unions because they didn't really need a living wage. Ah ha.

And then in a flash she saw why, even as a little girl she'd never liked the end of the film, where Judy, back in country mouse Kansas, keeps saying "there's no place like home, there's no place like home," and her whole experience is explained away as nothing more than a dream, literally a dream, the result of a crack on the head delivered at the height of the tornado ("A device to establish psychological verisimilitude," she'd heard it explained in her course). But really it had an even more insidious function. It was the power elite's way of making the people buy a lie, what she'd heard described in her history class as the fascist ethic: We'll show you how to dream. We'll show you what you really want and what you don't. We'll show you what's real and what isn't. And we'll do this in such a way as to convince you that it's all your own idea. That was the point of all that phoney gift giving toward the conclusion, she now saw, where the wizard, unmasked, distributes to everyone not what they were there to get, and what they'd earned, but what the movie suggests is the next best thing—at which, of course, the characters are all delighted. That is they are *said* to be delighted. Even if the power structure is exposed, in other words, it doesn't have to come across with anything, because everybody already has what they want—that is all the half-people do, the nonpeople, like scarecrows and workers and Blacks and tin men and women. *Women.* Above all women. Of *course* evil is represented in the film by a woman, and as one *out*side the system rather than in it, and therefore as an evil that is easily recognized and that may be joyfully destroyed. By natural means, too (she'd never noticed the significance of *that* symbolism before); the Wicked Witch is melted by a bucket of water, the source of all life. Her destruction, the destruction of all strong individual women, was thereby shown to be part of the order of things, no more than the way nature intended it. It made her furious. It reminded her of something she'd heard in a history lecture, that the Nazis had used the Jews just the way Western Civilization had used the Nazis: to convince themselves it was possible to settle something with force. It all went together. It all made malicious, hateful sense. A handful of sequins, a couple of jokes, and a few catchy songs. That's all it took for the power structure to pervert the American Dream into an instrument of oppression. That's all it took to convince people that the way it was convenient for a priviledged few to *keep* the world running was the way the world really was.

"Home is where the heart is," she'd heard a boy behind her say in disgust as the lights came up, "and be grateful for what you have and everybody gets what they want. American Dream my ass."

And she'd winced, she was ashamed to remember, in spite of her revelation. She'd been offended.

But on the way back to her dorm, remembering her instructor's sneer at Judy Garland, she'd been able to place her prudishness for what it really was. The truth *was* crude, crude and ugly, and of course she'd been conditioned against it. Nice girls don't think like that, she'd been made to believe. Nice girls don't talk like that. Nice girls let themselves be lied to, be made slaves. And nice girls loved it. Shit is what it was! Just plain shit! And of course the truth had offended her when she'd heard it, even now, even given what she'd begun to understand. The depth of her deception, the full extent of her violation, appalled her. How easy she'd been to take advantage of as a child. And she'd bought it, year after year, the whole bag of tricks, curled up against her father who was buying it too, buying it just as unknowingly as. . . .

"*Just* as unknowingly?" she put it to herself, and the realization had stopped her dead, right in the middle of the rain.

No.

Not just as unknowingly. Not her military father. Not unknowingly at all, in fact.

He'd known. He *had* to have known. My God, he. . . .

Why, he was *part* of it. Her own father. A member of the industrial-military establishment. He was part of it!

Her own father, who'd forced her and her sisters to see him as a "sir," who saw her as his "girl"! *His* Avery! Avery, the Clockwork Country Mouse!

The thought of the videocassette she'd unwrapped just that morning, her mindless gladness, had driven tears to her eyes.

So that's the way it was. That's how it was.

But there were no tears now she noted, as she crossed her room to stand at the window. She could see all the way to downtown Pittsburgh from her dorm room high in the Tower. The city was rimmed by hills, she knew, though she could not see them, that opened to sky and stars, though these too were hidden by the rain.

There were no tears now. Quite the contrary, as a matter of fact. Her mind was like ice.

Very well then. If that's the way it was, why then that's how it was. They'd not find her so easy from here on in.

Assignment 12

Not all of the newly sighted that von Senden examined, however, responded to what they saw or to being able to see in the same way. Annie Dillard is struck by another set of attitudes in von Senden's report:

On the other hand, many newly sighted people speak well of the world, and teach us how dull is our own vision. To one patient, a human hand, unrecognized, is "something bright and then holes." Shown a bunch of grapes, a boy calls out, "It is dark, blue and shiny. . . . It isn't smooth, it has bumps and hollows." A little girl visits a garden. "She is greatly astonished, and can scarcely be persuaded to answer, stands speechless in front of the tree, which she only names on taking hold of it, and then as 'the tree with the lights in it.'" Some delight in their sight and give themselves over to the visual world. Of a patient just after her bandages were removed, her doctor writes, "The first things to attract her attention were her own hands; she looked at them very closely, moved them repeatedly to and fro, bent and stretched the fingers, and seemed greatly astonished at the sight." One girl was eager to tell her blind friend that "men do not really look like trees at all," and astounded to discover that her every visitor had an utterly different face. Finally, a twenty-two-year-old girl was dazzled by the world's brightness and kept her eyes shut for two weeks. When at the end of that time she opened her eyes again, she did not recognize any objects, but, "the more she now directed her gaze upon everything about her, the more it could be seen how an expression of gratification and astonishment overspread her features; she repeatedly exclaimed: "Oh God! How beautiful!"*

The same "extensive field of light" in which for one patient everything appears "dull, confused, and in motion," for another, just as "dazzled by the world's brightness," so dazzled in fact that she keeps her eyes shut for two weeks, gives rise eventually to the repeated exclamation: " 'Oh, God! How beautiful!' " The revising process, in other words, being introduced to and having to learn ways of knowing the world different from the ways in which they had been experiencing it, seems understandably to have meant conflict for all the newly sighted. But not all of them responded to the experience in the same way.

Similarly, not all people respond to the revising process of education the same way or with a single attitude, even when the process is successful. Here, for example, is an essay in which someone analyzes his experience as a child of one culture responding to the demand that he become a man in another. Richard Rodriguez was educated in Catholic primary and secondary schools in Sacramento, California and later attended Stanford University. "The Achievement of Desire" he later rewrote into a chapter of a book entitled: *Hunger of Memory: The Education of Richard Rodriguez* (New York: Bantam Books, Inc., 1983).

The Achievement of Desire: Personal Reflections on Learning "Basics"

NOT LONG AGO in a ghetto classroom, I attempted to lecture on the mystery of the sounds of our words to a roomful of diffident students. (" *'Summer is i-cumen in. . . .'* The music of our words. We need Aretha Franklin's voice to fill plain words with music—her life. Don't you hear it? Songs on the car radio. Listen!") In the face of their empty stares, I tried to create an enthusiasm. But the girls in the back row turned to watch some boy passing outside. There were flutters of smiles, blushes of acne. Waves. And someone's mouth elongated heavy, silent words through the barrier of glass.

---

*Annie Dillard, *Pilgrim at Tinker Creek, op. cit.*, pp. 30–31. Reprinted by permission of Harper & Row, Publishers, Inc.

Silent words—the lips straining to shape each voiceless syllable: *"Meet meee late errr."* By the door, the instructor kept smiling at me, apparently hopeful that I would be able to spark an enthusiasm in the class. But only one student seemed to be listening. A girl around fourteen. In that grey room her eyes glittered with ambition. She kept nodding and nodding at all that I said; she even took notes. And each time I asked the class a question, she jerked up and down in her desk, like a marionette, while her hand waved over the bowed heads of her classmates. It was myself (as a boy) I saw as she faced me (now a man early in my thirties).

I first entered a classroom unprepared and barely able to speak English. Twenty-one years later, I concluded my studies in the stately quiet of the reading room of the British Museum.

Thus with two sentences, I can outline my dramatic academic career. It will be harder to summarize what sort of life connects both of these sentences. For though I was a very good student, I was also a very bad student. I was a "scholarship boy,"[1] a certain kind of scholarship student. Always successful. Always unconfident. Exhilarated by my progress. Yet sad. Anxious and eager to learn—the prized student. Too ambitious, too eager—an imitative and unoriginal pupil.

Certain factors important for my success are easy enough to mention. In the first place, my older brother and sister were very good students; they influenced me. (They brought home the bright, shiny trophies I came to want.) And, I attended an excellent grammar school. (Due to a simple geographical accident, our house in Sacramento neighbored one of the wealthiest sections of town; I went to a school, as a result, where I was the only "problem student" in class.) And, my mother and father always encouraged me. (At every graduation, they were behind the stunning flash of the camera when I turned to look at the crowd.)

As important as these factors were, however, they inadequately account for my advance. Nor do they suggest what an odd success I managed. Only moderately intelligent, I was highly ambitious, eager, desperate for the goal of becoming "educated." My brother and two sisters enjoyed the advantages I had and were successful students, but none of them ever seemed so anxious about their schooling. I alone came home, when a new student, for example, and insisted on correcting the "simple" grammar and

---

[1]For reasons of tone and verbal economy only, I employ the expression, scholarship *boy,* throughout this essay. I do not intend to imply by its usage that the experiences I describe belong to or are the concern solely of male students.

pronunciation mistakes of our parents. ("Two negatives make a positive!") Regularly, I would ask my parents for help with my homework in order to be able to pull the book out of their hands, when they were unable to help me, and say, "I'll try to figure it out some more by myself." Constantly, I quoted the opinions of teachers and trumpeted new facts I had learned. Proudly, I announced in my family's surprised silence—that a teacher had said I was losing all trace of my (Spanish) accent.

After a few months, I outgrew such behavior, it's true. I became more tactful. Less obvious about my ambitions. But with always-increasing intensity, I devoted myself to my studies. There never seemed enough time in a day "to learn"—to memorize—all that I wanted to know. I became bookish, a joke to my brothers, and puzzling to my parents. ("You won't find it in your books," my brother would sneer when he often saw me reading; my father opened a closet one day and found me inside with my books.) Such ambitions set me apart, the only member of the family who deserved the pejorative label of scholarship boy.

What I am about to describe to you has taken me twenty years to admit: *The primary reason for my success in the classroom was that I couldn't forget that schooling was changing me, and separating me from the life I had enjoyed before becoming a student.* (That simple realization!) For years I never spoke to anyone about this boyhood fear, my guilt and remorse. I never mentioned these feelings to my parents or my brothers. Not to my teachers or classmates. From a very early age, I understood enough, just enough, about my experiences to keep what I knew vague, repressed, private, beneath layers of embarrassment. Not until the last months that I was a graduate student, nearly thirty years old, was it possible for me to think about the reasons for my success. Only then. At the end of my schooling, I needed to determine how far I had moved from my past. The adult finally confronted—and now must publicly say—what the child shuddered from knowing and could never admit to the faces which smiled at his every success.

I

At the end, in the British Museum (too distracted to finish my dissertation), for weeks I read, speed-read, books by sociologists and educationists only to find infrequent and brief mention of scholarship students, "successful working-class students." Then one day I came across Richard Hoggart's *The Uses of Literacy* and saw, in his description of the scholarship boy, myself. For the first time I realized that there were others much like me, and I was able to frame the meaning of my academic failure and success.

What Hoggart understands is that the scholarship boy moves between environments, his home and the classroom, which are at cultural extremes, opposed. With his family, the boy has the pleasure of an exuberant intimacy—the family's consolation in feeling public alienation. Lavish emotions texture home life. *Then* at school the instruction is to use reason primarily. Immediate needs govern the pace of his parents' lives; from his mother and father he learns to trust spontaneity and nonrational ways of knowing. *Then* at school there is mental calm; teachers emphasize the value of a reflectiveness which opens a space between thinking and immediate action.

It will require years of schooling for the boy to sketch the cultural differences as abstractly as this. But he senses those differences early. Perhaps as early as the night he brings home some assignment from school and finds the house too noisy for study.

> He has to be more and more alone, if he is going to "get on." He will have, probably unconsciously, to oppose the ethos of the hearth, the intense gregariousness of the working-class family group. Since everything centres upon the living-room, there is unlikely to be a room of his own; the bedrooms are cold and inhospitable, and to warm them or the front room, if there is one, would not only be expensive, but would require an imaginative leap—out of the tradition—which most families are not capable of making. There is a corner of the living-room table. On the other side Mother is ironing, the wireless is on, someone is singing a snatch of song or Father says intermittently whatever comes into his head. The boy has to cut himself off mentally so as to do his homework as well as he can.[2]

The next day, the lesson is as apparent at school. There are even rows of desks. The boy must raise his hand (and rehearse his thoughts) before speaking in a loud voice to an audience of students he barely knows. And there is time enough and silence to think about ideas ("big ideas") never mentioned at home.

Not for the working-class child alone is adjustment to the classroom difficult. Schooling requires of any student alteration of childhood habits. But the working-class child is usually least prepared

---

[2]Richard Hoggart, *The Uses of Literacy* (London: Chatto and Windus, 1957), p. 241.

for the change. Unlike most middle-class children, moreover, he goes home and sees in his parents a way of life that is not only different, but starkly opposed to that of the classroom. They talk and act in precisely the ways his teachers discourage. Without his extraordinary determination and the great assistance of others—at home and at school—there is little chance for success. Typically, most working-class children are barely changed by the classroom. The exception succeeds. Only a few become scholarship students. Of these, Richard Hoggart estimates, most manage a fairly graceful transition. They somehow learn to live in the two very different worlds of their day. There are some others, however, those Hoggart terms scholarship boys, for whom success comes with awkwardness and guilt.

Scholarship boy: good student, troubled son. The child is "moderately endowed," intellectually mediocre, Hoggart suggests—though it may be more pertinent to note the special qualities of temperament in the boy. Here is a child haunted by the knowledge that one chooses to become a student. (It is not an inevitable or natural step in growing up.) And that, with the decision, he will separate himself from a life that he loves and even from his own memory of himself.

For a time, he wavers, balances allegiance. "The boy is himself (until he reaches, say, the upper forms) very much of *both* the worlds of home and school. He is enormously obedient to the dictates of the world of school, but emotionally still strongly wants to continue as part of the family circle" (p. 241). Gradually, because he needs to spend more time studying, his balance is lost. He must enclose himself in the "silence" permitted and required by intense concentration. Thus, he takes the first step toward academic success. But a guilt sparks, flickers, then flares up within him. He cannot help feeling that he is rejecting the attractions of family life. (There is no logic here, only the great logic of the heart.)

From the very first days, through the years following, it will be with his parents—the figures of lost authority, the persons toward whom he still feels intense emotion—that the change will most powerfully be measured. A separation will unravel between him and them. Not the separation, "the generation gap," caused by a difference of age, but one that results from cultural factors. The former is capable of being shortened with time, when the child, grown older, comes to repeat the refrain of the newly adult: "I realize now what my parents knew. . . ." Age figures in the separation of the scholarship boy from his parents, but in an odder way. Advancing in his studies, the boy notices that his father and mother have not changed as much as he. Rather, as he sees them, they often remind him of the person he was once, and the life he earlier shared with them. In a way he realizes what Romantics also know when they praise the working-class for the capacity for human closeness, qualities of passion and spontaneity, that the rest of us share in like measure only in the earliest part of our youth. For Romantics, this doesn't make working-class life childish. Rather, it becomes challenging just because it is an *adult* way of life.

The scholarship boy reaches a different conclusion. He cannot afford to admire his parents. (How could he and still pursue such a contrary life?) He permits himself embarrassment at their lack of education. And to evade nostalgia for the life he has lost, he concentrates on the benefits education will give him. He becomes an especially ambitious student. "[The scholarship boy] tends to make a father-figure of his form master" (p. 243), Hoggart writes with the calm prose of the social scientist. His remark only makes me remember with what urgency I *idolized* my teachers.

I began imitating their accents, using their diction, trusting their every direction. Any book they told me to read, I read—and then waited for them to tell me which books I enjoyed. I was awed by how much they knew. I copied their most casual opinions; I memorized all that they taught. I stayed after school and showed up on Saturdays in order "to help"—to get their attention. It was always their encouragement that mattered to me. *They* understood exactly what my achievements entailed. My memory clutched and caressed each word of praise they bestowed so that, still today, their compliments come quickly to mind.

I cannot forget either, though it is tempting to want to forget, some of the scenes at home which followed my resolution to seek academic success. During the crucial first months, the shy, docile, obedient student came home a shrill and precocious son—as though he needed to prove (to himself? to his parents?) that he had made the right choice. After a while, I developed quiet tact. I grew more calm. I became a conventionally dutiful son; politely affectionate; cheerful enough; even—for reasons beyond choosing—my father's favorite. And in many ways, much about my home life was easy, calm, comfortable, happy in the rhythm of the family's routine: the noises of radios and alarm clocks, the errands, the rituals of dinner and going to bed in flannel pyjamas.

But withheld from my parents was most of what deeply mattered to me: the extraordinary experience of my education. My father or mother would wonder: "What did you learn today?" Or say: "Tell us about your new courses." I would barely respond. "Just the usual things. . . ." (Silence. Silence!) In place of the sounds of intimacy which once flowed easily between us, there was the silence. (The toll of my guilt and my loss.) After dinner, I would rush away to a bedroom with papers and books. As often as possible I resisted parental pleas to "save lights" by coming to the kitchen to work. I kept so much, so often to myself. Sad. Guilty for the excitement of coming upon new ideas, new possibilities. Eager. Fascinated. I hoarded the pleasures of learning. Alone for hours. Enthralled. Afraid. Quiet (the house noisy), I rarely looked away from my books—or back on my memories. Times when relatives visited and the front rooms were warmed by Spanish sounds, I slipped out of the house.

It mattered that education was changing me. It never ceased to matter. I would not have become a scholarship boy had it not mattered so much.

Walking to school with classmates sometimes, I would hear them tell me that their parents read to them at night. Strange-sounding books like *Winnie the Pooh*. Immediately, I asked them: "What is it like?" But the question only confused my companions. So I learned to keep it to myself, and silently imagined the scene of parent and child reading together.

One day—I must have been nine or ten years old at the time—my mother asked for a "nice" book to read. ("Something not too hard that you think I might like.") Carefully, I chose one. I think it was Willa Cather's *My Antonia*. But when, several weeks later, I happened to see it next to her bed, unread except for the first few pages, I was furious with impatience. And then suddenly I wanted to cry. I grabbed up the book and took it back to my room.

"Why didn't you tell us about the award?" my mother scolded—though her face was softened with pride. At the grammar school ceremony, some days later, I felt such contrary feelings. (There is no simple roadmap through the heart of the scholarship boy.) Nervously, I heard my father speak to my teacher and felt my familiar shame of his accent. Then guilty for the shame. My instructor was so soft-spoken and her words were edged clear. I admired her until it seemed to me that she spoke too carefully. Sensing that she was condescending to them, I was suddenly resentful. Protective. I tried to move my parents away. "You must both be so proud of him," she said. They quickly answered in the affirmative. They were proud. "We are proud of all our children." Then, this afterthought: "They sure didn't get their brains from us." I smiled. The three of them laughed.

But tightening the irony into a knot was the knowledge that my parents were always behind me. In many ways, they made academic success possible. They evened the path. They sent their children to parochial schools because "the nuns teach better."

They paid a tuition they couldn't afford. They spoke English at home. ("*¡Hablanos en* English!") Their voices united to urge me past my initial resistance to the classroom. They always wanted for my brothers and me the chances they never had.

It saddened my mother to learn about Mexican-American parents who wanted their children to start working after finishing high school. In schooling she recognized the key to job advancement. And she remembered her past. As a girl, new to America, she had been awarded a diploma by high school teachers too busy or careless to notice that she hardly spoke English. On her own she determined to learn how to type. That skill got her clean office jobs and encouraged an optimism about the possibility of advancement. (Each morning when her sisters put on uniforms for work, she chose a bright-colored dress.) She became an excellent speller—of words she mispronounced. ("And I've never been to college," she would say smiling when her children asked about a word they didn't want to look up in a dictionary.)

When her youngest child started going to high school, my mother found full-time employment. She worked for the (California) state government, in civil service positions, positions carefully numbered and acquired by examinations. The old ambition of her youth was still bright then. She consulted bulletin boards for news of new jobs, possible advancement. Then one day saw mention of something called an "anti-poverty agency." A typing job. A glamorous job—part of the governor's staff. ("A knowledge of Spanish desired.") She applied without hesitation and grew nervous only when the job was suddenly hers.

"Everyone comes to work all dressed up," she reported at night. And didn't need to say more than that her co-workers wouldn't let her answer the phone. She was only a typist. Though a fast typist. And an excellent speller. There was a letter one day to be sent to a Washington cabinet officer. On the dictating tape my mother heard mention of "urban guerrillas." She typed (the wrong word, correctly): "gorillas." Everyone was shocked. The mistake horrified the anti-poverty bureaucrats who, several days later, returned her to her previous position. She would go no further. She willed her ambition to her children.

After one of her daughters got a job ironing for some rich people we knew, my mother was nervous with fear. ("I don't want you wearing a uniform.") Another summer, when I came home from college, she refused to let me work as a gardener. "You can do much better than that," she insisted. "You've got too much education now." I complied with her wish, though I really didn't think of schooling as job-training. It's true that I planned by that time to become a teacher, but it wasn't an occupation I aimed for as much as something more elusive and indefinite: I wanted to know as much as my teachers; to possess their confidence and authority; even to assume a professor's persona.

For my father, education had a value different from that it had for my mother. He chuckled when I claimed to be tired by reading and writing. It wasn't real work I did, he would say. "You'll never know what real work is." His comment would recall in my mind his youth. Orphaned when he was eight, he began working after two years in school. He came to America in his twenties, dreaming of returning to school and becoming an engineer. ("Work for my hands and my head.") But there was no money and too little energy at the end of a day for more than occasional night-school courses in English and arithmetic. Days were spent in factories. He no longer expected ever to become an engineer. And he grew pessimistic about the ultimate meaning of work or the possibility of ever escaping its claims. ("But look at all you've accomplished," his best friend once said to him. My father said nothing, and only smiled weakly.)

But I would see him looking at me with opened-mouth curiosity sometimes when I glanced up from my books. Other times, I would come upon him in my bedroom, standing at my desk or bookshelves, fingering the covers of books, opening them to read a few lines. He seemed aware at such moments of some remarkable possibility implied by academic activity. (Its leisure? Its splendid uselessness?) At the moment our eyes met, we each looked quickly away and never spoke.

Such memories as these slammed together in the instant of hearing that familiar refrain (all scholarship boys hear) from strangers and friends: "Your parents must be so proud." Yes, my parents were happy at my success. They also were proud. The night of the awards ceremony my mother's eyes were brighter than the trophy I won. Pushing back the hair from my forehead, she whispered that I had "shown" the *gringos*. Years later, my father would wonder why I never displayed my awards and diplomas. He said that he liked to go to doctors' offices and notice the schools they had attended. My awards got left in closets. The golden figure atop a trophy was broken, wingless, after hitting the ground. Medals were put into a jar. My father found my high school diploma when it was about to be thrown out with the trash. He kept it afterwards with his own things.

"We are proud of all of our children."

With more than mere pride, however, my parents regarded my progress. They endured my early precocious behavior—but with what private anger and humiliation? As their children grew older and would come home to challenge ideas both of them held, they argued with a son or daughter before submitting to the force of logic or superior evidence with the disclaimer: "It's what we were taught in our time to believe." These discussions ended abruptly, but my parents remembered them at other times when (smiling, unsmiling) they said that education was going to our heads. More importantly, both of them noticed how changed the family had become. My father himself retired into quiet, speaking to his children in paragraphs of single words or short phrases. My mother—the woman who joked that she would die if she ever stopped talking—softly wondered: "Why can't we be more of a family? More in the Mexican style?" She asked the question of all her children. But the last one surely from whom she would have expected an answer was her youngest son, the child who was so quiet at home, but had so much to say to high school instructors and his best friend's mother—a college professor.

When the time came for me to go to college, I was the first in the family who asked to leave home. My departure only made physically apparent the separation that had occurred long before. But it was too stark a reminder. In the months preceding my departure, I heard the question my mother never asked except indirectly. In the hot kitchen, tired at the end of her workday, she demanded to know, "Why aren't the schools here in Sacramento good enough for you? They were for your brothers." In the middle of a long car ride, never turning to look at me, she wondered, "Why do you need to go so far away?" Late at night, ironing, she said with disgust. "Why do you have to put us through this big expense? You know your scholarship will never cover it all." But when September came, there was a rush to get everything ready. In a bedroom, that last night, I packed the big brown valise. My mother sat nearby sewing initials onto the clothes I would take. And she said no more about my leaving. Nothing.

Months later, two weeks of Christmas vacation: the first hours home were the hardest. My parents and I sat in the kitchen and self-consciously had a conversation. (But lacking the same words to develop our sentences and to shape our interests, what was there to say? What could I tell them about the term paper I had just finished on "the universality of Shakespeare's appeal"?) I mentioned only small, obvious things: my dormitory life, weekend trips I had taken, random and ordinary events. They responded with news of their own. (One was almost grateful for a family crisis about which there was much to say.) We tried, finally we failed, to make the conversation seem like more than an interview.

II

From an early age, I knew that my father and mother could read and write both English and Spanish. I had seen my father make his way through what, now I suppose, must have been income tax forms. On other occasions I waited apprehensively while my mother learned of a relative's illness or death from letters airmailed from Mexico. For both of my parents, however, reading was something done out of necessity and as quickly as possible. Never did I see either of them read an entire book. Nor did I see them read for pleasure. Reading materials around our house were those of a nonliterate household: work manuals, prayer books, newspapers, and recipes. As Hoggart explains:

> . . . At home [the scholarship boy] sees strewn around and reads regularly himself, magazines which are never mentioned at school, which seem not to belong to the world to which the school introduces him; at school he hears about and reads books never mentioned at home. When he brings those books into the house, they do not take their place with other books which the family are reading, for often there are none or almost none: his books look, rather, like strange tools. (p. 242)

Each school year would start with my mother's instruction: "Don't write in your books so we can sell them at the end of the year." Teachers at school echoed the comment, but only in part: "Don't write in your books, boys and girls. You must learn to treat them with care and respect."

In the classroom, the written word possessed great authority, and reading and writing were central activities. Reading especially. "You'll learn to speak English well, if you practice your reading," a teacher told me. (She never explained how I had been able to speak Spanish at home without ever learning to read it.) In class, there were grammar books, spellers, elementary readers, and an odd phonetic alphabet to consult during the first months of instruction. "READ TO LEARN," read the poster over the teacher's desk in September. Every course had its own book. And what one read in a text was unquestioned. "OPEN THE DOORS OF YOUR MIND WITH BOOKS," the sign on the wall commanded in March. I privately wondered: What was the connection between reading and learning? And did an idea become an idea only when it was written down? Later, in June: "CONSIDER BOOKS YOUR BEST FRIENDS." (Friends?) Reading was only a chore.

I needed to look up whole paragraphs of words in a dictionary. Lines of type were dizzying—the eye having to move slowly across the page, then down, and across. . . . The sentences in the first books I read were coolly impersonal. Toned hard. Only informative. But mostly what bothered me was the silence reading required. To shield myself from it, I read in a soft voice. Until: "Who is doing all that talking to his neighbor?" an instructor shouted when my whispering punctured the silence of an afternoon reading period. Immediately, a tutorial was arranged with an ancient nun.

At the end of each schoolday, for nearly a year and a half, I would meet with her in the tiny room which served as the school's library, but was actually a storeroom for used textbooks and a vast collection of *National Geographics.* Everything about our sessions pleased me. The smallness of the room. The vague sounds of a few children, playing, screaming far away. The sound of the janitor's broom hitting the edge of the wall, as it came down the long hallway outside the door. The soft green of the sun, lighting the wall. And the old woman's face, blurred with a white beard.

Most of the time, we took turns reading. I began reading from some elementary text. The drab, ugly sentences: "The boys ran after the ball. . . . He wanted to go to the party. . . . The girls flew the yellow kite against the big, blue sky." Then the old nun would read from her favorite books, usually biographies of early American presidents. She playfully ran through complex sentences, mysteriously making written words sound friendly. Listening to her dramatic readings, I sensed for the first time some possibility of a fellowship between a reader and a writer and even a bond between readers, a communication never intimate like that I heard spoken words at home convey, but one profound and intensely personal nonetheless.

The nun ended the session one day by asking me why I was so reluctant to read by myself. I tried to explain my fears, said something about the way written words made me feel all alone— almost like, I wanted to add but didn't, when I spoke to myself in a room just emptied of furniture. She studied my face as I spoke; she seemed to be watching more than listening. Then in an uneventful voice, she replied that I had nothing to fear. Didn't I realize that reading would open up whole new worlds? A book was a kind of magic carpet. It would introduce me to new people and transport me to places and ancient times I never imagined existed. She gestured toward the bookshelves. (Bare-breasted African women danced and the shiny hubcaps of the automobiles on the back covers of old *Geographics* gleamed in my mind.) I listened respectfully, but her words were not very influential. I was thinking of another consequence of literacy, one I was too shy to admit but deeply trusted. Books were going to make me educated. That confidence enabled me, a few months later, to overcome the initial difficulties of reading by myself.

In the third grade, I embarked on a grandiose reading program. "Give me the names of important books," I would say to startled teachers. They soon discovered I had in mind "adult books." I ignored their suggestions of anything I supposed to be written for children. (Not until I became a college student, as a result, did I read *Huckleberry Finn* or *Alice in Wonderland.*) Instead, I read books like Franklin's *Autobiography* and Hawthorne's *Scarlet Letter.* And whatever I read was for "extra credit." Each time I finished a book, I carefully reported the achievement to a teacher and basked in the praise my effort earned. Despite all of my reading, however, there seemed to be more and more books I needed to read. At the library, I literally trembled when I came upon whole shelves of unfamiliar titles. I read and I read. Librarians, initially worried when they saw me check out the maximum ten books at a time, started saving books for me they thought I would like. Teachers would say to the rest of the class, "I wish all of you took reading as seriously as Richard."

At home my mother would find me reading at times when I was supposed to be asleep or helping around the house or playing outside. She would ask, sometimes puzzled, or mad, or worried, or simply deeply curious: "What do you see in your books?" (Was reading some hobby like knitting? Was so much reading good for a boy? Was it a sign of fabulous intellect? Was it an evasion of responsibility?) Always she wondered: "What do you see . . . ?"

What *did* I see in my books? I had the idea that they were crucial to my academic success, though I couldn't have said exactly how or why. In the sixth grade I concluded that what gave a book its value was some major idea or theme it contained. If that core essence could be found and then memorized, I would become learned like my teachers. I decided to record in a notebook the themes of the books I had read. After finishing *Robinson Crusoe,* I wrote that its theme was the "value of learning to live by yourself." When I completed *Wuthering Heights,* I noted "the danger of letting emotions get out of control." Re-reading these moralistic appraisals left me disheartened. I couldn't really believe that they were the source of the value of reading. For many more years, however, they comprised the only means I had of describing to myself the educational value of literature.

In spite of such earnestness, reading was in various ways a pleasurable experience. I had favorite writers—although ironically those I most enjoyed reading were the writers I was least able to value. When I read William Saroyan's *The Human Comedy,* for example, immediately I was pleased by the narrator's warmth and the charm of the story. But as quickly I became suspicious. A book so easy and pleasurable couldn't be very important, I decided. Another summer, I determined to read all the novels of Dickens. I loved the feeling I received after the first hundred pages of being at home in a complicated fictional world, and I was bothered by the way I was pushed away from the novel, at its conclusion, when the fiction closed tight, like a fortune teller's fist, with the futures of the major characters neatly concluded. I never knew how to take such feelings seriously. Nor did I suspect that these experiences could be part of a novel's meaning.

There were other pleasures reading provided. Each time I completed a book, I realized a feeling of great accomplishment. I would run my fingers along the edge of the pages and marvel at how much I had achieved. Around my room, the growing stacks of paperback books reinforced my assurance. Gradually, too, I came to love the lonely company of books. Early on weekday mornings, I would get up to read. I felt a mysterious comfort then, reading in the dawn quiet—the grey silence interrupted only by the churning of the refrigerator motor a few rooms away or the sounds of a city bus beginning its run. On weekends, I read in an uncrowded corner of the neighborhood library or, if the weather was fine, I would take my books to the park. Warm summer evenings were my favorite time to read. Neighbors would leave for vacations and have me water their lawns. I would sit for hours on their porches or in backyards, reading to the crisp, cool whirling sounds of sprinklers.

I entered high school having read hundreds of books. I was able to say something about Meister Eckhart and Jane Austen and Engels and James Baldwin. I sensed the shape of Western thought. My habit of reading also made me a confident speaker and writer of English. In these several ways, reading brought me success as my first teachers had promised it would. But I was not a good reader. Merely bookish, I lacked a point of view when I read. (Rather I read in order to acquire a point of view.) I vacuumed books for epigrams, scraps of information, ideas, "themes"—anything which would fill the hollow within me and make me feel more educated. When one of my teachers suggested to his drowsy ninth-grade English class that a person could not have a "complicated idea" until he had read at least two thousand books, I heard the remark without detecting either its irony or its complicated truth. I determined instead to compile a list of all the books I ever had read. Harsh with myself, I included only once a title I might have read several times. (How, after all, could one really read a book more than once?) And I included only those books over a hundred pages in length. (Could anything shorter be a book?)

There was yet another high school list. One day, I came across a newspaper story about the retirement of an English professor at a nearby college. The article was accompanied by a list of "the hundred most important books of Western civilization." "More than anything else in my life," the teacher told a reporter with finality, "these books have made me all that I am." That was the kind of remark I couldn't ignore. I clipped out the list and kept it for the several months it took me to read all of the titles. But most books I barely understood. While reading Plato's *Republic*, for example, I needed to keep consulting the book-jacket comments to remind myself what the text was all about. Nonetheless, with the special patience of a scholarship boy, I looked at every word of the text and by the time I reached the last page, I convinced myself that I had read the *Republic*. In a ceremony of pride, I solemnly crossed Plato off my list.

III

The scholarship boy pleases most when he is young. To teachers, he offers great satisfaction; his success is their proudest achievement. Many other persons offer their help. A businessman hears the boy's story and promises to underwrite the cost of his college education. A woman leaves him her entire library of several hundred books when she moves. His progress is even featured in a newspaper article. Everyone is very happy for him. They marvel. ("How did you manage . . . so fast?" they ask.) From all sides, there is lavish praise and encouragement.

Altruism alone cannot explain the pleasure—the ambiguous reaction—of all those who want the boy's success, but only if he remains, in some way, unchanged. The scholarship boy for a time offers complex delight. When he is young, the boy seems to straddle two great opposing cultures. Struggling for academic success, he still seems a child of the working-class and thereby suggests a remarkable possibility: the ancient dream of reconciling a way of life that is primarily active with one that is primarily reflective. Few persons who expect such a spectacular achievement from the boy probably are conscious of doing so. Their expectations become apparent, however, when they are finally disappointed, when the scholarship boy grows older and changes too much.

By the time he makes it to college, the boy hears less praise. Sometimes, he may even detect a trace of scorn on the faces of some who watch him. It is initially puzzling. In college, he behaves very much as he has always. If anything is different, it is that he dares anticipate the successful completion of his work. At last he feels comfortable and secure in the classroom. But this is precisely the source of the dissatisfaction he causes. To many persons who watch him, he appears suddenly too much the academic. There may be some things about him which still recall his beginnings—his shabby clothes; perhaps the hint of an accent; his persistent poverty; or his complexion (in those cases when it symbolizes his parents' disadvantaged condition)—but they only make clear how far he has moved from his past. He has used education to remake himself.

Many hope for someone quite different, a boy-man who would not be substantially changed by his schooling. An independent student. A working-class child, *and* an academic success. Someone impatient with his teachers when he hears them construct their lofty abstractions. A passionate pupil. Questioning. Scornful of his classmates' ignorance of the way "real" people live. A boy who would graduate a man with sharpened intellect and the knowledge of books but still be someone able to return home, still his parents' son and recognizable by "his people" as one of their own.

Instead there is the scholarship boy!

How many persons, I wonder, could have seen me in college and graduate school without feeling great disappointment? (The student whose surname was Rodriguez! The student with dark skin! The son of immigrant parents!) I had by that time become no different from other students around me. But though no different from them, I was more disappointing. The seminar room jargon coming from me sounded especially odd. (Bubbles at the tip of my tongue: "*Topos* . . . negative capabilities . . . vegetation images in Shakespearean comedy." All clearly borrowed opinions: something from Leavis, something else from Empson or Coleridge. No thought of my own.) I spoke by then without trace of a Spanish accent. (I spoke and read French and Italian better than I could Spanish.) My eyes watched the instructor. My voice caught as I offered an answer. And when I was finally praised, there was an inevitable blush of contentment, a smile of modest pride on my face.

When he is older and so little of the person he was survives, the scholarship boy makes apparent his profound lack of self-confidence. Richard Hoggart complains:

[The boy] tends to overstress the importance of examinations, of the piling-up of knowledge and of received opinions. He discovers a technique of apparent learning, of the acquiring of facts rather than of the handling and use of facts. He learns how to receive a purely literate education, one using only a small part of the personality and challenging only a limited area of his being. He begins to see life as a ladder, as a permanent examination with some praise and some further exhortation at each stage. He becomes an expert imbiber and doler-out; his competence will vary, but will rarely be accompanied by genuine enthusiasms. He rarely feels the reality of knowledge, of other men's thoughts and imaginings, on his own pulses: he rarely discovers an author for himself and on his own. . . . He has something of the blinkered pony about him. (p. 243)

This is criticism more accurate than it is fair. The scholarship boy *is* a bad student, but in large part the reason he is so bad is that he realizes earlier and more acutely than most other students—than Hoggart himself!—that education requires radical self-reformation. As a very young boy he knows this; he knows it too well. He cannot forget that the academy is responsible for remaking him. That is why he depends on it so much. He becomes, in obvious ways, the worst student, the great mimic, the last student who ever feels obliged to voice an opinion of his own. But he would not be so bad—nor would he become so successful—if he did not accurately perceive that the truer synonym for "education" is not "learning" but "imitation." And that education is mainly a long, unglamorous, and even demeaning process of acquiring skills and habits of mind—a nurturing never natural to the persons we were once, before first entering the classroom.

Those who would take the scholarship boy's success—his failure—seriously would be forced to realize how great is the change any academic undergoes, how far they have moved from their pasts. It is easier to ignore such considerations. For good reason is little mentioned about the scholarship boy in pages and pages of educational literature. Instead, one hears proposals for increasing the self-esteem of students and encouraging early intellectual independence. (The platitudes ignore altogether the function of imitation in a student's life—and the fact that the "best" students must also be those least independent.) Self-styled radical teachers complain, meanwhile, that ghetto schools attempt to mold students and that they stifle native characteristics. But the much more acute critique should be just the reverse: not that schools change students too much, but that while they might promote the scholarship boy, they change most students barely at all.

There is no specific pedagogy of the ghetto to glean from the story of the scholarship boy. There is, however, a much larger lesson. At once different from most other students, the scholarship boy is also the archetypal student. He exaggerates the difficulty of being a student, but his exaggeration reveals a general predicament. Others are changed as much as he. They too learn by imitation. They develop the skill of memory long before they become truly critical thinkers. And when they read Plato for the first several times, it is with awe rather than a deep comprehension.

The impact of schooling on the scholarship boy is only more apparent—to the boy himself and to others. Finally, although he may be laughable, "the blinkered pony," the boy will not let his critics totally forget their own "failure." He ends up too much like them. When he speaks, they hear themselves echoed. In his pedantry, they face their own. His ambitions are theirs. If his failure was singular, they would readily pity him. But he is much more troubling than that; they would not scorn him if this was not so.

Nearing the end of my education, I looked back and, for the first time, recalled my past with nostalgia. The same longing fills Hoggart's scholarship boy. Hoggart's description of the boy's nostalgia, however, is stripped of sympathy and coated with scorn:

> He longs for the membership he has lost, "he pines for some Nameless Eden where he never was." The nostalgia is the stronger and the more ambiguous because he is really "in quest of his own absconded self yet scared to find it." He both wants to go back and yet thinks he has gone beyond his class, feels himself weighted with knowledge of his own and their situation, which hereafter forbids him the simpler pleasures of his father and mother. (p. 246)

Hoggart judges this nostalgia a result of two failures. The scholarship boy senses that he will never be fully accepted as an equal by other academics. Additionally, he remains still the uncertain scholar, unable to master the skills and tasks of the classroom.

This fate does not resemble, however, what happened to me. When, as a graduate student, I arrived in London to write my dissertation on English Renaissance literature, I was confident of having at last become an academic. But the exhilaration that confidence brought dimmed as, after only a few weeks in the British Museum, it grew clear that I had joined a lonely community of scholars. Around me each day were heads partly hidden by piles of pages and books. Some persons I sat beside day after day, yet we passed silent at the end of each day, strangers. Still, although we were strangers, we were united by a common respect for the written word and the value we placed on scholarship. We did form a union, albeit one primarily theoretical.

More profound, but more troubling, was the bond I felt with the writers of the books I consulted. Whenever I opened texts which had not been used for years, I realized that my special interests united me to a handful of other academics. We formed an exclusive (eccentric!) company, separated from other persons who would never care or be able to understand our concerns. Again, this was a lonely and impersonal society. The reward of my membership in such company seemed suddenly thin compensation for the loss of my intimate society of childhood. (The pages I turned were dusty and stiff.) Who, I began to wonder, would ever read what I wrote? And, was my dissertation much more than an act of social withdrawal? The questions seemed unanswered by the dank silence of the Museum reading room.

Meanwhile, my file cards accumulated. A professional, quick and efficient, I knew exactly how to look for information I needed. I could quickly determine the usability of what I read. But whenever I started to write, I knew too much—and not enough—to be able to write anything but sentences that were little more than cautious and timid, strained brittle under the heavy weight of footnotes and qualifications. I seemed unable to make a passionate statement. I felt drawn by professionalism to the edge of sterility, capable of little more than a pedantic, lifeless, and unreadable prose.

Then the nostalgia began. After twenty-one years, school years spent trying to forget the attractions of my past, I suddenly yearned for the time in my life when I was not so alone with my ideas; when ideas didn't seem so removed from experience; when ideas were felt; and—most of all—when there was the solace of an intimate company. Yearning became preoccupation. Memories beckoned, then flooded my mind. (A sudden embrace. The early idea of death in the child's massacre of hundreds of ants. The whispered sound of Spanish at night. . . .) Less and less time was spent on the dissertation; more was spent reading sociologists. I needed to understand how far I had moved from my past—to determine how fast I would be able to recover something of it once again.

Then I came home. After a year in the library, my first months I worked as a laborer, shirtless and exhilarated by sensations of sweating and fatigue, my hands confident with a shovel. Those first few months back in America I lived with my parents, deeply relieved by how easy it was to be with them both. Although we had little to say, I noticed suddenly (watching carefully for evidence) the thin, firm strands of the unconscious which bind generations. (Of course, people had been right, I concluded, when they recognized that my mother and I laughed the same way. And, could it be possible that when my father spoke Spanish, he sounded a tone that I also achieved when I wrote English?) After the early relief, this return, however, brought a later suspicion, nagging until it led to a certain realization, that I had not side-stepped the impact of the years of my schooling. My desire to do so was the measure of just how much I remained an academic. *Negatively* (for that is how this idea first occurred to me): my ability and need to think so much (so abstractly!) about my life and my relationship to my parents was already indication of a long education. My mother and father, by comparison, did not pass their time thinking about the "cultural" meaning of their experience. It was I, who had been taught to conceptualize experience, who described their daily lives in an idea. And yet, *positively:* the ability to use abstract ways of thinking about experience had allowed me to shape into desire what would have been only indefinite longings in the British Museum. If, because of my schooling, I had become separated from my parents, my education had also given me in the end a way to speak and to care about that fact.

My best teachers in college and graduate school, years earlier, had tried to prepare me for this conclusion, I think, when they described pastoral and Romantic literature. I noted all that they said. I even memorized it. "The praise of the unlettered by those who are highly educated is one of the primary themes of 'elitist' literature." But, "The importance of the praise given the unsolitary, richly passionate life is that it simultaneously reflects the value of reflective life."

I heard it all. But there was no way for any of it to mean very much to me. I was a scholarship boy then, busily laddering my way up the rungs of education. To pass an examination, I wrote down what my instructors said. It took many more years of learning and reading (my inevitable miseducation), as I slowly came to trust the silence and the habit of abstracting from immediate experience—moving away from a life of closeness and immediacy I remembered in my parents, growing older—before I turned, unafraid, to desire the past, and thereby achieved what had eluded me for so long, the end of education.*

*Richard Rodriguez, "The Achievement of Desire: Personal Reflections on Learning 'Basics,' " in *College English* (November 1978), pp. 238–254. Coypright © by The National Council of Teachers of English. Reprinted by permission of NCTE.

In your first paper for the course, Assignment I, the working paper that has just been returned to you, you addressed the subject of some change you expected or hoped your experience with college would help you to make in your life. You were talking, in other words, about how you believed that college could give you a way of seeing things that you didn't have then, about what you might have to pay to get this new way of seeing, what might make it worth it anyway, in spite of what you might have to pay.

You've had more experience with college than you had when you wrote your first paper—experience made up in part of what you have read and written and heard in this course, as well as in others.

What do you now say about how your college education can change the way you see things, about what you might have to pay for this change, and about what might make the change worth it— even knowing what you know about what it might cost? There are complications now for you that were not apparent in that first paper you wrote? Dangers or risks you may not have been aware of? Resources to draw on of more value, things in the future more worth hoping for (thinking of what you've read and written, what you've heard said and said yourself) than can be articulated with a simple moral vocabulary or in the commonplaces about education? Richard Rodriguez, you will notice, makes use of a concept he takes from a writer named Richard Hoggart, the concept of "the scholarship boy," in order "to frame the meaning of [both his] academic failure and success."

Begin your paper by evaluating that working paper you wrote in 50 minutes at the beginning of the course. As you see things now, what exactly were you saying then? What does that saying say about you as a see-er? This section of your essay is to be a close reading of your working paper rather than an easy dismissal of it.

Then, readdress the same question you dealt with in Assignment 1 in such a way as to enable what you'd call a good reader, but not a member of this class, to put this second section of your essay alongside your working paper and say of the pairing:

What I like about these two papers put side by side is the way they are an example not of someone's simply *claiming* to have learned something, but of somebody's *showing* such learning. The way this writer uses her experience with both the material of the course and beyond makes it clear that she is doing a lot more than just trying to guess what someone else thinks she ought to say about the meaning of a college education for her.

This is the last paper you will write for this course and as you can see it is an opportunity for you to put some things together for yourself, whatever it is you care to connect in whatever order you choose. But if you consider the way your audience is specified above, you will see that you should also think of this essay as a kind of research paper. You have read and written and heard rather a lot this term, both in this course and out of it. This is your research material, and in adapting it to your own purposes you will be performing operations similar to those you will use to study other subjects in college. This final essay, then, will be an individual statement. But as is the case with any piece of good research writing, it is an opportunity also for you to show what you owe to others in having worked something out for yourself.

For this reason it would be wise to consider carefully what sort of approach to the writing of this paper would best enable you to see what you want to put together with what and in what sorts of arrangements. You have been given experience with various ways of going about the writing of a paper, and have begun, at least, to develop some sense of what sort of approach to writing seems to work best for you. Are you the kind of writer, for example, who would do most justice to this project by first developing a set of notes? And if so, notes on what in this case? And of what sort? Or are you someone who works best by launching immediately into the writing of a draft, who uses the pouring of thought after thought onto paper as a way of finding a key question or discovering a focus? Or perhaps you will decide to use some combination of these approaches.

The approach you take to writing this paper ought to be one which will enable you to create the best piece of writing on the subject of this assignment that you can produce. Do *not* submit any notes, any early drafts, any outlines with your final draft. This paper will speak for you in speaking for itself and *vice versa*.

Your paper must be typed.

Be sure to turn back in a copy of that first paper you wrote with the paper you write addressing Assignment 12.

Seeing Assignment 12

BETTY'S PAPER FOR ASSIGNMENT 1

Though it probably seems strange to say so, the change I hope for most coming back to college has to do with an attitude toward myself. I don't mean that I consider myself stupid or even uninformed. It's just that it's important to me to finish what I start.

I am the mother of two small children, the second of which started school just this September. My husband has a job at Westinghouse that he's good at. Westinghouse seems to like him. I don't have to work now the way I did when we were first married. I could just stay home now if I wanted. I don't think I'd get fat or just disappear either. I'd probably watch some television, but I've never been addicted to it and I've always liked to read.

~~But it~~ On the other hand, my being here doesn't come ~~for free for~~ for sure. We've had to cut some corners financially. I have to arrange my day so that I get time away from both my kids and my husband to study. I'm not preparing for a better job than I could have right now if I went back to work as a paralegal secretary.

So why am I back after leaving college the middle of my sophomore year over ten years ago to get married and build a home? That's a good question. It's a better one than I thought it was when I started this paper. I need ~~somebody~~ ~~pro~~ discipline. I read, yes, but ~~I need to~~ (time)

    talk (people)

    ~~To nobody to my~~

    ~~security~~ (for me

    color in my

Time!

BETTY'S ASSIGNMENT 12 (OPENING)

From what I could remember of what I wrote, I thought my paper for Assignment 1 was going to look

a lot worse to me than I think it does. I don't mean
I think it's a great piece of writing. It isn't
finished (I never dealt with the third question of
the Assignment at all). And the end of the paper is
a mess. But still, I like some of the things the
paper tries to do, and I like some of the things it
doesn't do, or rather that I got scared off doing.
Maybe this is more private than public, more a
matter of what the words in the paper mean to *me*
because I wrote them than what they might mean to
someone else. I'll know that better when I finish
this. That I think is the main thing I've gotten
from the course, by the way: whoever else I may be
writing to or for, whether a teacher or a class or
as is the case with the second part of this essay,
someone outside both (supposedly) to whom I'm to
show what I've learned this term, I'm still my most
important reader.

Let me take what I like about what the paper
doesn't do first because that's easier to talk
about.

I was tempted in doing the paper that day in
class to stay with "the commonplaces about
education," and I would have I think had it not
been for the course description and our class
on it, and the warnings in Assignment 1 (" . . . no
one with any sense would pretend . . . that cliches
say what needs to be said"). Frankly, I was
terrified. So even though I didn't then begin to
know what the course *was* going to be, I knew some of
the things it *wasn't* going to be. That's why I
questioned "the commonplaces about" why to come to
college as I did in the paper. I'm *not* here because

I think I'm dumb and that college is going to make me smart. I'm *not* here to get a better job. I'm *not* here because I think if I stayed home I'd become a nothing. Ironically, I brought those negatives in because I was playing things safe. I was turning on "the commonplaces" said by the good student (which I've always been) by trying to be *my teacher's* kind of good student, the kind of good student I thought he was after. The irony of *that* irony, however, is that my "trick" took me to the best sentence in the paper (for me), the one where I respond to myself asking why I'm back in college with: "It's a better question than I thought it was when I started this paper." How I used language in the paper, even though my motives for it were hardly commendable, had changed how I saw something. Even in an in-class nothing piece of writing.

The most interesting thing for me in the paper, however, (I guess this involves some "*not* doing" too) is the way I get to what I never really get to: those notes at the end. I was running out of time and was terribly frustrated with myself. I can see that "on the other hand" isn't quite the way to open my next to last paragraph, and I'd have done better to put the last sentence of that same paragraph earlier. My handwriting gets sloppier, and the second reference to "time," in block capitals with an exclamation point, is almost a scream. What I like, however, is what's *in* those notes at the end, what I've kept on the table for consideration when it comes to the question of why I'm back in college and what I've swept off the table by crossing it out. I made some real choices in doing that, I think, choices that I didn't even know I was making, but choices that I've been helped to see the importance of from a number of things I've read and been through this term: three of the assignments specifically, a couple of conversations (two in our study group, two out of it), a project I've taken on for my art history course, and a novel called *Prince of Tides* by Pat Conroy. In this paper I want to try to say . . .

LOU'S PAPER FOR ASSIGNMENT 1

dependant → individ.
lose security → freedom/adult
pain

sheltered dep. → free, self-reliant, control
(par. authority)

means   pain / stress from change.

but   Adulthood worth it →

One positive change that college will help me to work in my own life will be to the This transition from a chil sheltered dependant to a free self-contai fully cognizent, self-reliant, free individual. This change will enable me to fully control my own life. I will no longer be regulated by the authority figures of my parents and relatives. This change, however, will be accompanied by a sacrafice

The payment for the transition into adulthood will be the loss of the complete security of childhood. Once total freedom is acheived, one becomes fully accountable as an individual for his actions. There will be many more payments, I am during the transition, in the form of stresses and agonies caused by stresses. These payments will be the inevitable results of changing, and of realizing that one has changed too much or that one is not changing quickly enough. These payments undoubtedly will be painful, yet the promise of self-awareness makes the goal of adulthood worth attempting.

Adulthood with its full freedom and responsibility, and cognizance, is a goal worth any price to me. When adulthood is attained, I will have the ability to live life fully and to be totally self-aware. This property of being self-aware is what I most desire from adulthood, and what makes the phase of change worth enduring.

LOU'S ASSIGNMENT 12 (OPENING)

The interesting thing for me about my first paper is what kind of a reader (and listener, and see-er, to coin a phrase) it says I was and sometimes still am. The easy way for me to handle the paper would be to say "boy, what a jag-off I was when I came in here and this is the evidence." But I'm not going to get anywhere by writing off my stuff as "garbage" the way the writer in Assignment 5 did. A very wise friend of mine says that people who don't deal with their own history are going to have to repeat it. I don't want to cop out either by saying "well, I was new to college and what can you expect." I was, sure. I was "pressed for time" too, the same way the woman in Assignment 8 was. But like her I have to admit "that's me in that first paper, some of me anyway." It's part of the "record" (a good word) not just of how I *saw,* but of how I sometimes still see, and that's why it's worth dealing with.

What I did to write that first paper was to make the question into what the course description calls a "yelled short order." I did this even before I started to write the paper (you can see my little "outline"), and everything I said in it follows that decision (except the bad spelling!). What I heard was "gimme a theme," and I said "O.K. Now *you* gimme an A." I blocked out everything that was said in the course description (and in the class discussion of it) about what a theme is, what a conversation is, what writing is. And I blocked

out the same things in Assignment 1. I guess I made
a choice to do that, but the really interesting
thing is that I didn't know I'd made a choice. I had
a purpose too, but I don't think I knew that
either. What I heard and saw was what would help me
do my number, go into my act. It's one of many acts
I've got down to a science, and they all have one
thing in common. They're all ways of my convincing
myself I'm doing life, but because they're just
routines, they're all ways of my doing a number on
myself.

I think I can see why now to talk about lies or
truth in writing, phoniness or honesty, is stupid.
I did tell some "lies" in the paper. (I don't have
"parents" because my father is dead. God only
knows where my "relatives" are. I don't think I've
exactly been a "sheltered dependent.") But all the
lies I told were true to my reading the Assignment
as a "yelled short order." When I did that, I set up
a system, just as closed as the system of physics
the way we discussed it in class. In that system it
is *true* to say I think I can become totally reliant
and totally free, that I believe I can live life
fully and be totally self-aware. I wasn't just
putting it on when I wrote that stuff. I really
believed what I was saying when I wrote it. I
really thought I knew what being totally
self-aware meant . . .